Rebels in the Wild

Rebels in the Wild

The Equality Colony and the Taming of American Capitalism

Robert Burns

Cover photo: Equality colonists with a banner of their newspaper, *Industrial Freedom*, 1898. Courtesy of the Center for Pacific Northwest Studies, Western Libraries Archives and Special Collections, Western Washington University. Frederick E. Smith papers.

Cover design: Libby Burns.

Formatted with Vellum

To Liz, for love and faith

Contents

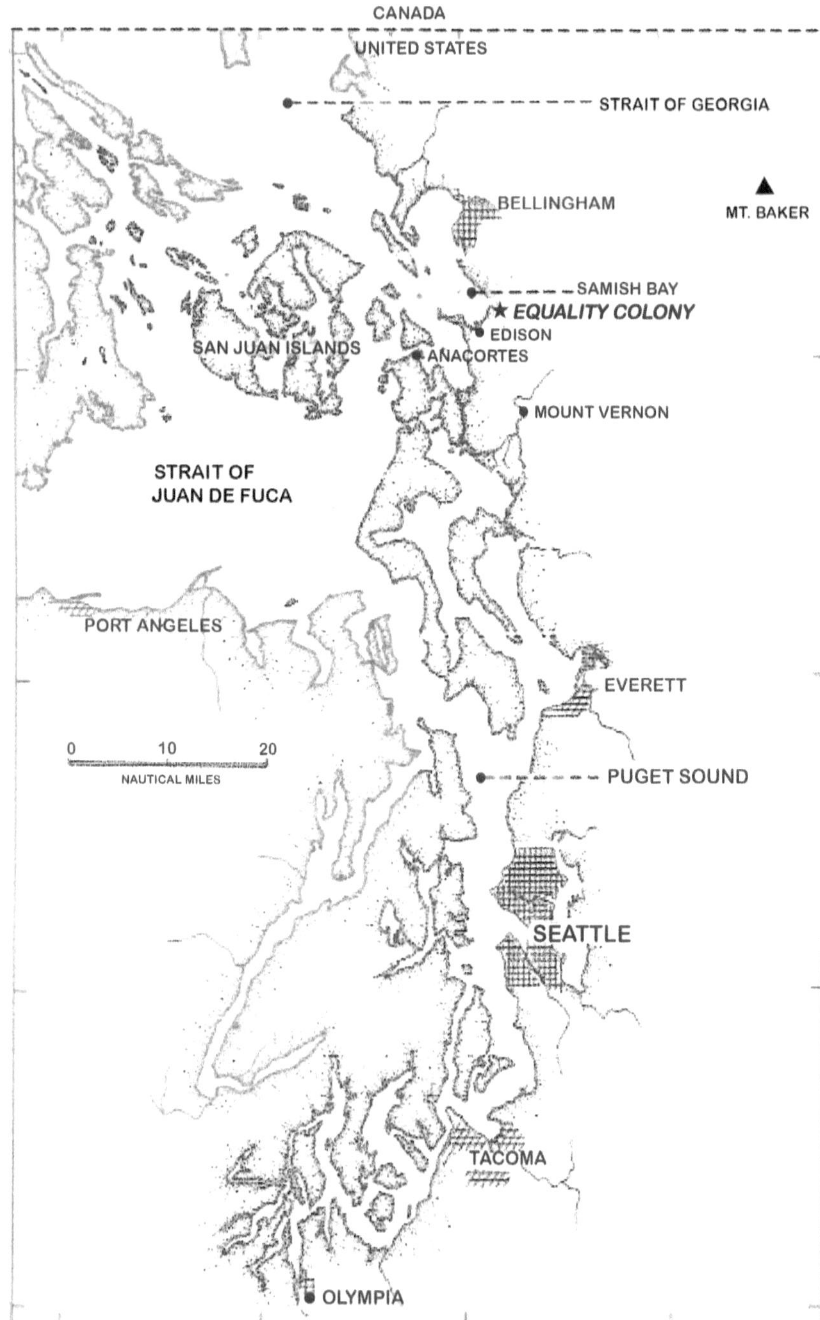

Map Adaptation by Libby Burns

Prologue

America was shrinking—its open spaces, its promise of opportunity, even its optimism—when a little band of dreamers headed west with a big idea. They gathered in a wilderness near Washington's Puget Sound, a raw frontier still welcoming of the ambitious and the rambunctious. There, among ancient stands of cedar and fir, on the cusp of a new century, they launched an attempt at revolution known to few alive today.

The year was 1897. The idea was that like-minded men and women could build from scratch a socialist community that would succeed so spectacularly that enlightened people across the state would replicate it. Once Washington had been captured for socialism, the rest of the country would follow—quickly, peacefully, democratically. Power would flow through socialist hands, breaking the grip of capitalism.

It was to be a march to Utopia, an imagined state of perfection, if only these radicals could agree what that should mean.

Eugene V. Debs, the socialist labor leader who gave the venture his early but tepid support, saw the goal as "simply trying to build up the people."[1] He thought of it as leveling the playing field in an economic system tilted in favor of industrialists who had shown they could crush labor revolts like the Pullman rail strike and boycott of 1894 that destroyed Debs' rail-workers union, landed him in prison, and led him to socialism.

Others aimed much higher, envisioning a bone-rattling shakeup of the social, political, and economic order. Democracy would stay. Capitalism would go, replaced by an economy based on collective ownership of the tools of prosperity—factories, mines, forests, railroads, and more. Every man and woman willing to work would be assured a decent home, a job, and a vote—essentials too often denied ordinary Americans of that era.

For this revolution to be realized peacefully, skeptics would have to be shown that socialism could work, not just in theory but in real life. And so was born the idea of creating a model commune—a starter colony. Washington, with a newly elected liberal governor, seemed the perfect host. It was new to statehood, thinly populated, blessed with natural resources, and possessed of a reputation for open-mindedness. Here lay the essence of the colony's initial appeal: it was a novelty—not the first socialist experiment but the first in the United States to put into practice a colonization-as-revolution strategy.

The arrivals on Puget Sound called their colony Equality, a name inspired by the pen of novelist Edward Bellamy, who wrote of an American economic system working in the wrong direction—toward oppressing the laborer and farmer and making the rich richer rather than fulfilling the Founding Fathers' promise of a fair shake for all. The colonists, like the novelist, envisioned an escape from the dark side of capitalism —the poverty, the despair, the indignity felt by those who saw themselves as wage slaves to corporate masters who would tolerate no restraint in their pursuit of profit. Never mind that most Americans embraced free enterprise, by habit if not by studied conviction; it was the economic bedrock on which the country had been built. Never mind that Bellamy himself saw little sense in dispatching a legion of starry-eyed socialists to the wilds of Washington.

"Stay at home,"[2] Bellamy advised.

The Equality colonists, however, were not the stay-at-home type. In some ways they were regular folk—patriotic, honest, of ordinary intelligence—with a rebellious streak more obvious in some. They shared a vague hope for better lives and a more just world but had little else in common beyond a belief that capitalists were making a mockery of democracy.

You won't find these rebels' names in history books; they are long forgotten. Faded, too, are memories of the final decade of the 19th century, a period largely ignored by writers and scholars as a backwater of American history. Many of these 1890s agitators were in their thirties, born during or shortly after the most transformative event in American history, the Civil War, and raised in a new age of industrialization. They were idealists, convinced that in an era producing one technological miracle after another—the light bulb, the telegraph and telephone, the moving picture camera, and much more—political miracles, too, were possible. A few were delusional; some were naive. They were not, however, cons or clowns. Among them: an accomplished civil engineer from Ohio, a St. Louis public school teacher, a self-taught Shakespeare expert from Massachusetts, a graduate of Georgetown Law School in the nation's capital, an Arkansas entrepreneur, and a hard-swinging lumberjack from mid-coast Maine.

They also included a few knuckleheads, like a "boy bandit" who got tangled up with a train-robbing gang. Some were a little loopy, like a young woman who fashioned herself a spiritualist and later was implicated in one of the stranger real estate scams of the 20th century.

They gathered from across a landscape battered by one of the worst economic storms in history, triggered by the third bank panic in as many decades. For most Americans, the nostalgic "Gay Nineties" were anything but cheery. They were a decade of extreme inequality: glittering wealth for a relative few; severe depression and farm failures for many. The country suffered through what economists call a double-bottom depression, with the second low point reached in 1897, the year of Equality's founding. Ordinary people were starving, if not for food, then for hope. Labor and industry were at war—in the coal and silver mines, on the railroads, and in the steel and textile mills.

As radicals saw it in the century's closing years, the main problem was that too much wealth and power rested in the hands of too few, like tycoons John D. Rockefeller and J.P. Morgan. The time had come to take a stand against what looked like plutocracy—government by the rich, for the rich. The longer they waited, the worse the injustice. Capitalism, they felt sure, was ripe for ruin.

They dared to dream big. An early arrival at Equality recalled in a handwritten account of his family's journey from Kentucky, "We were going to abolish wage slavery and provide plenty for all, assuring to each the full fruits of the product of his or her labor."[3] At its core, that vision and the story of the Equality colony reflect the timeless struggle to defend human dignity and the endless and essential search for a better way to organize society.

"Great scheme if it works,"[4] a skeptic wrote in the early months. To some it seemed a sure thing. One enthusiast wrote in the hopeful spring of 1898: "Just imagine Equality in two or three years if nothing greater than an earthquake strikes it."

The scheme did not work, not as imagined. Equality stood for ten years but crumbled under the weight of pressures more subtle than an earthquake: incompatible ideas and the irresistible human urge to look out for Number One. The colony was built on a brotherly pledge of "all for one, and one for all," but in the end, self-interest proved the stronger instinct. Some remained loyal to the idea of creating a socialist society—a cooperative commonwealth, they called it—but others proved to be unbending individualists with unworkable ideas. In frustration, they turned on one another, at first gently, then violently.

The Equality colonists failed in the sense that their community withered like a parched plant, as did the idea of converting the whole country—or even the state of Washington—to socialism. Once dead, Equality was quickly buried. And yet, the men and women who gave it a go are testament to a remarkable era of radicalism that foretold America's 20th century break with full-on free enterprise—what could be called the taming of capitalism.

In ways long lost in the American memory, the impulses that created Equality foreshadowed the birth of the social welfare state and the emergence of a national consensus on empowering a hands-on government to promote the common good. Ideas denounced as radical, even un-American, in the 1890s became conventional wisdom a few decades later. The eight-hour workday, for example, became the national standard only after years of agitating for more humane working conditions. Similarly: a federal income tax and minimum wage, voting rights for women, public works programs, limits on child labor, guardrails against Wall Street excesses, and legal protections for labor unions. Social safeguards dismissed at the turn of the 20th century as a perversion of capitalism became not just the law of the land but cultural anchors—notably the Social

Security Act of 1935, providing old-age and survivor benefits and aid to dependent mothers and children. A generation later came Medicare, offering health insurance for the elderly, and Medicaid for low-income people.

This history is especially resonant in the 2020s with the rise of a regressive radicalism aimed at returning the United States to wide-open capitalism, reminiscent of the 1890s when the rich were rewarded and the rest were dismissed as parasites on the state.

What follows is the most complete story yet told of the Equality colony—the unlikely cast of characters who envisioned, built, and then abandoned it, and the radical ideas that shaped their dream and changed the country.

Chapter 1

A Radical For All Reasons

George E. Boomer was a born hell-raiser, the rascally sort who not only defied authority but spit in its eye. Radicalism fit him as neatly as a tailored suit, which begins to explain how he slipped so easily into a crusade against capitalism. That, and the fact that he sported a contrarian streak as wide and deep as the white pine forests of his native Maine.

In boyhood, Boomer despised the life of a cotton mill worker, so he quit to learn the printer's trade. Newspaper publishing and labor organizing became his passions, and he so endlessly promoted the cause of the working stiff that some wondered whether his middle initial might stand for Everlasting. The man never tired of rousing the rabble. Of the righteous campaign to kill capitalism he declared, "It is war to the knife" —mortal combat.

Still, it probably surprised some when, in the spring of 1898, at age thirty-five, George Ellsworth Boomer[1] became a fugitive from the hanging noose, a rebel on the run.

As a writer of overripe opinion columns for the nation's

most-read socialist newspaper, Boomer had gone too far this time with an indelicate jab at the American flag. "A painted rag on a stick," he called it. He was intending to scold the public schools for choosing to teach kids more about national symbols like the flag than national needs like a better-working economy. To Boomer, patriotism was loyalty to social progress and to the Constitution, not allegiance to a banner or acceptance of a world view built on boasts of American superiority.

"Teaching little children to bow themselves low before a painted rag on a stick while refusing to teach them how to bring about better conditions over which the flag should float is ridiculous, criminal and debasing,"[2] he wrote under his ill-fitting pen name, Uncle Sam.

Boomer's indiscretion was not original. As far back as 1854, newspaperman Horace Greeley's *New York Tribune* had called the flag "hate's polluted rag," and a generation later, Walter W. Vrooman, an eccentric labor agitator with whom Boomer briefly collaborated, was arrested in Allegheny City, Pennsylvania, for declaring in the public square that the flag was a "rag" on a pole. "Threats of bodily injury were thrown at him,"[3] a local newspaper reported, but the offended stopped short of fitting Vrooman for a rope collar.

By the time Boomer used the term, in April 1898, the national mood had transformed. Congress was about to declare war on Spain, stirred to action by a suspicious explosion that had sunk the *USS Maine* in Havana harbor two months earlier, killing 260 sailors and marines. The American public had been whipped into a patriotic frenzy and Boomer's insult was one too many for folks in the Kansas coal town of Girard, where his newspaper was published. His "painted rag" comment triggered such outrage that townsmen[4] came calling with a hanging rope, or so the story was told in newspapers from coast to coast. Heeding a timely tip, Boomer escaped out the rear of his Girard office and hustled two dozen miles north to the town of Fort Scott near the Missouri border. There he hopped the rails for a thirteen-dollar ride to refuge in the deep woods of the Pacific Northwest.[5]

"*So Badly Scared He Flees from the State,*" a Kansas newspaper sniped with glee.[6]

Boomer's destination was Skagit County, Washington, on a stretch of ancient timberland where a finger of the Cascade mountain range touches a fertile tideland along Samish Bay, about thirty miles south of the Canadian border and seventy miles north of Seattle. In these wilds in the northwestern corner of what was then the Union's most northwestern state, life was uncluttered and uncomplicated. As recently as the 1850s it had been nearly untouched by white men. Even in the closing years of the 19th century, communication marvels such as the telephone had barely reached these parts; in the city of Mount Vernon, the county seat, only one home had a phone in 1897.[7]

For thousands of years the Samish River valley had been a homeland of the Coast Salish, whose tribal territories bordered the Salish Sea, a vast, crescent-shaped inland waterway stretching south from the Strait of Georgia in British Columbia, through Washington's San Juan Islands, to the southern tip of Puget Sound. Now this secluded spot was home to Equality, the newly formed socialist colony whose leaders' vision of brotherly bliss had been promoted in radical circles but notably ignored by Boomer's socialist newspaper, the *Appeal to Reason,* mocked by its critics as the "Appeal to Treason." Publisher Julius A. Wayland had soured on colonizing for socialism after recently starting and abandoning a utopian community in the hills of central Tennessee.

At Equality, Boomer was welcomed, if not for his firebrand reputation, then for his widely known socialist credentials and his mastery of that great social equalizer of 19th century America, the printing press. In an era when metal type was set by hand, he had a maestro's touch; he composed each page with the precision of a master pianist.

Boomer's timing could hardly have been better. Colony leaders were hurrying to start a weekly newspaper as their megaphone for socialism, but mechanical problems tripped them up. His presence would add technical knowhow and a splash of color. To Equality colleague William McDevitt, Boomer was, in the lingo of the time, "a man of parts," or multitalented. He may have known that Boomer was also skilled on the piccolo, the tiny woodwind as shrill and insistent as his personality. McDevitt saw Boomer as "probably at that moment about the most useful member we could have acquired."[8]

Shortly, Boomer resumed his column-writing, but he stayed only six months. Equality's socialists were too sedate for him—a problem he might have sensed even before he got there.

On the five-mile wagon ride to the colony from a Great Northern rail stop called Belfast, at the western edge of a grassland known as Jarman Prairie, Boomer fell into conversation with a seat mate, Lewis M. Ayer, who coincidentally had arrived at the same time after journeying from his home in Minnesota. Ayer had come to scout Equality for friends in Minneapolis who were thinking of joining. What he saw troubled him.

"The most radical elements are drifting to them,"[9] Ayer concluded after meeting Boomer, who was an unapologetic preacher of the socialist creed and an unrelenting critic of capitalism but hardly a flame-throwing anarchist. Boomer was the classic ink-stained wretch in an era when newspapering was truly a craft and the printed page was such a dominant form of communication that even small towns had multiple papers.

Skilled pressmen and typesetters were in demand regardless of their politics, and throughout the 1890s Boomer carried his anti-capitalist ideology and mechanical knowhow from print shop to print shop, from city to city—from Providence, Rhode Island, to Wheeling, West Virginia, to the Maryland towns of Easton, Cambridge, and Cumberland, and then, fatefully, to Girard, Kansas.

Ayer, a leader of the liberal People's Party in Minneapolis who later ran for state office as a socialist, said Boomer told him he intended to publish a new magazine called *The Red Flag*. To Ayer this was, well, a red flag—another sign that extreme radicalism posed a "menacing danger"[10] to this socialist experiment in the shadow of the Cascades. After his visit, Ayer wrote a stinging critique of the colony suggesting it was doomed, with or without Boomer. Ayer dismissed the colonists as earnest but misguided fools; they were in over their heads and already suffering the effects of internal dissension. He ended with this: "My advice to one and all: Keep away from Equality."

As accidental acquaintances on that wagon ride from Belfast, Boomer and Ayer embodied a problem that confounded Equality's leaders from the get-go: Progressive people who sympathized with the idea of colonizing for socialism could not always embrace it in practice. For some, like Ayer, Equality was too radical; for Boomer and others, it was not radical enough. This split mattered little at first. More people arrived at the colony's door than it could readily accommodate; tents and off-site lodging had to be arranged. Over time, however, divided views about Equality's path and purpose had real consequences: infighting, paralysis, bursts of violence, and, finally, a "reign of terror" that literally reduced to ashes these radicals' rickety framework for a socialist century.

Chapter 2

Defying Human Nature

Equality colony looked at first like a new opening, a portal to progress at a time of diminished hope among working-class people like Boomer who hungered for answers to what polite contemporaries called "the labor question." If capitalism was so great, why were so many able bodies out of work while the idle rich grew richer? To the builders of Equality, the answer seemed obvious: Capitalism was *not* so great; only socialism could close the employment and wealth gaps.

It was not that simple.

From its first day, Equality was a gamble and not a well-calculated one. Success in the form of revolutionary change was a long shot, as even some of the colony's most optimistic leaders knew. They understood that with Republicans and Democrats holding the political high ground in a country suspicious of radicalism, this underpowered little enterprise on the fringe of the socialist movement, in a far corner of the country, was a heavy underdog. Still, they could hope.[1]

"All must know that beyond these mountains lie the beautiful fields of golden opportunity," one leader[2] wrote wistfully as the colony's fortunes faded and its troubles accumulated like a long winter's snowpack on a Cascade peak.

The colonists never reached the summit of their ambition, and socialism as an institutionalized movement eventually slipped into irrelevance. Yet for most of its existence from 1897 to 1907 Equality was a functioning (sometimes just barely) community in splendid isolation. It had its own homes, schoolhouse, governing council, fruit orchard, farm, print shop, saw and shingle mill, grist mill, creamery, cooperage, beeyard, fishery, and more. The cycle of life brought births, weddings and funerals. There was a post office and a weekly newspaper with a national following. The population peaked at about 340 and included European immigrants as well as direct descendants of original New England colonists. Approximately thirty souls still rest in an abandoned and unmarked cemetery which, like the colony's fuller history, fell into neglect and was nearly forgotten.

Still, from their own words and the time-worn shards of their shattered dream, the Equality settlers' original aim is clear. They hoped to demonstrate that, freed of what they saw as the destructive effects of capitalist competition for wealth and power, people could live in peace and harmony and end their dependence on a wage system that seemed like slavery. They wanted to show that labor's burdens as well as its fruits could be shared fairly, if not equally. Everyone would chip in. No one would lord over them, and no individual would profit at the expense of others. They hoped to live as one, long before John Lennon imagined a brotherhood of man with "all the people sharing all the world."

This would require not just extraordinary patience, unselfishness and inventiveness, but also an ability to defy human nature by putting common interests ahead of personal ambition.

At first, good intentions prevailed.

Adult residents volunteered for, or were assigned to, work groups supervised by a man or woman chosen by vote. Men did most manual labor, such as tree-felling, stump-pulling, milling, horseshoeing, construction, and the planting and harvesting of crops. Women were assigned mostly to meal service, laundry, classroom teaching, sewing and childcare. None of those chores was easy. There was no electricity or running water, and several hundred meals had to be prepared and served each day from a communal kitchen. The laundry was done by hand at an old logging camp cabin on a nearby creek. Every able-bodied person eighteen years and older was required to work eight hours a day, six days a week. Some voluntarily worked longer. The women's eight hours were split between colony labor and domestic chores—an acknowledgement, rare in those days, that housework was in fact work.

There was to be no idleness; slackers were subject to expulsion. Once the colony became self-sustaining, industries like crop farming, mining, stock raising, brick making, fish processing, and the canning of fruits and vegetables would generate income to grow the enterprise and connect a statewide network of socialist colonies.

There would be little need for money. Basics like schooling, housing and medical care were provided collectively. In old age, a member in good standing but unable to work would be fully supported by the group. Instead of cash wages, members were given the equivalent of five cents an hour in scrip—a paper currency in several denominations bearing a picture of the breaking dawn with the inscription, "Labor alone creates wealth." The scrip was used to pay for meals—ten cents each—and could be exchanged for goods offered at the colony store.

In Equality's early months, visitors could be easily impressed. One returned to his eastern Washington home in Spokane and declared, "I never saw so enthusiastic a company of men and women."[3] A Seattle hotel cook dropped in for a few days to see what the fuss was about; he became an admirer but not a convert. "Their sociable way of living seemed a continual picnic, something of a mixture between a country hotel and an old-fashioned Methodist camp meeting," he wrote.[4]

Such scenes of serenity were notable in a part of the country known for violent collisions between hard living and hard luck. Skagit County at the time was the sort of place where a young bartender deliberately fired a bullet into his head one summer night and the coroner's report summed up the suicide in two words: "rum & women."[5]

Equality colony had no jail, no saloon, no church. It was not Utopia, but order was to be ensured by harmony among like-minded men and women. Alcohol was allowed, but temperance was preferred; some of the colony's leaders were teetotalers and had little patience for drinkers. (There was booze aplenty in the nearby town of Edison, which explains the cry heard among some in the colony's farm fields at quitting time: "I'm going to Edison for my medicine.") Many of the colonists were God-fearing, but as a group they opposed organized religion; one prominent member said he believed in Christianity but not "churchianity." Those who worshipped did so privately or in small groups; some attended Catholic or Protestant services in Edison or in other nearby communities.

The colony's main decision-making body was the General Assembly, whose venue was the schoolhouse and whose seats were open to every adult member in good standing. This included women in an era when most Americans considered them undeserving of voting rights. The Assembly was designed to replicate the original New England colonies' town meeting form of direct democracy—as distinct from representative democracy—and to go one better by including women. Inclusiveness, however, held a different meaning in an era when non-whites were an afterthought in American political life; there were few, if any, Black people living anywhere near Equality at a time when they made up just one-half of 1 percent of the state's population.[6] Race relations may not have been a topic for discussion, but prejudices common to that period were clearly evident. One promotional article about Equality, written by an unidentified member and published in a Nebraska newspaper, compared "wage slavery" to chattel slavery.[7] While noting that enslaved people of the American South were subjected to "evils unknown" in the history of servitude, the writer offered the (now jarring) view that a slave's life had been rewarding in some ways. "He lived, as a rule, without fear of want, a valued member of society, useful to his fellows, sure of an opportunity to labor, under conditions for the most part wholesome, generally inspired with love and admiration for his master and family, and often tenderly cared for by them."

Colony membership for local Native Americans—mainly the Samish and the Lower Skagit tribes of the Coast Salish peoples, who were the original inhabitants of the very land on which Equality was built—was almost certainly never a serious consideration.

The General Assembly met every week or two, constructively at first. By egalitarian design, an elected officer presided but held no executive powers. Anything was up for discussion, no matter how trivial. This form of self-government fit the colonists' idea of pure democracy, and it ensured that elected work supervisors, women as well as men, were held to account. It didn't take long, however, for some to conclude that this democracy was altogether *too* pure. It yielded unending debate, scatter-shot decisions, unstable work management, and friction so intense that pettiness and impatience triumphed over progress. Rival factions formed, with destructive results.

Equality colony was not the first attempt in the United States to build a socialist or utopian community. It was not even first in the Puget Sound region. Yet it stood apart for the boldness of its ambition to usher in a radically new order while preserving democracy.

Political philosophies and theories aside, the best recruiting tool of Equality-style socialism was its promise of individual housing, advertised as the foundation of this community. At the time, a little fewer than half of Americans owned a home, and the percentage would not top fifty until 1950.[8] At Equality, each home was to be built and held in trust by the group, to be occupied by the individual colonist in perpetuity—no rent, no mortgage, no taxes. This was their idea of what came to be called the American Dream: a home and a job for every individual—security achieved in harmony with the common interest.

And so, it was unfortunate that when the homebuilding was delayed and families unhappily remained for months in overcrowded communal apartment buildings, a rumor made the rounds in nearby towns—where suspicion of radicals ran high—that these socialists were sharing not just their labor and their dining tables but also their beds. This "free love" accusation was born of ignorance, yet it stuck to the colonists like pitch on a pine.

The colonists couldn't shake the gossip, but they hoped to at least disabuse skeptical neighbors of the other popular notion about socialists—that they were bomb-throwing anarchists and traitors. In fact, these radicals were peaceful and loyal. Violence had no place in their vision of a socialist future, although it eventually intruded with a vengeance. They had in mind a gentle revolution that would flow logically from the power of their example.

As strange as the Equality project seemed then and may appear now, it wasn't cooked up by crackpots around a campfire. This was not a foreign plot, an anarchist scheme, a cult, or a criminal enterprise. It certainly was not a seditious conspiracy like the January 6, 2021, assault on the United States Capitol by right-wing extremists trying to overturn the result of a presidential election.[9]

Equality was a lawful, though poorly executed, attempt at peaceful revolution by earnest Americans backed by a truly national organization, albeit one that proved to be less capable, less unified, and far more fragile than its founders had expected. If the Equality colonists were guilty of anything, it was naivety, bad timing, and poor judgment. They could be faulted, too, for unwarranted optimism, as their own newspaper once acknowledged.

"To them the sun is always shining, and the rain is not even damp," it declared with pride one year into the project. The colonists, it said, were "some of the most optimistic souls on earth."[10]

Optimism would not get them far. It could not substitute for a workable plan to implement their ideas and advance their cause. They lacked consensus but not confidence. As one early arrival put it, every Equality member knew for certain that his or her approach was the only correct one. Said another, "As socialists, most of us were 'pulled before we were ripe.' We thought we had reduced socialism to a science before we had mastered the alphabet thereof."[11] This left abundant room for false starts, friction, and what might best be called fantasies.

One of Equality's original leaders imagined it as "Shangri-La"—a remote, idyllic hideaway. To another it was "an embryo garden of Eden" in a fertile landscape with potential to "equal the far-famed valley of the Nile." Yet another saw Equality as a revolutionary pathway to a "higher civilization." Critics saw it in starker terms. One in hindsight called it "Satan's nest," and another, a "nest of socialist crime." For yet another, only slightly less alarmist, the colony was a "grand visionary farce."[12]

Doubters had their reasons. The very idea of ditching free enterprise to create a radically new economic system from scratch seemed outlandish, even disloyal. And yet, in the last years of the 19th century, a small but not insignificant number of ordinary Americans were ready to reconsider whether the capitalist way was the right way—and if it was, whether it was too flawed to fix. As one man in rural Washington state put it during the economic depression of the mid-1890s—the worst in American history to that point— "It is hard to get a dollar here, but these are the times that make men think."[13]

Most Equality leaders thought it was time to end, not just reform, capitalism. They envisioned a more humane system, one that at least ensured a job for every able-bodied adult, one that gave every willing worker a chance to pay his way. Central to their diagnosis of what ailed the United States was a belief that 19th century capitalism in its largely unconstrained form was wrong because it was unjust, even ungodly. Tinkering at the edges would not do.

If revolution was the intended destination, however, no one at Equality was quite sure how to get there. There was no road map or signpost, there was only a starting point—Washington. Details would be worked out as they went along, but the basic idea was that a networked economy based on collectively owned and cooperatively managed industries and farms would replace traditional economic competition. Washington's natural resources—arable land, navigable waters, and abundant seafood, timber, and minerals—would be shared to benefit all.

The organization that gave birth to Equality was the Brotherhood of the Cooperative Commonwealth—the Brotherhood, or BCC, for short. The founder, Norman W. Lermond, believed it essential that the Brotherhood establish socialism in one state at a time rather than spread resources over an entire region. He expressed his strategy in military terms, harkening to an earlier revolution. "As Washington, when he drove [British Gen. Sir William] Howe out of Boston harbor, concentrated his troops on one hill, so we must concentrate our forces in one state and drive out the enemy—competition," he wrote in 1896.[14] Lermond knew history, but time would show that he lacked an understanding that effective leaders, whether in war or in civic affairs, must build a kind of intimacy with those in their charge.

Success on the socialist front would breed more success, Lermond figured. The domino effect would do the rest. One state after another would fall to socialism, peacefully converting the entire country. Democracy would not just be preserved; it would be perfected. A stressed-out society would find relief. Gone would be the festering discontent and the indignity of unemployment. Gone, finally, the curse of poverty.

This was an illusion. What was real and vivid was the disappointment with capitalism that weighed on many people of meager means and fragile hopes in the 1890s. For some, like Lermond, this was largely a philosophical struggle, a moral issue. For others, like many who answered his call to colonize on Samish Bay, the seemingly failed economic system was a threat to their very existence, or at least to their dignity and sense of self-worth.

By the time Equality took root, a growing minority of Americans were rethinking two bedrock tenets of capitalism.

First: free enterprise should be granted unlimited scope—in other words, business and industry should be allowed to do almost anything that fattened profits, unrestrained by government regulation and certainly not required to answer to organized labor. Second: government should play no role in managing the economy. The "invisible hand" of self-interest and natural competitive instinct, as described by Adam Smith in the 18th century, would guide and align the forces of supply and demand.

Only recently, in 1887, Congress had created the first small crack in those foundational beliefs by applying the Constitution's commerce clause to regulate interstate railroad rates—a first step toward addressing the problem of railroad monopolies. For years, rail barons had opposed federal rate controls. Put another way, the so-called champions of free enterprise wanted to preserve their freedom to kill off competition by manipulating rates—a hypocrisy not lost on socialists and other advocates of public ownership of railroads.

Bigger efforts to constrain capitalism would emerge during the Progressive era, from roughly 1900 to the First World War, building on ideas that late-19th century radicals like Lermond and Boomer promoted with little success. This emergence of progressive reform marked a fundamental departure, a change in governing philosophy whose benefits and limits are still debated in the 21st century. To what extent, for example, should government regulate land use? Impose rules on workplace and motor vehicle safety? Set and enforce public health, educational and environmental standards? Govern access to abortion services? Put limits on child labor? Set a minimum wage? Control gun ownership?

At what point does the hand of government become too heavy?

These are questions for a debate that in the 2020s is often

dominated by people who condemn government activism as devilish socialism, a bugaboo to be feared at every turn, to be equated with disloyalty. That attitude sells easily in a political marketplace filled with impulse buyers conditioned to regard socialism as a dirty word and social welfare as social weakness.

Socialism gained a bit of traction, temporarily, as attitudes toward work evolved in the late 19th century, a period when people increasingly found themselves in the kinds of jobs where the only future they saw was growing old—on the factory floor, in the coal mine, at the slaughterhouse—with little or no promise of economic security. Even farmers—the salt of the earth and providers of the nation's daily bread—were questioning the morality of unconstrained capitalism. Common sense, if not desperation, told them there must be a better way.

In Kansas, the epicenter of farmer discontent, the worry could be heard at the State Agricultural College (now Kansas State University), where a faction of the board of regents wrote in the fall of 1894 that the true culprit was the economic system, not the farmer.

"He has produced enough of the useful and necessary things of life that with fair equitable exchange would bring prosperity in place of poverty, comfort in place of humiliating drudgery, and content and patriotism in place of unrest and dissatisfaction," they wrote.[15]

Farmers' Alliance, a Nebraska newspaper that amplified agrarian anger, took it a step further: "The simple fact that, despite a generation of hard toil, the people are poor today, mortgage-ridden and distressed, is sufficient evidence that the whole system under which they have lived is a lie and an imposture."[16] It lamented a "cruelly unjust system" moving the country toward the day when there would be no viable middle class, only the very rich and the very poor.

George Boomer, the rabble rouser from Maine, made the same argument, in his typically provocative way: "I do see and announce," he told striking textile weavers in Providence in 1893, "a time when nearly all capital will be in the hands of the few, and the many, the working people, will arise in their frenzy and their suffering and level [demolish] existing institutions." It was during this speech that he warned that labor and industry already were in a death struggle.

"It is war to the knife," he said, "and the strongest man will win."[17]

Setting aside his apocalyptic bluster, Boomer was right to worry about wealth inequality in America at a time when its true dimensions were only beginning to come into focus. He was right, also, to suggest the disparity would grow. The rich-poor gap widened throughout the second half of the 19th century and into the early 1900s. It did not reverse course (and then only temporarily) until the period of major shocks—the First World War, the Great Depression and the Second World War—and the introduction of progressive policies like an income tax structure in which rates rise as incomes rise, as well as estate and inheritance taxes.

Inequality of wealth and income confounded many Americans of Boomer's era, but to Henry Demarest Lloyd, an acclaimed journalist, author, and social activist who gave Equality a small assist at its birth, it boiled down to this: "The millions produce wealth; only the tens have it."[18] The problem, in other words, was not wealth. The problem was its concentration.

Lermond, the founder of Equality, made the wealth gap the centerpiece of his argument against capitalism. In his view, this disparity was a product of a dog-eat-dog society that ought to be transformed to "a new and diviner system of civilization."[19] As his language suggests, he believed this with an almost religious fervor.

Socialists for years had decried wealth inequality, but the complaint was based more on observation than calculation. It wasn't until the 1890s that national survey data became detailed enough to begin to illustrate the gap. The man who first crunched the numbers and made them public was an obscure government economist and statistician, George K. Holmes. His work provided the first detailed evidence that the wealth gap was more than a socialist talking point. Writing in *Political Science Quarterly* in 1893,[20] Holmes extrapolated from sample data in the 1890 federal census to calculate that 71 percent of national wealth was owned by 9 percent of America's families. (A remarkably similar wealth gap persists today. In 2022, the latest reading by the nonpartisan Congressional Budget Office, the share of wealth in the top 10 percent of families stood at 69 percent.) By Holmes's reckoning, fully 20 percent of wealth in 1890 was held by just 3,800 of the nation's 12.7 million families.

Holmes arrived at his numbers by analyzing a first-of-its-kind set of Census Bureau data on home and farm ownership and mortgages. The findings surprised him. He hadn't realized the distance that had developed between the country's wealth winners and its also-rans. His commentary on this was telling; it reflected a tendency among many Americans—in those days and today—to admire the rich and doubt the rest. "It is probable," he wrote, "that the concentration of wealth has gone too far," but this was inevitable. It had reached this stage, he wrote, largely because of "defects of human nature" among the less able, and the resulting poverty was simply "a penalty of shiftlessness, improvidence" and laziness among the masses. As he saw it, the poor got what they deserved—very little besides hardship. "A large element of the population [is] unfitted to save or to earn much, and unqualified to use and keep considerable wealth," he wrote. And yet he worried that this trend toward wealth concentration was irreversible without more progressive tax policies.

Economic inequality never produced Boomer's predicted "frenzy," let alone a serious threat of violent revolution, but it remains a stark feature of American society in which the bottom 50 percent of households own just one percent of national wealth.[21] It draws millions of voters to Democratic presidential candidates who argue—as did socialists and populists in the 1890s—that the economic system is unfairly skewed against working people and that corporate giants, billionaires, and the titans of Wall Street wield too much power.

In the 1890s, the feeling of being left behind in an unfair race to riches was motivation for movements like Lermond's to defy convention and to explore new pathways to equality. It was after all, a breakaway decade. As one Lermond associate put it, "The '90s were quite irreverent to mere tradition, mere custom, mere formality, mere deportment."[22] A California school teacher said the very idea of creating an Equality colony "made me wish to shake off the dust of worn-out customs, conventionalities and opinions and cast in my lot with the pioneers of the new civilization."[23]

What the *Farmers' Alliance* called a divide between the millionaires and the masses soon came into sharper relief. In 1893 the country suffered a bank panic, followed by a severe and prolonged economic depression. More than 150 railroad companies went bankrupt, banks called in loans and collapsed by the hundreds, the flow of credit dried to a trickle, and investors panicked. Businesses failed daily. A farm crisis deepened. An absence of reliable statistics makes it hard to know how many people were out of work, but the unemployment rate may have hit 20 percent in 1894. In retrospect, this was not an isolated setback but rather a culmination of what economists have called a "long-wave depression" that began with the bank panic of 1873 and did not fully resolve itself until about 1900.

The American economic system—capitalism itself—seemed to be teetering. Might it fall?

Millions gave up on Democrats and Republicans. An attempt to force change at the ballot box by promoting a third national political party, the People's Party, whose members were commonly called populists, gained momentum in the early 1890s but failed utterly in the 1896 election; Republican William McKinley easily defeated William Jennings Bryan, the Democratic candidate endorsed by populists. The People's Party never recovered.

Sensing opportunity, progressives of a more radical bent pointed to a new possibility, one that might achieve lasting change where populism had failed. The time seemed right to show what socialism could do.

It was put-up-or-shut-up time.

Chapter 3

A Bug Man And His Big Idea

The road to Equality colony began about as far from Puget Sound as you can get without leaving the continental United States. It started, figuratively and literally, in coastal Maine, where the big idea germinated and its cultivators set forth on a late-winter day to bring it to full flower.

The Maine-Washington connection was a quirk of history, although it so happens that the Pine Tree State and the Evergreen State have more in common than bountiful forests. Both have long been havens for free thinkers and unconventional ideas, which in Washington's case has meant attracting a stream of innovators and its share of oddballs.

Pointing the way to Washington was an imaginative socialist from mid-coast Maine, Norman W. Lermond. If not an oddball, he certainly was a free spirit. He was an ecologist long before the term gained popular usage in the United States in the 20th century; he was a tree planter and conservator, a tender of gardens, and a collector of seashells and bird eggs.[1]

Like a striking number of others who veered from the main

currents of life to pursue the socialist cause in the late 19th century, Lermond came from a family rooted in classic American values. There was nothing radical about his parents. He acquired his unconventional views on his own. He was a visionary, but he sometimes failed to see that success depended on connecting his big ideas to little details—a trait that would prove his undoing.

Judging from his writings, the most intimate of which became public in 2004, long after his death, Lermond was led to socialism by instinct and inquisitiveness. Curiosity turned to conviction when he became smitten with a utopian novel that tickled his imagination and prompted him to question his assumption that the dark side of capitalism was an unstoppable force. The book convinced him that poverty and other social ills could be minimized—maybe even eliminated—in an economy based on collective rather than private ownership.

Political philosophy shaped but did not define Lermond. Above all else, above even socialism, Lermond cared about nature—birds, plants, insects and more. He was a self-taught naturalist with an almost unnatural fascination with wildlife. As a two-year-old, he was found gripping a live snake between his tiny teeth, substituting for his rubber pacifier. Late in life, he immodestly compared himself to John Burroughs, one of the great naturalists of the late 19th and early 20th centuries, with whom he shared not just a love of nature but deep doubts about organized religion. The two even looked alike in long, white beards. Lermond was fond of saying that some called him "The John Burroughs of Maine."

Lermond developed a lifelong interest in malacology—the study of snails, mussels, and other mollusks, of which mid-coast Maine has an abundance. He also traveled to Florida to hunt and collect liguus (tree snails) in the Everglades, and on Florida's Gulf Coast he discovered a species of bivalve seashell that was officially named for him —the Caecum lermondi.

From his devotion to this hobby would emerge Lermond's most successful brainchild and his most enduring legacy—the American Malacological Union (now the American Malacological Society), created in 1931 to promote the study of mollusks. By one account, he conceived and developed the idea with a colleague over a series of chop suey dinners at a restaurant near Harvard Square in Cambridge, Massachusetts. It was fitting, then, that when his autobiography, which was unfinished when he died in 1944, turned up more than fifty years later its discoverer was a malacologist thumbing through archives of the Department of Mollusks at Harvard's Museum of Comparative Zoology.

Lermond's love of the natural world led him to believe that he had a special understanding of human nature, too. "Man is made what he is by his environment," he wrote in 1896. Thus, in his view, a social system built on faith in cutthroat capitalism drives men to "trample one another under foot" and reduces them to "the lower order of animal life." He did not share the widely held belief that economic competition is the essential fuel that powers innovation and enables prosperity. He believed a truly civilized and productive society was possible only if predatory capitalism were replaced by humane socialism.

Among radicals who shared this view—that capitalism was built on un-Christian selfishness—was George D. Herron, a Congregationalist pastor and messianic socialist who earned a flash of fame in 1890 for a radical sermon, "The Message of Jesus to Men of Wealth," in which he declared, "A civilization based on self-interest and securing itself through competition has no power within itself to secure justice."[2] Such a society, he warned, is built on a foundation more dangerous than dynamite. Herron was a leading voice in the Social Gospel movement, which sought to apply Christian ethics to social problems, advocating for economic justice as a moral imperative. Herron did not join Lermond's Brotherhood but became an honorary member. In a thank-you note written from Grinnell, Iowa, where he was chairman of the Department of Applied Christianity at Iowa College (now Grinnell College), Herron told Lermond: "I am in deepest sympathy with the ends to which you are struggling, and with the heroic efforts you are making."[3]

Norman Wallace Lermond was born July 27, 1861, in a house that predated the Revolutionary War and stood on a farm near the neighboring towns of Warren and Thomaston in Knox County, Maine, at the confluence of the St. George and Oyster rivers. During his schoolboy years, he lived in Boston and in Hartford, Connecticut, later returning to Maine, where his old-stock American roots reached back to colonial times. His father, Omar W. Lermond, was a farmer and seasonal shipyard worker whose father, David Lermond, fought in the War of 1812. Omar's great-grandfather, Alexander Lermond, came to New England with his parents from Londonderry, Ireland, in 1719. They were among Scottish families who migrated to the north of Ireland in the 1600s; those who subsequently came to the United States are often called Scotch-Irish.

The Lermonds settled first in the Massachusetts Bay Colony, at Milton, with other Scotch-Irish immigrant families. In 1736 they moved to Maine, which was a district of Massachusetts and would remain so until it gained statehood in 1820. During the Revolutionary War, the Lermonds helped found the township of Warren, whose boundaries include a village of the same name as well as the Lermond family farm. The name was a tribute to Dr. Joseph Warren of Boston, a leader of colonial resistance to British rule and the man who summoned Paul Revere for his midnight ride to Lexington in 1775; Warren was killed two months later in the battle for Bunker Hill.

Norman Lermond's mother, Rebecca, was born in Scotland and immigrated to the United States in 1854.

In his autobiography, Lermond highlighted the fact that he was born just days after the first major land battle of the Civil War, at Bull Run in northern Virginia. He didn't mention it, but his hometown was hardly a hotbed of enthusiasm for fighting the southern rebels. Of seventy-two men drafted from Warren in 1863, only one served. Some found willing substitutes; others were exempted for disabilities and for other legitimate reasons. Twenty-four of the seventy-two draftees, including Lermond's father, Omar, paid a $300 "commutation" fee to avoid service, according to a Warren town history published in 1877.[4]

Without mentioning his father's views on the war, Norman Lermond hinted in his autobiography that Omar had opposed it. When the boys at grammar school played a game of pretend politics, each acted as a "second edition" of his father, and little Norman was counted among the "Copperhead" Democrats—the party's anti-war faction.

Norman never served in uniform. The Civil War was long over when he came of age; the war against Spain began while he was in Washington state and ended shortly after he returned to Maine. Nor did he ever marry; his two great loves were Mother Nature and socialism.

By his own account, Lermond had an almost idyllic childhood. It revolved around bugs and books, to which he was drawn like a bee to a blossom. He spent much of his youth in the Roxbury section of Boston, where he was exposed to literary achievers and notable social reformers whose influence on his thinking can only be imagined. "One day," he recalled of his grammar school years, "I was examining the flower of a horse chestnut tree when who should come along and stop to examine the flower but Rev. Edward Everett Hale." Hale, who lived near the Lermonds, was author of "The Man Without a Country," the classic short story with a Civil War-era message about the importance of loyalty to country.

Lermond also spent two years at a boys' boarding school in Hartford, Connecticut, run by John Stevens Cabot Abbott, a minister and Bowdoin College classmate of Nathanial Hawthorne. Lermond recalled him reading to the boys from Harriet Beecher Stowe's abolitionist novel, *Uncle Tom's Cabin*; she happened to live in Hartford at the time. Lermond also remembered visits by Abbott's nephew, Lyman Abbott, a liberal Roxbury theologian and Social Gospel advocate who edited Christian journals on social and industrial reform. In important ways, Lyman Abbott's views became Lermond's, particularly regarding the dangers of corporate power, which Abbott believed had dangerously weakened American democracy.

Lermond was nine when his parents moved the family from Maine to Boston in 1870 to run a boarding house on Centre Street, not far from Roxbury's historic John Eliot Square. In his early teens, after returning home from Hartford, Lermond joined a neighborhood debate club and became a frequenter of the city library, where he recalled borrowing "book after book, mostly on natural history and philosophy." These experiences nurtured his belief that knowledge, like nature, should be accessible to all. This idea would help shape his utopian dream.

Bugs, too, were often on his mind. At Boston's English

High School, he spent a full year writing an essay on aphids and other gall insects, with accompanying drawings and specimens. It won first place in a contest sponsored by Harvard University. He spent his prize money on a canoeing and camping trip with friends down the Concord River to Concord and Walden Pond. At Concord the boys visited an elderly Ralph Waldo Emerson, the poet and essayist. "All his talk was about Thoreau," Lermond recalled of their conversation, referring to Henry David Thoreau, the naturalist and transcendentalist.

After high school, Lermond got his first job at the Bartlett second-hand bookstore on Boston's Cornhill, a 19th century mecca for the city's literary crowd. Later he worked as an office boy, writer and ad salesman for the *Boston Telegram*, a monthly trade journal for telegraph operators, and then as an accountant for a railroad. The work-a-day world, however, was never a good fit. Lermond's realm was philosophy, grounded in his love of nature and energized by his dream of improving the human condition.

In his unfinished autobiography, Lermond recounted his boyhood and young adult years in great detail but, strikingly, made no mention of a series of life-altering tragedies. He was a teenager in Roxbury when tuberculosis, a common killer in his day, invaded the Lermond home on Dorr Street and took three family members in three successive years—an 18-year-old sister, then a 21-year-old brother, and then their mother, Rebecca, forty-four. And there was more. Four years later his father, Omar, drowned, apparently by suicide.

The elder Lermond had moved back to Maine about two years after his wife died, leaving Norman in Roxbury. While employed as a mechanic at a fish cannery in Port Clyde, Omar disappeared without a trace one summer night in 1884.[5] He had slipped away in a rowboat, alone and unnoticed in the darkness enveloping Port Clyde's quiet harbor. Six weeks later his body was found a couple of miles north, floating in the waters off St. George peninsula. A rope was found tied around the decomposing body, with evidence that the other end had been attached to a rock that pulled him to a watery grave.

These personal losses may have left the 23-year-old Norman searching for a vision of a better world.

Less than a year after losing his father, Lermond returned to Maine to take up farming on the original family estate, which his forebears had named *The Willows* for the famously flexible trees they planted along the property boundary. It was here, ten years later, that he conceived of the Brotherhood of the Cooperative Commonwealth. With strong leadership, he wrote, it was destined to "lead us out of the wilderness." The agenda was simple: advance the cause of socialism by educating the masses while also establishing colonies in a single state to demonstrate socialism's practical value. This was a departure from the socialists' usual approach of focusing on electoral politics as the path to power. Lermond didn't ignore politics, but he believed that electoral success would come only after the average voter had seen socialism's real-life merits.

If a single event ignited Lermond's enthusiasm for socialism, it may have been an encounter with a family friend in 1890 at *The Willows*. The friend was visiting from Boston and told Lermond of the city's burst of excitement over Edward Bellamy's new novel, *Looking Backward: 2000-1887*. Bellamy foresaw an American Utopia in which there was no economic competition and thus no cycle of boom and bust, no unemployment and thus no poverty, no global rivalry for resources and thus no war. In this imagined 21st century egalitarian paradise, greed and class distinctions disappeared. Gone was the age when "money alone commanded all that was agreeable," as Bellamy put it. The material world had transformed to a humane, peaceful world.

"(It) appealed to my imagination and aroused my interest," Lermond wrote. His aunt's friend later sent him a paperback copy, and he read it in one sitting. Then he read it twice more, "so extremely fascinating was the subject."[6]

"Bellamy's blueprint of a new and very different civilization, and economic, social, and political system and government, opened for me a whole new world," he wrote.[7]

Lermond became a socialist, and the book became a sensation. It was the biggest seller of its time. This was a surprise even to Bellamy, who previously had labored in obscurity as a newspaper writer. The suddenness of his fame was captured in a comment two years later by Frances E. Willard, national president of the Woman's Christian Temperance Union. She recalled that after reading *Looking Backward*, she wrote to the book's publisher to ask "who, when and where this Edward Bellamy might be."[8] The response: "We do not know, except that his letters are mailed from Chicopee Falls, Mass."

Bellamy, who wrote *Looking Backward* from his hometown (now the city of Chicopee) in western Massachusetts, said a few years after publication that he initially imagined the story as a literary fantasy— "a fairy tale of social felicity"[9]—not a roadmap to revolution. As he progressed in the writing, however, he came to believe that he had stumbled upon a formula for a new social order in which the government absorbed all private enterprise and consolidated it into one giant trust, operated for the shared benefit of all. He thought of this not as socialism, which seemed to him a vague term suggestive of undue foreign influence, but rather as "nationalism," since its central mechanism was the nationalization of industries. He imagined not a sudden and violently explosive revolution but a phased, peaceful transition from unconstrained capitalism to an egalitarian utopia.

With its emphasis on civility, harmony and equality, *Looking Backward* struck a chord in readers from coast to coast and around the world. Bellamy clubs, and then Nationalist clubs, sprang up across the United States to propagate the novel's ideas and in some cases to translate them into political action. Naturally, the infatuation was not universal. It drew criticism from both ends of the political spectrum. On the left, Percy Daniels, a Kansas farmer who would be elected lieutenant governor in the populist wave of 1892, wrote that Bellamy's utopia was pie in the sky and irrelevant to his generation. "There is no road to his paradise," Daniels wrote.[10] "It is beyond our reach." From the right came William T. Harris, a former superintendent of St. Louis public schools whose philosophy of education and freedom was highly influential in this period. In 1889, while serving as United States commissioner of education, Harris wrote a critique of *Looking Backward* in which he likened Bellamy's plan for cleansing society of its economic ills to throwing the baby out with the bathwater. In disposing of what Harris called the "incidental evils" of free enterprise, Bellamy would also expel a more essential item —the right to private property. This would prove more repressive, Harris argued, than the worst examples of despotism.[11]

When Lermond undertook to make a reality of Bellamy's imagined utopia by establishing the first in a network of socialist colonies, he didn't realize that he and his collaborators were imitating Bellamy's book title. They were looking backward, trying to build on the foundation of an idea that by the close of the 19th century had outlived its appeal.

Colonizing as a means of proving socialism's potential had a certain logic but was out of sync with the times. The political climate was shifting as the United States approached a new century and became an expansionist power with its defeat of Spain in the Caribbean and in the western Pacific in 1898, and its annexation that year of Hawaii and acquisition of the Philippines, Guam and Puerto Rico. The very idea of domestic colonies and other separate societies had become passé. As one newspaper put it in 1899, "America is too cosmopolitan a country to be the home of 'colonies' of any nature."[12]

Bellamy himself recognized the evolving political environment. In *Equality*, his sequel to *Looking Backward*, he made clear his view that a successful transition from capitalism to socialism, or nationalism, was not possible if it depended on the creation of a network of cooperative colonies. He seemed to foresee Lermond's Equality experience. Many "noble and enthusiastic souls" stumbled down the colonization road with the best intentions, Bellamy wrote, but it was a dead end.

"Economically weak, held together by a sentimental motive, generally composed of eccentric though worthy persons, and surrounded by a hostile environment which had the whole use and advantage of the social and economic machinery, it was scarcely possible that such enterprises should come to anything practical unless under exceptional leadership or circumstances," he wrote in *Equality,* which he completed in the summer of 1897, just weeks before Lermond launched his colony project and one year before Bellamy succumbed to the tuberculosis that had tortured him for years.

Lermond's thinking was stuck in the 1880's and early 1890s when the traditional political parties seemed incapable of reviving hope among a dispirited working class. In 1891 he had been a founding member of the People's Party of Maine, considered radical but not socialist. A year later he welcomed the birth of a national People's Party, which favored government ownership of railroads but not the complete nationalization of industry. His enthusiasm for populism did not last, however. To his dismay, the 1896 People's Party presidential nominating convention in St. Louis endorsed the Democrats' candidate, William Jennings Bryan, rather than nominate its own. Lermond, who attended as a member of the Maine delegation, saw this as a death blow to the People's Party. He was not wrong. "I returned to Maine disgusted, a disillusioned but a wiser man," he wrote.[13]

The populists' Bryan endorsement was not the only reason Lermond left St. Louis in a foul mood. He had failed in a more personal way. He and other socialists met there for a "national cooperative congress," held separately but in parallel with the People's Party convention. Lermond wanted to present a blueprint for building his Brotherhood of the Cooperative Commonwealth, or BCC, as the unifier of a fragmented socialist movement. He figured that pitching his idea in St. Louis on the same weekend as the populists' convention would yield a splashy, public embrace. He was wrong.

The populists became consumed by a contentious and protracted nomination battle, and because he was a populist delegate, Lermond, too, was distracted. There would be no endorsement of his brainchild. The Brotherhood's arrival on the national scene would have to wait.

Lermond thought he had prepared the groundwork for St. Louis by road-testing ideas for unifying the socialist movement. In 1895, he wrote to *Twentieth Century,* a socialist magazine in New York, to promote the possibility of "unifying all social reformers into a brotherhood or association to the end that in union we might gain strength and hasten the dawn of the new day." This solidarity, Lermond seemed certain, would "give to the world an object lesson and prove by practice that our theories are correct and practicable." The editors of *Twentieth Century* were not impressed. They especially objected to

Lermond's claim that an organization of such grand ambition could succeed based entirely on voluntary donations. "Sentiment alone will not suffice," they advised Lermond.[14]

"We hope to present to our readers at a not distant day a much more practical plan than this of Mr. Lermond," they wrote.

Practical or not, Lermond pressed on. He set up a small BCC office near his home in October 1895, but the Brotherhood existed only on paper for many months until he widened his circle of support through a letter-writing campaign. Soon he began to believe he could transform his local group into a national organization with revolutionary aims. "The country must be stirred from center to circumference," he wrote.[15] Once a first state was colonized for socialism, he added, "the example thus set would be contagious, and neighboring states would not be slow to follow in the same road."

In his account of American radicalism during this period, Howard H. Quint called Lermond a "letter-writing dynamo" who bombarded prominent reformers with appeals for help.[16] A frequent target was Henry Demarest Lloyd, the newspaper journalist and social reformer who denounced monopolists as "corporate Caesars"—merciless tyrants. Playing up the anti-monopolist theme, Lermond stressed to Lloyd the logic of bringing socialists together in a network of BCC colonies in a single state. Spread too thinly, they would be at the mercy of monopolists, "who, whenever they sense the danger, will crush these colonies like so many eggshells," he told Lloyd in April 1896.[17]

Lloyd didn't put much stock in colonizing or in Lermond's one-state-at-a-time strategy. In an earlier exchange with a Lermond colleague, Lloyd had predicted that monied interests would stop at nothing to destroy the Brotherhood.

Despite his doubts, Lloyd expressed sympathy with

Lermond's hopes and donated a modest amount of seed money. But he turned away pleas for bigger donations and declined Lermond's request that he serve as the BCC's first president. Lermond was openly disappointed. "What shall we do," he wrote to Lloyd at the journalist's home in Winnetka, Illinois, north of Chicago, "if all our prominent leaders decline to serve? This move never can be made a success unless we have men at the head in whom the people have full confidence."[18] Clearly, Lermond knew star power was essential for his Brotherhood's success.

This helps explain why the lost opportunity in St. Louis was so troubling. On the plus side, Lermond used his time there to good advantage in other ways. He met with a Tennessee delegate, Alfred S. Edwards, who was editor of a widely read socialist weekly, *The Coming Nation.* Edwards agreed to give Lermond space to publicize his ideas. Also in St. Louis were Charles F. Taylor, a Pennsylvania populist delegate and Philadelphia orthopedic surgeon who soon became the Brotherhood's first treasurer, and Morrison I. Swift, a California socialist agitator, editor, and pamphleteer who served briefly as chief national recruiter. Swift shared Lermond's view that capitalism, stripped of its well-dressed charms, was nothing more than organized robbery. In a matter of months, however, Swift gave up, convinced that the Brotherhood was an exercise in escapism, doomed to die in the political wilderness. He accurately foresaw the disillusionment that would erode and eventually destroy Equality's community spirit. "When the first unthinking enthusiasm subsides, the contributors will begin to demand results, which the colony organizers will be unable to show," he wrote.[19]

St. Louis likely was where Lermond met Helen M. Mason, a local reformer who was active in a St. Louis branch of the Woman's Christian Temperance Union, the leading voice in a national movement to prohibit alcohol use. She would soon become an important Lermond ally and go on to play a central, even heroic, role at Equality in its formative first year.

Lermond used the columns of *The Coming Nation* to spell out his philosophy and his hopes for the Brotherhood.

"A change, sooner or later, must come; a change that forever will banish the chaotic competitive system and usher in the millennium, when the love of money shall be changed to love of right, of justice and of our fellow man," he wrote.[20] "The competitive system drives men to trample one another under foot. It is essentially beastly in its nature."

In late summer, he offered more specifics: "We must own and operate coal mines, oil wells, electric plants, sugar refineries, shoe shops, cotton and woolen mills, iron mines, foundries and mills," and more, with efforts concentrated in "one section of the country."[21] He did not mention Washington. "Almost any state west of the Mississippi or south of Ohio" would do nicely, he said. "The results could not fail to astonish the most enthusiastic socialist dreamer."

Notably, Lermond in his writings rarely mentioned "equality," though it formed the philosophical backdrop of his Brotherhood and became the name of its first colony. Lermond's rhetorical focus was on economic failings and injustices—the economic *inequalities* of his day—rather than on the more positive, if elusive, idea of achieving economic and social equality.

Lermond quickly attracted hundreds of like-minded socialists, but he wildly overestimated the level of interest among the broader public. He figured at least 100,000 people would heed the BCC's call to join its network of socialist colonies, and perhaps another 400,000 "stay-at-home" supporters would contribute a portion of their earnings to sustain their pioneer brothers and sisters. With each member chipping in $100, a network of colonies in a single state could be capitalized at $10 million—plenty, he believed, to buy land, machinery, mines, tools "and everything necessary to establish industrial plants for the production of all wealth needed by a highly civilized and progressive people." Even a base of 10,000 socialists instead of 100,000, would do the trick, he figured. His math may have been credible, but his optimism was not. In the churn of people coming and going at Equality during its ten-year lifespan, the total number may have topped 1,000, but at any given time the resident population never exceeded 340. Even the "reserves"—those non-residents who were dues-paying BCC members—never topped 4,000.[22]

Lermond persisted. A proposed BCC constitution was published in *The Coming Nation* in August, and the following month it won ratification in a mail-in vote among members. The BCC was now in business. The constitution said the Brotherhood welcomed into its ranks "any person of good moral character" who agreed that a socialist system "offers the only solution to present chaotic conditions." In addition to pledging one's word and honor to this cause, the only other obligation of membership was monthly dues of ten cents.

By October, Lermond was calling himself the provisional national secretary of the BCC. He had a treasurer but hardly needed one. A financial statement listed cash holdings of $32.27, of which Lloyd donated nearly a third. Lermond used most of the money on postage, printing and related promotional efforts. To his credit, over the course of 1896 he managed to gather the rhetorical if not financial support of moderate socialists across the country. Among them was the Rev. Myron W. Reed, a Denver preacher, Christian Socialist, and associate of Edward Bellamy.[23] Reed agreed to serve as the Brotherhood's figurehead president, even though he thought the colonizing should begin in Utah, where he believed the Mormons would be helpful, instead of Washington, where "the climate is not over-desirable."

Also on board was another Bellamy acquaintance, Frank Parsons, a well-known Boston lawyer, academician, and author who argued for a wide range of liberal economic and political reforms. He had exchanged letters with Bellamy in 1896 to arrange the author's appearance at the St. Louis "cooperative congress," an event for which Bellamy had little enthusiasm; in his letter he referred to it as "your circus."[24]

Parsons signed on to the BCC board of directors as "dean" of its education and publicity program. He was an example of a socialist who admired Lermond's initiative but gave the colony plan a weak embrace. In Boston he was consumed by what seemed like more urgent work with other social and economic reform groups and with his teaching. Parsons offered the BCC his name's drawing power, but not much else. He never set foot on the Equality site.

In 1897, the year Lermond sent a surrogate to Washington to start the colony, Parsons began splitting his time between Boston University, where he was a law school lecturer, and Manhattan, Kansas, where he taught history and political science at the State Agricultural College. There he became entangled in a fight for academic freedom that showed the strength of his convictions.[25] In 1899, Parsons and several other faculty members, plus the college president, were fired for daring to expose students to ideas like populism and socialism, alongside capitalism. The Republican-dominated board of regents deemed this a "perversion of the college." In other words, Parsons and the others had defied political correctness by embracing the notion that higher education should offer students a chance to hear and explore a full range of ideas. Parsons explained this principle in a face-to-face meeting with the regents who were about to fire him:

> Let me tell you, gentlemen, kindly but frankly, that the movement of progressive thought in this institution cannot be stopped by any change of professors. This great body of earnest, open-minded students will go on thinking for themselves. The questions of the day will boil and surge in their literary societies, their classes, their boarding houses and their private rooms. They will read and think and speak, and the new thought will grow, and no board, no party, no power can stop it.

If timing is everything, Equality's chance of success was nearly nothing. The year of its founding coincided with two developments that captured the public's imagination, distracted many from their troubles, and undercut the appeal of Lermond's message.

The first was news of the Klondike gold strike in the Canadian Yukon, which stirred hopes of instant wealth and a quick escape from the mid-90s depression. (The discovery was made in August 1896, but word didn't spread widely in the outside world until the summer of 1897 when the first steamers bearing tons of gold and tales of fortune reached the port cities of Seattle and San Francisco on a tidal wave of publicity.) The very week that Lermond set his colonizing plan in motion in late summer 1897, a Maine newspaper that he likely read regularly carried on its front page a remarkable dispatch from Puget Sound about a blind rush to the Far North. "Nobody wants to know how to get back from Klondike or how much money will be made," it said.[26] "They all expect to get rich."

The second development was the emergence in late 1897 of faint signs of economic recovery amid efforts by the new McKinley administration to talk up the national mood and rekindle optimism. Also, political tensions with Spain over Cuba's struggle for independence pumped up American patriotism and lowered the public's tolerance for radicalism.

This convergence of events could not have been foreseen when, in early 1897, the Lermond plan began to take shape. From his headquarters in Maine he recruited staff assistants, including Helen Mason, who arrived from St. Louis on March 5. This freed him to scout sites for an initial BCC colony. He had previously thought of Colorado, Washington, California and Texas as potential hosts, but after visiting Tennessee and Arkansas, he was leaning toward Arkansas when a sudden turn of events changed his thinking.

Eugene Debs, the most recognized voice of American socialism, was causing a stir. He had led the American Railway Union until his imprisonment at Woodstock, Illinois, for defying a court injunction against the 1894 Pullman rail strike. He emerged from prison a socialist— "baptized in socialism in the roar of conflict," as he put it years later[27]—and became an advocate for building a socialist commonwealth, beginning in a Western state. With a national following far beyond what Lermond might hope to attain, Debs toured the Far West in early 1897 and proclaimed his support for beginning this socialist transformation in Washington. His intent, formalized in Chicago in June, was to do this through a new organization, the Social Democracy of America, which he would create by combining remnants of his railway union with Lermond's Brotherhood and other disaffected socialists.

Lermond traveled to Debs' home in Terre Haute, Indiana, to meet with Debs, and then to Chicago to witness the birth of the Social Democracy. In Lermond's recollection, he and Debs strode onto the stage in Chicago, arm in arm. But there would be no true synergy and no agreement to merge the two organizations. Upon returning to Maine, he and the BCC board of trustees decided to go their own way, without Debs. They declared Washington their colony target—putting the Brotherhood in direct competition with Debs. As a Seattle newspaper put it, the BCC simply "threw Eugene V. Debs overboard."[28]

By calculation or coincidence, Debs and Lermond were right to think of Washington as fertile ground for growing socialism. The state turned out to be more receptive than most to radical politics. In 1912, at the peak of the Socialist Party's national popularity, Washington had more dues-paying party members than any other Western state and the second-highest number in the nation as a percentage of its population.[29]

Debs told reporters in Chicago that upwards of 100,000 men and women could be enlisted by September to begin the migration to Washington, although nothing remotely like that happened and it's unclear whether Debs truly believed his own rhetorical flourishes.

Talk of putting an army of socialists on the march had the expected unsettling effect on mainstream America. "Fear has been expressed already," one Michigan newspaper reported, "that the mobilization of large bodies of men might result in many deeds of violence. Many have said the country would be thrown into a civil war."[30]

Fear not, said Debs. "Each colonist must be sound mentally and physically, and he must understand thoroughly what he is going out there for." He counseled patience but foresaw quick success. He was quoted in the New York *Daily Tribune* as predicting, with exaggeration designed to capture headlines, that once word of his colony project began to spread, "in twenty-four hours the state of Washington will be a socialistic community." John R. Rogers, the state's reform-minded governor, (who coincidentally was a native of Maine) now sensed political opportunity. He wrote to Debs suggesting he build his colony on semi-arid lands along the Palouse River in southeastern Washington.[31] Rogers figured that if each socialist newcomer chipped in just twenty-five cents a month the state's development budget would soon be brimming with possibilities. Not incidentally, an influx of liberal voters couldn't hurt his own political fortunes.

The Rogers idea drew immediate jeers from the state's newspapers, portending a rocky road for the socialists.

"Gov. Rogers would import into this state a drove—a saturnalia of cranks, a parliament of lunacy, a congress with a bomb in its coattail pocket and the fist of anarchy in its eye," the staunchly Republican *Whatcom Reveille* wrote. "These men would rob thrift and manacle enterprise and dance like dervishes on the ruins of any organization of law and order."[32]

The Rogers proposal went nowhere, as did Debs' idea of uniting all socialists in his Social Democracy. Like many socialist leaders of that era, Debs and Lermond were talking past each other. Debs agreed to lend his name to the BCC for recruiting purposes, but this was an empty gesture. He lost interest in colonization and abandoned his Washington project. He pivoted to national electoral politics and never looked back.[33]

Without Debs, Lermond's venture by late summer 1897 was off to a shaky start. Sensing hazards ahead, he turned to a fellow Mainer and trusted associate, Ed Pelton, to serve as his "special agent," or miracle worker, on Puget Sound.

Chapter 4

Equality is Born

Ed Pelton knew little about the Pacific Northwest but a lot about hard work. No one at Equality topped him in that department. He did a little of everything, from peeling potatoes and baking bread to digging ditches and catching every imaginable form of flak from unhappy colonists. It fell to him, also, to rustle up financial donors and to occasionally entertain the colony's dozens of children, leading them in singing games like "Drop the Handkerchief" and "Pig in the Parlor."

There was almost nothing Pelton would not do for Equality, and when his voice fell silent three years into the colony's life, its future died with him.

Born in Lincoln County, Maine, in July 1855, George Edwin "Ed" Pelton was an eighth-generation descendant of an Englishman who crossed the Atlantic in about 1630 and settled in colonial Boston.[1] Over the centuries, Pelton men were mariners, farmers, carpenters, and soldiers. Peltons had what a family historian called a "tendency to migrate to new lands and to serve their country in times of war." Ed's great-great-grandfather, Moses Pelton, was killed by the British during the Continental Army's retreat from New York City in 1776; Ed's father, George Washington Pelton, served in artillery in the Civil War, and Ed's youngest brother, Charles H. Pelton, served in Puerto Rico during the Spanish-American war and in Europe in the First World War.

Ed never joined the military, but he held true to the Pelton tradition of searching out new lands. In the 1870s, he and several family members left Maine to try their luck as loggers in Michigan and later in Minnesota. Timber companies were pushing west to the Great Lakes region in the post-Civil War period as decades of intense logging had diminished New England forests. In the early 1880s, the Peltons resettled in Todd County, in central Minnesota. Here the eastern forests meet the western prairies, and the landscape reveals hallmarks of the Ice Age—kettle lakes formed thousands of years ago by retreating glaciers. The Peltons, including Ed and three siblings, lived in Grey Eagle, a village on the Northern Pacific line, wedged between Bass and Trace lakes, about ninety miles northwest of Minneapolis.

Ed carried to Grey Eagle a ruffian's reputation. A close colleague of later years recalled that prior to discovering socialism Pelton was "a sport, wasting his precious powers in riot and revelry, associating with the low and debased." While details are incomplete more than a century later, Pelton seemed to reinforce that legend on November 25, 1885.[2]

On that fateful Thanksgiving eve, Ed and younger brother Ernest, who was twenty-five and newly married to a local woman named Lydia Anna "Annie" Walker, decided to settle a score with a Grey Eagle farmer, Jeremiah M. Woodman. Several months earlier, Woodman had accused the Pelton brothers of stealing timber from private land. The Peltons angrily denied it. The timberland was owned by an absentee speculator who had enlisted George G. Howe, a brickyard owner from the nearby town of Clarissa, to manage it. Howe in turn hired Woodman to watch for trespassers.

Once Woodman made his accusation, there was little chance the dispute would end well. Ernest Pelton confronted him beside a vacant building on a Grey Eagle street that Wednesday night in November. According to an eyewitness, Pelton demanded Woodman take back his accusation, "or I will knock the face off of you." Woodman refused. Pelton punched him in the face twice, probably not knowing Woodman had a pistol in his pocket. It was a .22-caliber seven-shot revolver.

"The flash and report of the pistol was almost simultaneous with the second blow," the local *Argus* newspaper reported in an account that portrayed Woodman as the aggrieved party.

Handwritten court transcripts of eyewitness testimony before a justice of the peace in the nearby town of Long Prairie tell the rest of the story. Pelton stepped back and said, "I am shot." Brother Ed, who heard the commotion from inside a nearby store, rushed to Ernest's side and punched and kicked Woodman before the night air crackled with another report from the pistol.

Woodman had managed to get off a second shot, this one meant for Ed.

"The bullet that was intended to kill him struck a rib just over the heart and glanced off without penetrating the body, making only a slight wound," the *Argus* reported.

Brother Ernest was not so lucky. The bullet from Woodman's first shot—a .22 Short rimfire cartridge—hit him square in the belly, nicked his gall bladder, severed his liver and intestine, and struck his spine. He died the next day, Thanksgiving. Ed was at his side and recalled his final words: "I am not sorry or afraid to die because it is in defense of my reputation."

Ed vowed to exact revenge; the newspaper reported that he

promised to kill Woodman, "if he has to follow him all over the world to do it." As it turned out, there was no payback, at least not of the violent kind. Nor was there justice—not from Ed's point of view. A county grand jury returned an indictment of second-degree murder against Woodman, but the case never went to trial. It languished for two years before the county attorney dropped it, citing insufficient evidence. What led him to that conclusion is lost to history; it is not explained in surviving court records.

The Grey Eagle tragedy surely shook Ed and may have soured him on the justice system, but it also seemed to steer his life in a tamer, more peaceful direction. He moved back to Maine, gave up drinking, married his dead brother's widow, Annie, and adopted her daughter Eva, who had been one month shy of her first birthday when her father died. Soon Ed shifted his focus to fighting for socialism, not with force but with his wounded heart, his pen, and his hope for a more just world. He was a new man. Reform zeal replaced boozy rowdiness, and he filled his days writing and talking the gospel of socialism.

FEW INVESTED as much sweat equity in Equality as Pelton. Even before the first structures went up, he gave Lermond's vision a fighting chance. Of average height at five feet, eight inches, Pelton was mustachioed with a square jaw and broad shoulders befitting his pugilist profile. He was among Lermond's earliest, most effective, and most trusted supporters, although the two eventually split over the basic question of how to govern Equality.

Pelton saw himself as a moderate socialist, not a revolutionary in the Karl Marx fold. He favored a gradual, peaceful transition away from capitalism, much like Bellamy had imagined. But as early as 1895, he saw risk in overthinking this. "Some say educate and wait, which would be excellent advice, but the enemy won't let us wait. We must act quickly or it will be too late." He disliked the very notion of class warfare, which in the eyes of some Equality comrades made him something less than a worthy socialist. William C. B. Randolph, who worked with Pelton at Equality for about a year, called him a "born non-conformist" incapable of unqualified support for any cause, including socialism. Randolph nonetheless credited Pelton with an inspiring drive to succeed. "Ed was always the first to pick up the ax or crosscut saw and lead whatever work needed most to be done, and he was the last man to quit."[3]

Pelton felt an urgency to start building the first colony, but he also cautioned against overlooking a parallel mission: to educate the Brotherhood's ideological opponents. Education, in fact, was one of the purposes stated in the BCC's constitution— "to educate the people in the principles of socialism." In Equality's second year of life, Pelton expressed the idea more colorfully: "A colony," he wrote, "is valuable in order to disabuse the minds of its neighbors of the idea that socialists are a lot of uncanny, fiendish nondescripts and half-human rapscallions and freaks."[4]

Lermond had employed Pelton on his Maine farm and had developed great faith in him— "the brainiest man in our ranks," he called him.[5] Pelton in 1895 had written a national manifesto calling on socialists to colonize one or more states, starting with California, where he believed the tide had already begun to turn in favor of "industrial cooperation."

Two years later, when Lermond had been sold on the idea of Washington as the hatchery for his plan and the BCC's organizational structure had begun to take shape, he dispatched Pelton to the Pacific Northwest as his "special agent." His instruction: buy land for the first colony and prepare to populate it. Writing later of this moment and referring to himself in third person, Pelton said he humbly accepted the assignment, "fully realizing his own unfitness owing to lack of both experience and ability." Also lacking was a realistic picture of the task ahead. Just days before heading West, Pelton told Lermond and the rest of the BCC faithful that the main reason for targeting Washington was not its great natural resources and "equable and healthful climate" but the miles it had already traveled on the road to socialism. "Already, nearly half of the voters of Washington are Socialists," he wrote in what surely was a gross exaggeration, even if the state had fairly earned a reputation for attracting radicals.[6]

On the first day of September 1897, Pelton set out from Rockland, a shipbuilding and fishing town on mid-coast Maine's West Penobscot Bay, never to return to his home state. He could not afford the cross-country train fare, so it was agreed the BCC would put him on an expense account of two dollars a day. Ever the pragmatist, he figured that "a poor agent was perhaps better than no agent."

In Washington, his first order of business was to size up a proposal to build Lermond's first colony near a logging town called Buckley, southeast of Seattle, in the shadow of Mount Rainier. A couple dozen BCC members had begun gathering there in August, ready to build as soon as a Lermond emissary gave the go-ahead. To their surprise, Pelton took one look at Buckley and turned thumbs down. The property was too pricey, too distant from water transportation, and too vulnerable to what he called capitalist "extortions" by the Northern Pacific Railway, which had made Buckley a regional hub in the 1880s and named the town for one of its superintendents, James M. Buckley.

In his own telling,[7] Pelton decided to venture north for

seventy miles or so to Skagit County on the upper Puget Sound. Lermond had mentioned the possibility of buying a Skagit sawmill that had been scouted by local socialists, but he failed to persuade Henry Demarest Lloyd to front the required $1,500, so prospects for colonizing there appeared dim. Nonetheless, Pelton traveled by steamboat on September 16 from Seattle to La Conner, a little port on the Swinomish Slough separating Fidalgo Island from the mainland. From there he walked the final fifteen miles to the village of Edison. He recalled passing "through a rough country, along the waterfront," which would have taken him by Bay View, a logging community and former Coast Salish village atop a ridge overlooking Padilla Bay at the saltwater edge of the Skagit River delta. This was scenery not unlike what Pelton had known growing up near Maine's rugged seacoast.

On September 17 he reached the marsh and river tidelands that ringed Edison at an oxbow in the Edison Slough, less than a mile northeast of the mouth of the Samish River.[8] Centuries earlier, the Samish likely had been among several slender channels that snaked through the lowlands as tributaries of the grander, glacier-fed Skagit River. In those pre-settler times, the Skagit may have flowed west to Padilla Bay from near the present-day city of Sedro-Woolley, where today it instead turns south.[9] A few miles north of Edison stands Blanchard Mountain, a 2,300-foot peak crowned by a west-facing promontory known as Oyster Dome. To the east, rising in the distance to nearly 11,000 feet, stands Mt. Baker, a great white volcano atop the North Cascade range and, to Baker's southwest, the strikingly jagged Twin Sisters, ascending like a stairway to the stars. To the west lie the forested and fabled San Juan islands and, on the Pacific horizon, the Olympic mountain range with its snow-capped peaks, alpine glaciers, rain forests, and lakes cradled in a wilderness of mist and shadow.

As an experienced woodsman, or axman, as he sometimes called himself, Pelton marveled at the panorama—trees, trees and more trees. Centuries-old forests of Douglas fir, western red cedar, Sitka spruce and western hemlock, some more than two hundred feet tall, once covered more than 80 percent of Skagit County's million-acre landmass.[10] Beneath this canopy, big game roamed: black bear, wolves, cougars, black-tailed deer and elk, under the watchful eye of bald eagles and other birds of prey. Shorelines were patrolled by mallard and pintail ducks, snow geese, and trumpeter swans.

Much of the old-growth timber still stood when Pelton first laid eyes on this land of emerald giants. In this dim solitude beside sea and forest he seemed inspired by what native Washingtonian poet Herbert Bashford called the liberating power of the Pacific Northwest's natural wonders—"a fascinating freedom not easily comprehended by those who have known nothing but the conventionalities of an older civilization."[11]

In those days this corner of the United States was an afterthought, if it was thought of at all. No white man was known to have settled here until about 1852, when William Robert "Blanket Bill" Jarman, an English adventurer, trader and seaman, arrived with his Native American bride on the east end of Samish Island near the mouth of the Samish River.[12] The legal door to white settlement was kicked opened in 1855 with the Treaty of Point Elliott, by which the Coast Salish peoples ceded territory—including the land on which Equality colony would be built—to the United States government in exchange for small reservation lands and promises of fishing rights and medical care. Adventurous men began to arrive from across the country and from Europe—in small numbers at first—to dike and farm the fertile tidelands, to log the hills, and to organize little trading posts like Edison, which traces its origin to 1869 and was formally established and named several years later. Small numbers were drawn, too, by talk of gold and silver in the foothills of the North Cascades. The attractions, however, did not include unmarried women, who were as scarce as a quiet saloon on payday.

Men like Lermond, who had not yet set foot in the new state of Washington and probably knew no one who had, could only imagine its otherworldliness. It seemed wild, mysterious, and unpredictable compared to those long-settled areas back East where life had hardened into familiar patterns which seemed "as incapable of change as the tides of Maine and the granite of New Hampshire," as author and historian Stewart H. Holbrook put it.[13]

Though unknown to most Americans then, the Skagit River valley was not entirely unheralded; an 1896 New York newspaper article referred to the Samish flats and other lowlands in Skagit County as "America's Netherlands," with dikes forming tide gates as tall as fifteen feet that drained the land so easily that crops were raised in soil below sea level.

In an early report to Lermond and the rest of the BCC faithful, Pelton sketched the scene:

> This is certainly an embryo garden of Eden, with its rich soil, surrounded and sheltered by mountains full of timber, stone and minerals, a mild climate, navigable waters, fish in abundance at your door, grand scenery on every hand, and high land all around on which to erect residences. It only requires a common-sense Socialistic colony to render it a veritable paradise.[14]

He concluded: "With a foothold here and a few thousands in ready money, we could gradually corral the whole region."

But there was a hitch. In fact, there were two.

The first problem, in Pelton's view, was Lermond's reluctance to join forces with Debs' Social Democracy while a union was still viable. Lermond believed Debs was too political and that partisanship would hurt the BCC, but it's unclear from the historical record whether this was the true reason for the split with Debs. At one point, Lermond wrote that it was Debs, not he, who decided that merging was a bad idea. Whatever the case, Pelton worried that without Debs, the Brotherhood was destined to "cut a small figure"—gain little influence and attain little success.

The second problem for Pelton was finding a suitable real estate deal. A local farmer, Carey Lewis, had shown him two attractive properties, but neither owner was "the kind of 'feller' we were trying to find" —a landowner willing to trade property for membership in the BCC. Disappointed but not defeated, Pelton chased down leads on nearby Lummi Island and elsewhere in the state and in Portland, Oregon, before concluding that a conventional cash purchase, rather than a trade, was the only realistic option. He returned to Skagit County and contracted in October with a local farmer, Mathias Decker, to buy 280 acres for ten dollars an acre.[15] He paid $100 cash up front, another hundred in November, and then scrambled to come up with the balance before a due date of January 15.

By December, Pelton was worried. Most pledges of financial support from BCC members across the country amounted to illiquid offerings of land, equipment, and other resources, rather than cash. (The BCC had not collected colony membership fees—$160 per family—since Equality did not yet exist.) Like Lermond before him, Pelton turned to Lloyd, the journalist friend of socialism.

"The time is so short," Pelton wrote Lloyd on December 14, "and there are so many 'slips between the cup and the lip' that I feel justified in endeavoring in every way feasible to meet the emergency. Now I do not like the idea of seeming a beggar, but this cause is the cause of humanity, and this is, we think, a sober, sensible business-like proposition." He asked Lloyd for a loan of up to $200 to help the BCC avoid losing its 280 acres.

As a measure of his desperation, Pelton felt the need to exaggerate the degree of sympathy among neighbors. "The people are mostly well disposed toward Socialism," he told Lloyd, "friendly though a little skeptical as to the feasibility of the scheme." Just weeks earlier, he had privately warned Lermond that most in the local population were hostile to socialism.

At stake, Pelton insisted to Lloyd, was not just the future of a colony but the fate of a nation.

"Our defeat may mean the closing of a safety valve that might, if kept open, prevent a fearful national explosion," he wrote, alluding to the pressure cooker of social discontent that he and Lermond believed could find safe release only in Washington's conversion to socialism. His allusion to a "national explosion" was a rough equivalent of the memorable metaphor John Steinbeck would use in 1939 to describe the swelling anger of America's poor— "... and in the eyes of the hungry there is a growing wrath. In the souls of the people the grapes of wrath are filling and growing heavy, growing heavy for the vintage."

Pelton and Lermond were in a rush for a reason. Gaining clear title to the land would demonstrate the seriousness of their work and convince fence-sitters to commit to the cause. A recruit in Minnesota, for example, was delaying his promised donation of cash and equipment until a land title was secured, and "others are holding back on the same account," Lermond said.[16]

By late December, the fundraising effort had succeeded, apparently without Lloyd's help, and Pelton paid the balance due of $2,600, plus $54.16 interest. Lermond had forbidden Pelton to take on BCC debt, even in land deals, but Pelton felt he had no choice. As he put it, "I decided that it was a desperate time; that desperate chances must be taken, and that it would be infinitely better to break a rule than to break the whole movement."

Pelton wasted no time getting to work, even as he realized that socialism was suspect here.

"So great was the prejudice against the word 'Socialist' at that time in this section that I deemed it inadvisable to attempt purchasing land in the name of the BCC," he wrote a year later. So, he made the deal in his name jointly with his wife on December 30 and transferred the deed to the BCC board of trustees the following day.[17] In May of the following year the BCC increased its holdings to 440 acres by buying an adjacent 160 acres on which stood an old orchard, paying $1,500. Another nearby 160-acre parcel was made available to the Brotherhood by a friendly local landowner[18] as a gifted source of timber.

To Pelton's delight, a newspaper in the nearby Skagit River town of Mount Vernon, the *Argus*, had a liberal-minded editor who championed the People's Party and occasionally printed short, uncritical articles about Equality. In the summer of 1898, it ran a lengthy column written by Equality's designated publicist to dispel misconceptions and explain the colony's socialist aims— "Our mission is 'peace and plenty,' not bomb-throwing and destruction"—and to promote its plans for growth. Less sympathetically, the *Argus* reprinted a San Francisco newspaper article that skewered Equality and its colonists for aspiring to a "happy-go-lucky" lifestyle and an "idleness" that would invite a communal descent into mischief and crime.

Among the few locally grown socialists were farmer Carey Lewis and his wife, Grace, a couple who could not be described as happy-go-lucky or idlers but might fairly be called eccentrics. Carey was given to unconventional hobbies hatched by what a colleague called his "exclusive" imagination. A local author who studied the history of Equality colony wrote of Carey: "He had an ear for any idea that sounded a little radical —theosophy, reincarnation, spiritualism, the Samish religion." Described by fellow colonists as patient and plodding, Lewis could be provoked to fisticuffs, which in coming months would cost him a piece of his scalp.[19]

Lewis, whose farm was about a mile east of Edison, had a green thumb; he reputedly was among the first in the Puget Sound region to grow loganberries, a hybrid of the wild blackberry and the red raspberry. He also had a knack for cultivating friendships with the area's Samish tribesmen, who have inhabited the area for more than ten thousand years and largely refused to move to the Swinomish reservation designated for them by the Point Elliott Treaty. Lewis would bring them samples of his fruits and vegetables, and whenever a tribesman returned from fishing, he would hang a salmon or two on the Lewis gatepost. This form of sharing could be seen, broadly if not exactly, as a melding of socialist instincts among men from different worlds. In Coast Salish culture, a deliberate redistribution of wealth was achieved by "potlatching," in which families or communities gave surplus food and other possessions to those in greater need. They viewed material wealth not as their end goal but as a means to high social status achieved through the act of giving.[20]

Lewis also learned to communicate with the Samish by using what was called Chinook Jargon, a kind of pidgin that blended Native American, English and French words and functioned as a trade language.[21]

Harry Ault, an Equality teenager from Kentucky, wrote that Lewis used plant-growing methods unfamiliar to easterners, and the results were spectacular. Ault claimed Lewis's strawberries were as big as a man's fist, his onions "as big as your hat and as sweet as apples," and his green beans so stout that pickers stacked them on their arms like firewood.[22]

Early in 1897, Lewis had organized a local Edison branch of Lermond's socialist Brotherhood, so when Pelton arrived that fall in search of a colony site, Lewis was eager to help. The property that Pelton ultimately chose was about two miles northwest of the Lewis farm, at a spot where the Samish River delta converges with forested hills just south and east of the hamlet of Blanchard. Pelton may not have known, but this was a capitalist stronghold; Blanchard was named for a father-son team of loggers, Dudley and George, who arrived in the 1880s as agents for an eastern lumber company and soon built their logging operation into the largest in Skagit County.

As a woodsman, Pelton would have recognized remnants of commercial logging operations on portions of his new property, including an abandoned camp, log bridges, a network of skid roads on which teams of oxen had dragged logs to a narrow rail line, and a smattering of split-cedar shacks once occupied by local tribesmen. This property originally was comprised of separate parcels of 160 and 120 acres. At the time they were recorded by the U.S. Surveyor General's office, in June 1872, only about three dozen white men, mostly European immigrants, inhabited this portion of the Samish River valley.[23]

On November 1, 1897, with his land purchase still pending, Pelton and about a dozen others gathered at the Lewis farmhouse to officially christen colony number one. They named it Equality after Bellamy's latest book, which was popular by standards of his day but fell far short of the global acclaim of *Looking Backward*. The Bellamy influence was apparent in the first building erected on colony land—a two-story, L-shaped log house with living quarters upstairs and a kitchen and dining hall downstairs. They called it Fort Bellamy.

Doubters be damned, Pelton and his early partners envisioned not just a village but an industrial city.

"We are the advance guard of a mighty host," Pelton declared, invoking the biblical image of an army of angels.[24]

Lermond and the other BCC leaders had not yet arrived, which meant the monumental task of carving a little empire out of the emerald forest and the marsh was left to foot soldiers in this march to utopia. Pelton and other early arrivals began laying the crude foundations of a functioning community. They rented small parcels to raise vegetables while colony land was being prepared. On the Lewis farm they erected a two-story, ten-room building, nicknamed the Hatchery, to serve as a reception lodge, or "incubator," from which would emerge new members of the socialist flock once colony housing had expanded to accommodate them. To provide additional temporary living quarters, they spruced up a bunkhouse at the abandoned logging camp and set up tents as short-term bachelor quarters.

Their grubby work by pickax, plow, shovel, crosscut saw, hammer, and tongs would prove to be the easier part. More difficult was building an edifice of community spirit, cooperation and trust.

Nothing here came easily. They faced privation, the onset of winter rain and mud, and a slippery slope of local mistrust. A shortage of funds was the first challenge, but second on Pelton's list of worries was the neighbors. In a report to Lermond at his headquarters in Maine on October 23, Pelton estimated that fewer than half the people in nearby towns would offer a "more or less hearty" welcome. The rest were ignorant, indifferent, or "bitterly, intensely hostile." He enclosed newspaper clippings as evidence that attitudes toward the socialists could be summarized as: "We don't want them, and we won't have them." That bothered Pelton but did not stop him. In his view, these critics spoke out of ignorance.

"Neither is there any way in which they can prevent our success except by physical force, unless we ourselves weaken and slink back," he wrote, hinting at his fear that when push came to shove, some Equality colleagues might not share his resoluteness. In mid-November, with the weather turning chilly and damp and the colony site still barely habitable, he seemed worried that Lermond, from his distant vantage point on the opposite coast, had yet to appreciate and communicate the urgency of the situation.

"Washington can be captured if the Socialists will only get here and take hold," Pelton wrote.[25]

They needed to get a jump on their local critics or risk allowing what Pelton called a "hostile, devilish element" to turn public opinion more decisively against them. Despite his concern, press coverage was not uniformly negative. A Tacoma newspaper, reporting in December from the small city of New Whatcom (now Bellingham), about a dozen miles north of Equality, praised the colonists. It said their "sturdy, industrious, intelligent appearance at once won favor among their new neighbors." It did not mention they were socialists. They were "not of the agitator style," the report said. "Their operations are carried on in that independent, straightforward but modest manner and material American spirit which appeals to the good will and good sense of all well-meaning people."

Even later, several months into the colony's life, Lermond and his followers were viewed by some locals as harmless oddballs, with the emphasis on odd. A short article in the colony newspaper recounted a conversation between an elderly man in Edison, where Lermond and his inner circle were renting rooms and office space, and an acquaintance in Mount Vernon, the county seat. "Well, how are your anarchists getting along?" the acquaintance asked. The Edison man bristled, insisting the other man never again "make use of such insinuations against our socialists." The worst he could say about the radicals was, "We are all agreeably disappointed with them." But at least they were not anarchists.[26]

Perhaps more typical of the attitude of the locals was the disdain that Blanche Smith expressed when a son years later asked why she held the colonists in low regard. The extent of her firsthand knowledge is unclear; she lived about a dozen miles from Equality during much of its existence, and in the colony's heyday her future husband Dell R. Smith and his brother Paul made guest appearances at Equality dances to play their mandolin and harp guitar.[27]

"The people who came there and started this, they were uneducated, funny [*meaning odd or mentally deficient*], radical people—every one of them," she said. In her view, they had forsaken their country by turning against capitalism. "It makes me sick to even think about it."[28]

She was right to call them radical but wrong to suggest this made them worthy of contempt.

Chapter 5

Radicalism: From Hope to Despair

During the United States' formative years and arguably throughout its history, men and women of conviction embraced radicalism, especially when economic forces threatened to steal their souls. Radical, however, does not always mean extreme. It can mean doubting convention and rejecting the status quo in search of new solutions.

Without being a zealot, a radical may resist what feels like oppression or insist on a defense of dignity. Such were circumstances in the first decades after the Civil War, when Lermond and many of his Equality colonists came of age. It was a time of restrained hope, lingering resentment over the war and its causes, and fear of a growing concentration of industrial wealth. The Reconstruction period is best remembered for political crisis, corruption, and the fleeting promise of a foundation for racial equality, but it also coincided with the creation of a truly national economy and new mobility for people and ideas. Previously isolated domestic markets took on a national scope, stitched together with threads of transcontinental rail that now connected the coasts. Big, lasting change ensued.

America's richest capitalists were ready for this transition. Much of the rest of society was not. For many this was a time of doubt, confusion, restlessness, and the emergence by 1890 of radical new questions. Why was the free-market economy so frequently in crisis? Who was to blame? What was weakening the culture of self-reliance that had long typified the American character? Why had so many ordinary people lost out on promises of prosperity and equal opportunity? Where were the hopeful new horizons—figuratively and literally?

The levers of economic power were now pulled predominantly in board rooms, and as their reach and power grew, corporations in the eyes of ordinary workers became not just big but beastly. "A vague and indescribable dread and suspicion of them pervade the minds of men," William W. Cook, a corporate insider himself, wrote in 1893.[1] More than a century later, acclaimed historian David M. Kennedy put it this way: The growth of huge corporations "swamped the hope of Americans both native-born and newly arrived that they would lead lives of economic autonomy and personal freedom."[2]

The laboring class felt squeezed, cheated, and disrespected as profit-hungry corporations cut wages unilaterally on the downside of each boom-and-bust business cycle in the final decades of the century. Labor unions were largely ineffective; those not strangled at birth were weak and fragile. (Workers' right to organize was not written into federal law until the 1930s.) Wage-earners came to believe, in the language of the times, that their sweat and muscle were being coined into fortunes by ruthless corporate barons.

As the journalist and historian Frederick Lewis Allen put it in *The Lords of Creation*, his account of the excesses of late-19th century capitalism, "There burned a fierce resentment against the inhuman conditions prevailing in most industries" and anger at employers' exploitive practices. Allen was far from the first to explore the problem. Upton Sinclair, a fervent socialist, struck a raw nerve in 1906 with his novel *The Jungle*, a wrenching indictment of an under-regulated meatpacking industry—its vile products and its evil treatment of the men and women who worked in the Chicago slaughterhouses.[3] Sinclair's revelations were so damning of a major industry that the first five publishers he approached rejected his manuscript as too explosive. And the industry, naturally, fought back. It launched an advertising counteroffensive and pressured Congress to stop or water down legislation aimed at regulating slaughterhouses.

THE IMPLICATIONS of heightened tension between the ordinary worker and the capitalist elite were recognized by some as early as the 1870s. It was captured in an obscure essay by Isaac Rehn, a Philadelphia painter, inventor and photographer. Yes, the nation was getting fabulously rich, he wrote in the summer of 1874, but the extent of wealth inequality was appalling. The suffering of those at the bottom of the heap—the ordinary wage earners—had become largely invisible to the rest.

"The glitter and show of affluence at points here and there in the social field may, and does, divert our attention from the surrounding misery, privation, and want," Rehn wrote.[4] He was describing what Mark Twain famously called the Gilded Age—that period when a shiny veneer of prosperity masked an underlying core of discontent.

This disillusionment hardened into radicalism in the 1880s, not just in industrial centers but on farms and ranches, where tough times were confounding ordinary people and transforming the political landscape.

As mechanized industrialization accelerated, so did the migration of jobs, and thus of people, from farms to urban areas. During the decade of the 1880s, agriculture's share of total employment dipped below 50 percent for the first time in recorded American history.[5] This was due in part to the introduction of more efficient, labor-saving farm equipment. Still, farmers sensed their collective voice growing weaker. They began to demand change at the state and national level, angered and baffled by the inexplicable fact that the harder they worked, the more crop prices disappointed and the harder it got to make a loan payment.

Farmers of the Great Plains had planted the seeds of their discontent in the Grange movement, which held equality and equity as core American values. With a surge in membership after the national financial crisis of 1873, the Grange fought against the monopolistic practices of railroads and the exorbitant prices charged by grain elevators, which were owned by railroads. Author Charles A. Madison called this protest movement, which anticipated the rise of the national People's Party, a "spontaneous and sporadic expression of despair."[6] Farmers, Madison wrote, had been reduced to "the drudges of an industrial society," and they summed up their anger in a slogan: "Ten cent corn and ten percent interest"—the pain of depressed crop prices made worse by exploitive bankers.

In that downward spiral, a distressed Nebraska farm couple decided to give the Equality colony a try. Their names were Joseph and Annie Billingsley. For them, the decision to throw in with a socialist movement out West was as much about personal crisis as political cause.[7]

The Billingsleys had lost their farm to hard times in Buffalo County, Nebraska, where, yes, the buffalo once roamed on a rich stretch of prairie along a southerly bend of the Platte River, whose valley served as the trailway for Mormons migrating west in the 1850s. The Billingsley farm was nine miles north of Gibbon, a town that happened to have its own place in the history of American colonization. With no connection to socialism, Gibbon was settled in 1871 by Civil War veterans brought there in Union Pacific railcars as part of a promoter's drive to populate U.P. lands, and to thus increase their value.

Joe Billingsley, born in western Pennsylvania on Leap Day in 1844, was a son of Irish immigrants whose distant forebears included English Quakers who had migrated to America in the early 1600s. Joe was thirty-five when he and his wife Margaret left the Billingsley family farm in Butler County, Pennsylvania, to join his brother-in-law in staking out two nearly adjoining farms in Nebraska. Like thousands of others drawn to the government's offer of free land, Billingsley in 1879 entered a claim under the Homestead Act for 160 acres on which he built a sod barn and a frame house that measured sixteen feet by thirty-two feet. Nearly five years later he received a patent for the deed of title, having "proved up" his claim by actively farming the land and living on it for the required minimum of five consecutive years—a requirement that in his case was shortened by nine months as credit for his service in the 137th regiment of Pennsylvania infantry during the Civil War.[8]

The Billingsleys raised hogs and had 140 acres in crops, including corn, oats and wheat. The farm was valued in 1885 at $5,100, about average in their district.

Much had changed for Billingsley since he first broke ground. His first wife, Margaret, died in early 1881, and shortly afterward a young woman from Wisconsin came into his life. She was half his age and twice as adventurous. Annie W. Torrey made the unlikely move from Geneva, Wisconsin, just north of Chicago, to the lonesome prairie of Buffalo County by following the path of an older sister, Helen, who had met and married a Nebraska merchant, Frank H. More, in Wisconsin in 1880. (A quirky historical footnote: Frank More was a first cousin of Jay Gould, the railroad magnate and financial speculator who is remembered as a foremost example of the excesses of 19th century capitalism—what some called bandit capitalism. The collapse of his investment company in September 1873 triggered panic on Wall Street and sent the nation into depression.)

Annie's mother was descended from Puritans who emigrated from England to settle on Cape Cod in Massachusetts Bay Colony in the 1630s. Her father's paternal grandfather, Josiah Torrey, fought in the Revolutionary War. Annie never knew her father, a schoolteacher and Civil War veteran; he died three months before she was born in New Jersey. Her mother then moved the family to Wisconsin, where, as a teenager, Annie left home to join Helen and Frank More at their first home in the Platte River Valley town of Shelton, Nebraska. Frank ran a clothing store several miles south of Billingsley's farm. Being near-neighbors, Annie and Joe soon crossed paths, and they were married in 1882. He was thirty-eight; she was nineteen. Joe had two sons by his first wife, and by the time the Billingsley farm faced financial crisis in the 1890s, he and Annie had added two sons and two daughters. The youngest, Hazel, would die just weeks after the family arrived at Equality.

In Nebraska, Joe and Annie were active in civic affairs. He served in many roles in Gardner township, including property tax assessor and justice of the peace, and he was a member of the Buffalo County board of supervisors. In 1894 he helped organize county financial relief for families suffering the most from crop losses. Both he and Annie were leaders in the local branch of the Farmers' Alliance, a national group whose progressive agenda attracted thousands of discouraged farmers and helped give rise to the People's Party. Considered radical at the time, the Alliance blamed railroads, eastern banks, and corporate monopolies for what looked like disintegration of the national economy.

In October 1890, the Alliance organized a protest parade of several hundred farm wagons and other vehicles on the streets of Kearney, the seat of Buffalo County. The local newspaper called it "the greatest gathering of farmers ever seen" in the Platte River town. A six-mule hayrack carried a banner: "In Republicans We Trusted, and Now We are Busted."

Like most small farmers on the Great Plains in those days, the Billingsleys were precariously dependent on bank loans. Interest rates were on the rise, crop prices were shaky, and lenders' patience was growing thin. Luck, too, was hard to come by, and the Billingsleys' finally ran out. In January 1896, the Iowa Loan and Trust Co. began foreclosure proceedings. Nearly two years later, after a court affirmed the Billingsleys' default on a $1,300 mortgage, the farm was auctioned off in a sheriff's sale on the doorstep of the courthouse in Kearney. Joe and Annie were washed up as farmers, their American dream wrecked. In the end, they were left with little but disappointment and heartache for their nearly twenty years of work.

The Billingsleys' failure was of a kind familiar to readers of the *Gibbon Reporter*, a Buffalo County weekly, which published a flurry of foreclosure notices that year. Farms across the county were being auctioned by court order. Fifteen such formulaic notices appeared in a single July issue of the *Reporter*. In the midst of this crisis, the newspaper took note of the human toll and the feeling among farmers of being trapped:

> The farmer packs his little all into an old wagon and with wife and babies starts east for the land of prosperity and high

> protection. He is soon met by a score of men on foot who have neither wagon, food nor money. He inquires where they are going. They answer, 'Out west to look for work; the east is as dead as a mackerel.'[9]

About three months after losing the farm, the Billingsleys packed their little all and started west. They never looked back. Life had taken a hard turn, leaving a divot in their dignity. Joe and Annie were ready for a radical change, ready to push back against what felt like oppression. Equality seemed a fair bet—a long shot perhaps, but a shot, nonetheless.

Radicalism is native to the American spirit. Dormant, suppressed, or unrecognized in many, it has surfaced in some of this country's most distinguished families. President Rutherford B. Hayes, for example, had a cousin named John H. Noyes, a spiritualist and socialist who founded a utopian commune at Oneida, New York, in 1848. Noyes may have been the most radical American of his time.

Hayes, a Republican, had a few radical thoughts of his own after leaving the White House. He worried about the concentration of wealth and power in the hands of what he called a predatory corporate elite, a worry shared by succeeding generations, including today's. An echo of Hayes' concern could be heard more than a century later in the January 2025 farewell address of President Joe Biden, who warned of an emerging American oligarchy—a "dangerous concentration of power in the hands of a very few ultra-wealthy people."

Writing in his diary on March 11, 1888, seven years after retiring to his Ohio estate, Hayes said labor unions, though troublesome, were not the main problem. "The real difficulty," he wrote, "is with the vast wealth and power in the hands of the few and the unscrupulous who represent or control capital."[10] He lamented the passing of the period when the government was—in a phrase made famous by President Abraham Lincoln at Gettysburg in 1863— "of the people, by the people, and for the people." It had become instead, Hayes wrote, "a government of corporations, by corporations, and for corporations."

"How is this?" Hayes asked, echoing a question on the minds of many. Unsure of the answer or of the future, ordinary people became fed up. Some simply gave up. Some launched or joined any number of reform movements, aiming not to establish a radically new order but rather to trim the sails of the captains of industry, whose powers had grown too great.

Others, perhaps more daring or more imaginative than the reformers—or perhaps just more desperate—drifted toward ideas you could call radical. Of course, in Hayes's day, an idea like government regulation of workplace conditions was considered radical. So, too, was the idea that a vast prosperity gap between the working class and the corporate elite was something other than an acceptable outcome of capitalism operating in high gear.

THE BELIEF that unfettered capitalism condemned a segment of society to unfair hardships had its roots in the period when small producers and craftsmen were overtaken in the economy by aggressive corporations dominating—some said monopolizing—key industries like transportation, banking, oil, and minerals. A telling example of this concentration of power was the Philadelphia & Reading Railroad, which achieved a near monopoly in the production and transport of anthracite coal in eastern Pennsylvania in the 1870s and was considered the largest corporation in the world. As a behemoth, the company was used to getting its way. It blocked efforts by mine workers to form unions, provoking complaints of "corporate tyranny" and all but inviting workers to unsheathe their ultimate weapon, the strike.

No such clash of that era was more consequential than the railroad strike of 1877, the first national labor action in United States history. It was a wrenching episode in which the strikers' desperation was captured in their battle cry: "In heed of our right and in defense of our families, we shall conquer, or we shall die." At its core, this passionate stand was a revolt against a corruption of democracy, or as the literary historian Vernon Luis Parrington put it years later, the twisting of democracy into a right to "use the government of the whole for the benefit of the few"—in other words, plutocracy, or government by the wealthy.

The strike was fueled by anger over a series of pay cuts and work restrictions imposed by railroad owners and managers. Coming in the fourth year of a deep economic depression, labor frustrations grew into what a historian of the period, Robert V. Bruce, called "thunderheads of fury,"[11] which soon erupted. Rail conductors, brakemen, and flagmen—at times joined by mill workers and other distressed laborers who felt they had nothing more to lose—launched a strike unlike any before. They halted much of the nation's rail traffic and pushed the country astonishingly close to the brink of social revolution.

"*The Great Struggle Between Capital and Labor,*" declared a headline in the *Daily Eagle* of Reading, Pennsylvania. The city was a hub of the Philadelphia & Reading Railroad and fell in the path of that violent unrest in the summer of 1877. At least a dozen people were killed on Reading's streets in a clash with state militia. The newspaper called it "one of the most terrible butcheries that has ever disgraced the pages of Reading's local history." The city's drug stores became makeshift operating rooms for the wounded and the dying.[12]

The trouble had begun in Martinsburg, West Virginia, and quickly spread to Baltimore, to Reading, to Pittsburgh and west to St. Louis and Omaha. Eventually, dozens of strikers, as well as hoodlums, knuckleheads and bystanders, were killed or wounded by state militiamen called to arms in a desperate bid to keep the trains running. At one point it was feared the violence would engulf lightly defended Washington, D.C., and some urged President Hayes to call for military volunteers as Lincoln had done in April 1861 after Southern rebels captured Fort Sumpter. Hayes resisted, but he did send federal troops to Baltimore and to other cities. This martial response met with mixed results. Riots were extinguished and the strike was defeated, but the cost was incalculably high: the loss of civilian lives and, over time, a hardening of feelings against big business.

In its assessment of widespread violence as far west as Ohio and who was to blame, the *Daily Eagle* in Reading minced no words.

"It was the corporations that struck the first blow," the paper said, "and though noiseless, it fell with terrible effect on the heads and home and hearts of hundreds of laborers." The strikers had been unfairly blamed— "met with force of arms, provoked to violence and then shot dead." The paper feared an approaching breaking point that would fracture the very core of society:

> America is a country of working people, and they will not see their fellows wronged and crushed continuously by despotic corporations without a resistance which the latter will repent having provoked.[13]

This was an example of the social powder keg that, two decades later, George Boomer would warn about and that Ed Pelton would fear could ignite a national explosion if there were no socialist "safety valve."

This theme of conflict between the haves and the have-nots —class warfare, some called it—was central to an emerging debate over the role of government, the limits of a laissez-faire approach to capitalism, and social justice. It colored the thinking of people who sympathized with the working class, despised what they called the corporate class, and would find an experiment like the Equality colony to be a worthwhile expression of their frustration with the customary order of life in the Gilded Age.

The plight of workingmen had an added level of complexity in much of the South in the first decades after the Civil War. Examples are abundant but often forgotten. Among the most striking are the "convict wars," notably in the Cumberland Mountain mining region of eastern Tennessee, where as early as 1877 the Tennessee Coal and Iron Company began "leasing" convicts offered by the state as forced labor to replace free workers pressing for improved work conditions.

By 1891, mine workers had lost patience with this "leasing" practice, which was common throughout the largely bankrupt South during Reconstruction and beyond; it gave state governments a new source of revenue, and mining companies gained cheap labor—mostly black men. Beyond the repulsive fact that it amounted to slavery, the practice stole a livelihood from displaced mine workers whose prospects were dim enough to start with. Workers revolted. They stormed the stockades housing convict laborers at a Coal Creek mine, freeing hundreds and setting off a two-year conflict that sometimes turned violent and prompted Tennessee's governor to call out the national guard.

By the mid-1890s, tensions were rising from a deeper well of despair that showed itself mainly in the agrarian Middle West and in factory centers like New York, Philadelphia, Chicago and St. Louis.

Radicalism was in the air.

The common thread in these trends, on the prairie and in the city, was the growing size, power, and domination of big business and the introduction of the factory system. This paralleled a diminishing of the independence, and consequently the dignity, of tradesmen and small farmers. The very concept of a self-reliant tradesman—an individual who could support his family by exchanging his work or wares for other products or services—was fading irretrievably, erasing a traditional way of life. Men who had been their own master—the wagon maker, the blacksmith, the clock maker, the shoe and harness maker, for example—were facing a dead-end. To keep food on the table, these artisans had to accept becoming mere wage earners —cogs in the great wheel of modern industry. As Edward Bellamy put it with a figurative flourish, "Small businesses, as far as they still remained, were reduced to the condition of rats and mice, living in holes and corners, and counting on evading notice" to avoid getting crushed.[14]

The psychological toll was heavy and hard to measure. William A. Peffer, a Kansan who was the first member of the People's Party elected to the U.S. Senate, put it this way: The mechanization and specialization of industry and agriculture was stealing men's individuality and pride. "These people ... go to their work at the blowing of a whistle or the ringing of a bell; they go to their meals and return by the same signs at stated times every working day," he wrote in his 1891 book, *The Farmer's Side*. Unaccustomed to this regimentation, their work was alienating them from themselves. Or as Ed Pelton put it, working for a wage was damaging to one's dignity if it meant submitting to the personal control of a "master" and consequently becoming "a mere machine with no thought as to the amount or value of his work, but with his whole mind bent on the amount of 'time' he is putting in."[15]

Rather than depending on his own labor and ingenuity, a hired factory man was increasingly reliant on his employer's business decisions, with no say in the process and little defense against the consequences. The factory owner knew nothing of his workers, nor they of him; to them he was little more than a myth. Nor were these men accustomed to acceding to pay cuts and layoffs like those that flowed from economic depression in the mid-1870s and again a decade later.

Large-scale industrial unemployment, and a resulting growth in the number of "tramps" wandering through towns and cities in search of work or shelter, was a new problem with no apparent solution—certainly not one emanating from the Congress or the White House. This, in a nutshell, was the "labor question" that vexed so many; it was the social crisis that radicals like Norman Lermond believed socialism could solve.

THE FACELESS, soulless band of corporations that seemed to control the economy had no reason to fear government resistance to their tactics, which increasingly included stifling or eliminating competition by forming cartel-like trusts and near-monopolies.

Trusts, sometimes called pools, were designed to restrain trade for the benefit of a group of former competitors. The most famous example was John D. Rockefeller's Standard Oil Trust, established in 1882 with the effect of choking off competition and concentrating wealth. There was no law against it, so why not? It worked. A trust is an arrangement by which stockholders in multiple companies that compete in the same industry transfer their shares to a single set of trustees who then control the component companies, allowing them to improve efficiency, limit trade, control prices, and, in some cases, destroy competition. This became a craze in the 1890s, particularly late in the decade.[16]

As strange as it might seem at first blush, socialists of the 1890s and early 1900s liked the trust concept, so long as the trust was publicly, not privately, owned. It was a form of cooperation, making it the enemy of the socialists' enemy—competition. In Bellamy's *Looking Backward* utopia, all industries were operated as one shared trust; this was his solution to the problem of wealth concentration and class warfare. Trusts would be a good thing, Boomer said in 1899, if removed from private hands and forced to function for the benefit of the masses rather than for the few. "When we change the ownership—the only thing in question—all the people will be benefitted," he wrote.[17]

"Let the Nation Own the Trusts," became a socialist slogan. Frank Parsons, the lawyer-professor who served on the BCC board of directors for the first eighteen months of the Equality colony's life, argued that trusts could not be destroyed because they adhered to a natural law— "union means strength and economy." Nor *should* they be destroyed. Instead, he argued, as did Boomer and other socialists, trusts should be taken from private hands.

"That alone can remove the antagonism of interest that lies at the base of our industrial evils," Parsons wrote.[18]

Passage of the Sherman Antitrust Act in 1890 may have given the impression that the government was tackling the trust issue, but in fact throughout the 1890s that law was enforced feebly, if at all. In 1895, for example, the U.S. Supreme Court ruled that the American Sugar Refining Company, one of the defendants in an antitrust case before the court, had not violated the law even though it controlled about 98 percent of sugar refining in the country. The prevailing view was that government had no business messing with business. If corporations combined to kill competition, so be it. Nor should Washington protect workers or dole out financial relief to the poor or the unemployed. To do so, it was argued, would only weaken the self-reliant and encourage the lazy.

Thus, there was no social safety net: no unemployment insurance, no minimum wage, no food stamps, no assured compensation for a worker injured on the job. The government provided pensions for war veterans and widows of the war dead, but pension coverage for civilian government employees was minimal until passage of the Federal Worker Retirement Act of 1920; similarly, private-sector pensions were not common until the early 1900s. Corporate interests, however, had long enjoyed their own form of welfare: government subsidies, land grants and protective tariffs on imports—not to mention their manipulation of legislators through corruption largely invisible to the average American.

THE RAIL STRIKE of 1877 was pivotal, but it was not the century's last big labor fight. It was, in fact, a watershed moment. From it flowed streams of new thinking about the wisdom of unconstrained capitalism and a cascade of violent confrontations between labor and industry. An example is the Haymarket affair of 1886 in which a labor rally in Chicago's old Haymarket Square ended in tragedy after city police rushed the loud but non-violent crowd. Someone threw a dynamite bomb that exploded near police, killing one officer and wounding several dozen. The police opened fire, killing one in a crowd of several hundred and wounding untold numbers, including a few of their own.

As Henry David wrote in his authoritative account fifty years later, the Haymarket episode stunned Chicagoans and dealt a lasting blow to labor's cause, in part because the public focused more on the never-solved mystery of who threw the deadly bomb than who shot the unarmed protesters. In the absence of proof, authorities successfully used testimony of a Pinkerton detective to portray the protesters as part of a broader, unproven anarchist conspiracy to overthrow the government; thus were the accused deemed guilty of murder, regardless of who actually threw the bomb. Of the eight protesters charged and convicted, four were hanged.[19]

Rather than deter radicalism, the hangings fueled it. Emma Goldman, for example, was an 18-year-old newlywed Russian immigrant living in obscurity in Rochester, New York, when she became enthralled, and then enraged, by the Haymarket convictions. When the four were hanged, she reacted with what she recalled years later as physical revulsion and an awakening. "I had a distinct sensation," she wrote, "that something new and wonderful had been born in my soul. A great ideal, a burning faith, a determination to dedicate myself to the memory of my martyred comrades and to make their cause my own."[20] She became an anarchist—the most radical and famous of her time.

The hangings also strengthened the voice of socialists with no extreme inclinations—men like journalist Henry Demarest Lloyd and Eugene Debs, the labor leader who said the hangings made the condemned men "the first martyrs in the cause of industrial freedom."[21]

Even so, many Americans became convinced that blame for the Haymarket violence lay with anarchists and socialists seen as guilty of plotting to destroy democracy. Thus began the first "red scare" in American history, more than half a century before Sen. Joseph McCarthy's better-remembered abuses of civil liberties in a 1950s campaign against an exaggerated threat of communist subversion of government and society—a political witch-hunt that demonized left-wing dissent.

Six years after Haymarket, conflict between labor and industry again reached a boiling point. Again, the Pinkerton detective agency and its guards, labor spies and strike-breakers played a role. The year was 1892 and the setting was a steel mill on the banks of the Monongahela River, several miles east of Pittsburgh. That summer, the Homestead steelworks, owned by Andrew Carnegie and run by Henry C. Frick, announced a wage cut and refused to negotiate. The workers resisted. Frick's men locked out the steelworkers and hired Pinkerton mercenaries to secure the plant. The steelworkers fought back, opening fire on armed Pinkerton forces. Seven workers and three Pinkerton men were killed; others were wounded by gunfire, and many were injured in hand-to-hand combat. The workers' union conceded defeat. Carnegie hired replacements, and organized labor had again suffered a stinging defeat, although this time the motives of the industrialists' and the role of their private armies raised enduring questions.

In the short run, these labor conflicts were failures from the workers' standpoint. Over time, however, the publicity opened eyes to corporate overreach and created a narrow crack in Americans' traditional resistance to strengthening the hand of government in the name of social justice. Eventually that crack widened, and the result was a bigger, more centralized and involved federal government bureaucracy. Some viewed this as progress in softening the hardest edges of capitalism. Others saw it—and many see it still today—as freedom's retreat and a kind of paternalism incompatible with democracy.

In that era, individualism was central to the nation's democratic faith. President Grover Cleveland spoke for the majority when he declared in 1887, in vetoing $10,000 in drought aid for Texas farmers, "Though the people support the government, the government should not support the people."[22] In this view, help for the needy should come from private pockets. Federal aid, he wrote, "weakens the sturdiness of our national character."

That philosophy held sway across much of the country. In the summer of 1893, the editorial board of the *St. Louis Post-Dispatch* mocked labor groups' argument—echoed by one of the newspaper's own employees, who would become a top assistant to Lermond at Equality—that the government should use taxpayer funds to create work for the jobless. The newspaper called this proposal "irrational, un-American and undemocratic."[23]

"If there is an idea which can be called distinctively the American idea, it is that the individual ought to rely solely upon himself without aid or hindrance from the government," it wrote. To argue otherwise, even in times of extreme distress, was to embrace "socialistic sentiment stimulated by an empty stomach."

Those who hungered for change, including socialist agitators like Boomer and Lermond, were angered not so much by the government's action as by its absence. They believed that Washington's hands-off approach condemned the poor to suffer in silence. Central to their thinking was the idea that government must act as a partner in advancing human progress, that government should be regarded as something more than a necessary evil. In this they had support, if only in the abstract, from the American Economic Association, an emergent group of new-school economists founded in 1886 by Richard T. Ely, a Johns Hopkins University political economist whose most famous student was a Ph.D. candidate named Woodrow

Wilson, future 28th President of the United States. "While we recognize the necessity of individual initiative in industrial life, we hold that the doctrine of laissez-faire is unsafe in politics and unsound in morals," the group said in its founding statement.

A quarter century later, Wilson won the White House and began reshaping the economic landscape by lowering tariffs, establishing the Federal Reserve system, limiting child labor, and creating the Federal Trade Commission.

As THE NATION struggled in the 1890s with questions of basic economic fairness, the American experiment in democratic self-government seemed in jeopardy. Parrington, the literary historian and university professor—himself a post-Civil War product of the Kansas plains—thought of this as a moment of national reckoning after the rich had gorged themselves for years on profits in a capitalist feast he called "The Great Barbecue."[24]

Parrington put it this way: When the big meal ended and the bill came due, the farmers found they had been "put off with the giblets while the capitalists were consuming the turkey." The farmers left the table feeling unsatisfied, and "a sullen anger burned in their hearts."

In Ohio, a businessman and social reformer named Jacob S. Coxey sensed the depth and breadth of this anger. He had accumulated a small fortune from farming, horse breeding and silica mining, and in late 1893 he hit upon this radical idea: A dramatic public demonstration, one that would capture and hold the nation's attention, might compel Congress to do what seemed like the obviously right thing—help the growing numbers of unemployed.

The following April he led several hundred men on a month-long, 400-mile march from his hometown of Massillon, Ohio, to the steps of the United States Capitol to demand action. Shocking in its audacity, this was the first significant protest march on Washington in history. To many onlookers, it seemed almost treasonous—a challenge to the established order, a radical stirring of political passions.

The marchers traveled southeast across the Allegheny Mountains and along the Potomac River, crossing to Maryland and passing through Rockville and Bethesda before entering the District of Columbia. Other groups of unemployed men set out from other points on the map, including Boston, Chicago and cities and towns in the Far West. This "petition with boots on," as some called it, succeeded in grabbing national attention, but not in the way Coxey had hoped.

Newspapers ridiculed the Coxey march as a parade of cranks, bums, and screwballs. They dubbed it "Coxey's Army," although the men were unarmed civilians committed to a peaceful protest. They preferred their movement be called the "Commonweal," an archaic term meaning the "common good," reflecting the central theme of their protest and contrasting their philosophy with that of the laissez-faire crowd. This distinction was important. It highlighted a clash of ideas: Was democratic government meant to be kept to a bare minimum, or should it promote the general welfare by an active exertion of its powers?

In the sensationalist fashion of the time, some newspapers falsely claimed Coxey's protest was orchestrated by anarchists bent on violence. Estimates vary widely but the group's numbers may have grown to one thousand upon reaching the capital on May 1. They made no disturbance and were armed only with requests that the jobless be put to work building and improving roads.

Police at the Capitol arrested Coxey and two associates. He insisted on a jury trial and was convicted of two "crimes"—carrying a banner on the Capitol grounds and walking on the grass. The judge branded Coxey a menace to the community and sentenced him and his two associates to twenty days in jail. (They served their time in cell number 67, which they dubbed "Camp Bastille" for the Paris prison that was stormed by an angry mob in 1789, ushering in the French Revolution.) It's possible that Coxey was in technical violation of the District of Columbia's keep-off-the-grass ordnance, although eyewitnesses, including an Associated Press reporter, testified in court that he never touched it.[25] It is hard to escape the conclusion that Coxey was prosecuted for his political views, which were out of sync with the times but also were a harbinger of change to come.

For Lermond and other radicals this was one more reason to convert anger to action under the banner of socialism.

Chapter 6

'On To Washington!'

In the final decade of the 19th century, the American scene was colored in several shades of socialism—few distinct enough to be widely recognized, none strong enough to threaten the two political pillars of capitalism, the Democrats and the Republicans.

Labels are tricky things, particularly when it comes to political philosophy, and it can be difficult to distinguish between factions of the American socialist movement of that period. Before they established a national party structure in 1901, the socialists were like a flood-prone river; they could shift direction, abandon old pathways, and even reverse course. Some sounded more like communists, favoring abolition of private property. Some defied labels. Some invented them. Some transformed themselves, but few found common ground, which was why Lermond made unity the first goal of his Brotherhood.

Lermond was not a communist in the ordinary sense, but his Brotherhood and the Equality experiment were not purely socialist, either. They embraced the central principle of communism: collective rather than private ownership of land.

On the other hand, they rejected ideas, such as the supremacy of a central governing authority, control of religious activity, and suppression of dissent, that would become hallmarks of 20th century revolutionary communist governments in the Soviet Union and elsewhere. Seen through the lens of politics in the 2020s, Lermond's Brotherhood was more in the mold of the democratic socialist, prioritizing social needs over private profits and aiming to replace capitalism rather than reform it.

Among socialist factions of the 1890s that focused mainly on ideals and a more equitable distribution of wealth, the most prominent were the utopians and the Christian socialists. More obscure were the Fabians, so called for their adherence to tactics of the British Fabian Society, which aimed to infiltrate socialist ideas into society through non-violent means—a sort of intellectual guerrilla warfare against capitalism. Then there were the syndicalists, for whom ordinary socialism was too tame. They argued for nationalizing all industries and making each the responsibility of a specific group, or syndicate; railroad workers, for example, would run all rail transportation. And, finally, there were the Marxists, devoted to the philosophy of Karl Marx and his *Communist Manifesto* and committed to the idea that capitalism works only by exhausting the earth and the worker, and that eventually workers will rise in violent revolt.

Socialists in the Marx mold were largely European immigrants, although they included native-born Americans like Hermon F. Titus, a preacher-turned-physician who came to Seattle from Massachusetts in 1893. Seven years later Titus started *The Socialist*, a rabble-rousing Seattle newspaper that became a showcase for prominent defectors from Lermond's Brotherhood. Marxian socialists of a more extreme persuasion than Titus spoke of overthrowing the capitalist system by force of arms, an approach firmly rejected by utopians like Lermond. This was long before the Bolsheviks in Russia staged a successful revolution in 1917 and established the world's first communist government, ultimately a failure.

Here, then, was the clearest split in the American socialist camp in the late-1890s: On one hand the Marxists, who condoned class warfare but were badly divided over how far to push it, and on the other hand the less radical agitators who favored a peaceful approach to replacing capitalism but lacked broad support. Those in the latter camp were often dubbed utopians; they disliked this label because they fancied themselves doers and saw the Marxists as mere talkers. The utopians felt sure that in time their non-destructive ways would show them, not the talkers, to be pathfinders to true freedom. As Lermond put it shortly after Equality got started: "The people are sick of talk. They ask for something practical, something tangible, an object lesson, a working model of the new theory."[1] The Marxists saw the utopians as fearful of upsetting the rest of society by stating what plainly was true—that revolutionary socialism, peaceful or not, *was* destructive. It was destructive because it aimed to eliminate the capitalist system.

Thus fractured, the socialist movement by the late 1890s was paralyzed but far from played out. Its most widely embraced idea, that workers must cast off the burden of being slave to a corporate master, gave life to a related notion: that it might be possible to find "industrial freedom" in which ordinary people collectively reaped the full benefit of their own work. This was what Lermond had in mind when Ed Pelton convened the inaugural meeting of colonists at Carey Lewis's secluded farmhouse on the Samish tidal flats on November 1, 1897.

No complete list of attendees at that first gathering survives, nor is there a full account of what was discussed. Record keeping was a matter of routine, but for unknown reasons a substantial amount of Equality's history—most official correspondence, financial records, and accounts of most meetings of the general assembly, and much more—has disappeared. Perhaps it was deliberately destroyed; maybe it was simply set aside and forgotten. The closest thing to an official record of who constituted the original Equality group is a brief item published in the colony newspaper in 1898 reporting that an initial ten had been voted in as full members, having fulfilled their obligatory six months' probation.

"As the colony is but six months old, they are the first members that came here," it said.

In addition to Pelton and Carey Lewis, the pioneer group included Lewis's brother, August R. Lewis, and men from Idaho, Missouri, Oregon, Illinois, Montana, South Dakota, and California. Several of these adventurous spirits had initially gathered at Buckley, the rejected colony site southeast of Seattle, in anticipation of Pelton giving it the BCC's blessing. When he instead chose the Skagit County site, they followed him there. They included John Helm, a Montana miner enthralled by the idea of making the colony a quick success.

"If one half of what has been subscribed [pledged] is paid in, we will make things hum inside of a year," Helm wrote home to Butte.[2] He was especially impressed that Carey Lewis, a man of modest means, had donated five acres of his own land; Helm called the gesture "the widow's mite," referring to the Bible story of the impoverished woman who willingly gave her last two mites (Jewish coins) to God's cause.

Also in the Buckley group was Manley Dunckel, a hard-luck former cattle rancher who had been chasing long-shot dreams since 1876, when he left Iowa to join a gold rush in the Black Hills of Dakota Territory.[3] Riches evaded him, and when his cattle ranch failed in the early 1890s he tried his hand at grocery sales in the mile-high mining town of Terry, near Deadwood. In 1896 his store went belly up, and a few months later his wife of thirty years died of heart failure. When he left for Puget Sound in September, a Deadwood newspaper wrote admiringly that this socialist was "putting his faith into practice."

The list of original Equality pioneers did not include Lermond or any of his inner circle, other than Pelton. That's because Lermond and his Maine brain trust waited several months before coming out West. This absentee leadership struck some as odd, if not suspicious. A supporter in Nebraska asked: "By the way, is it not inconvenient, to say the least, to have the secretary of the colony live 3,000 miles away? Is there not some kicking about it?"[4]

When Lermond's group did come, it unintentionally stirred more suspicion by setting up shop in the nearby village of Edison rather than on colony grounds. Lermond and his associates took rooms in an Edison hotel, which they dubbed Freedom Hotel. With this physical separation from the colonists, Lermond was highlighting the difference between Equality's narrow, local mission and the broader, national role of the BCC. On paper, that made sense; on the ground, it would become a sore point that festered and set the stage for conflict to come.

During the final months of 1897, before tensions had time to build, families and single men made their way to the colony site from all points on the map—many by rail, some by wagon, and one by bicycle.

"On to Washington!" became their rallying cry, borrowed from the Coxey marchers with a different Washington in mind.

One enthusiast turned poetic.

On to Washington. Raise the cry,
For the dawn of peace is nigh.
Spread the news throughout the land,

Of the Brotherhood's noble plan.
Labor shall indeed be free,
And find at last true liberty.[5]

By year's end, Equality's population stood at fifty-eight, including thirty-six women and children.

Among the early arrivals at Equality was a Missouri farm couple, Oliver Hazard Perry Darr and his wife Naomi, and their eight children. From their home in Freeman, about thirty miles south of Kansas City, they sent ahead their membership fee in two installments. Their paper receipts were signed by Lermond at his BCC headquarters in Maine. Below his signature was a printed promise that membership entitled the payer to "a home and employment" —an assurance that some colonists would soon attack as fraudulent.

Darr was a neat fit for Equality. A grandson remembered him as "a dreamer looking for a perfect world."[6] It was a quest possibly rooted in childhood; he was orphaned as an infant. He might have inherited an adventurous spirit from his great-grandfather, Conrad Darr, who in 1802 traveled from his home in Pennsylvania to stake a claim in what was called simply the "Ohio country," soon to become the Union's seventeenth state. There, in Butler County, about thirty miles north of the Ohio River, Conrad Darr established a town that still bears his name —Darrtown, originally Darr's Town, near a creek called Darr's Run.

Most arrivals had learned of Equality through the socialist grapevine, mainly by reading radical papers like *The Coming Nation*, although a few mainstream papers also found Equality newsworthy. On December 9, the Seattle *Post-Intelligencer* reported that eleven families and thirty single men— "the advance guard of the socialists"—had settled on "a splendid piece of land, part marsh and part timber." Under a front-page headline, "*Socialist Colony is in Washington*," it wrote: "The new colony has crept in almost unheralded." The next day, the *Post-Intelligencer* ventured a guess at Equality's fate, forecasting with prescience that once the initial excitement died down, trouble would boil up:

> As the colony grows, the diversity of labor and the disproportion of work accomplished by those who are industrious and those who are lazy, by those who are intelligent and capable and those who are dull and slow at learning, will become more marked, and the members will drift apart by reason of different tastes, different caliber and different aims.

To its further credit, the *Post-Intelligencer* noted in a follow-up story three days later that people in neighboring Edison were circulating a false rumor that the newcomers were "free lovers."

"This is decidedly wrong and an injustice to the members," it reported.

In those puritanical times, the term "free love" was usually intended as a smear, an accusation of sexual decadence and moral depravity. To its practitioners, it meant love free of legal and religious constraint; it was a social movement powered by the idea that the government has no business sticking its nose in anyone's romantic affairs, be it marriage, sexual relations, or birth control. This notion was central to anarchists' counterculture philosophy, as expressed by Emma Goldman. "I believe in free love," she declared in 1897.[7] "I believe that love between man and woman should be the only bond to bind them, and that if they choose to live together or to separate it is no one's affair but their own."

In Equality's case, the "free love" accusation was aimed at a practice that became known decades later as "living in sin"—adult couples living together outside of conventional marriage. There were, however, no such arrangements at the colony until 1904, when a man of unconventional impulses, Alexander Horr, arrived from New York City with a live-in partner, Jenny Horr. The couple referred to themselves as husband and wife, likely having been joined in a common law marriage, which was recognized in New York state law until 1902.[8]

Talk of radical promiscuity at Equality, however, started long before the Horrs came on the scene. It so upset and embarrassed some colonists that when visiting Edison they would remove their BCC lapel button (red for the men, white for women, blue for children) and avert townspeople's gaze—behavior that likely served only to reinforce the rumor.

In fact, most of the colonists were as sexually conservative as their critics; they valued the institution of marriage. On the other hand, Lermond, a lifelong bachelor, had ideas about free love and state-sanctioned marriage that he expressed publicly only later. Three years after he had given up on Equality, Lermond revealed an intellectual interest in the anarchist movement and endorsed "freedom in marriage," which he did not explain in detail. He simply said it meant people should be as free in their sexual relationships as "birds of the air."[9]

Sexual standards aside, the moral issue that drew people to Equality was exploitation of the wage earner by the wealthy and the persistence of poverty in a land of great riches.

In nearby New Whatcom, the *Daily Reveille* was thoroughly unimpressed by this sudden influx of radicals. It announced their arrival without favor, flourish or hype. "*A New Colony Arrives*," was its page-one headline. "They are not rich in worldly goods and have the rope harness and battered wagons and flea-bitten nags of the camper who is eternally on the wing in the middle states," it said. Prairie schooners brought them, it added— "from Texas and Kansas and Nebraska and other prairie states mainly."

James A. Peek and his family arrived by wagon from southern Oregon in October 1897, well stocked for a fresh start. Their provisions included 100 pounds each of dried apples and dried peaches, 300 pounds of beans, 75 quarts of canned fruit, and an assortment of garden seeds. Peek likely was the unnamed Oregonian whom Lermond remembered many years later as having arrived with a large supply of dried prunes, a source of sustenance that stuck in memories long after Equality was gone. Lermond recalled eating them "meal after meal and day after day, until we got fed up with prunes!"

Peek said he came prepared because he was in it for the long haul.

"I have been a worker in the cause for a long time and wish to devote my life to it," he said.[10] That devotion was baked into his offspring; son Debs Peek, born in 1896, almost certainly was named for the revered labor leader.

Other early arrivals included several Kansas families who had been on the road together since May. "They wandered weeks in Arkansas, then went to Texas, and are now in Oklahoma," *The Coming Nation* reported in early October, leaving the impression that the Kansas wanderers had been lost or confused. Pelton later said they had, in fact, been "scattering the socialistic seed" and encouraging interested families to pool their resources for a rail charter to Puget Sound. Pelton quoted from a letter received from one of the Kansans, Henry W. Halladay, expressing confidence that success was at hand.[11]

"It seems that Socialism has a stronger hold on the people at this time than ever before," Halladay wrote. It certainly had a grip on him—one that would last a lifetime. It also grabbed a few members of his extended family; a nephew, Henry B. Huff, and his family in Oklahoma followed the Halladays to Equality.

Henry Halladay's patience with capitalism wore thin as the farm economy and his family's financial condition weakened in the late 1880s. He came to believe the country needed a good shaking up and that Equality was the place to start. He became one of the colony's most devoted members; he was the first supervisor of agriculture and later served as president. For his versatility, he paid a price: he lost part of a foot while cutting timber, and later he sacrificed a finger at the saw mill.[12]

Looking back after so many years, it can be treacherous to speculate about why people like Halladay were willing to uproot their families and travel hundreds of hard miles to join a cobbled-together commune with an uncertain future in an unfamiliar corner of the country. The personal financial risks were obvious, as a socialist in Nebraska noted in a letter to Equality's leaders in 1897. A married couple in his town was inclined to join the colony but worried about the potential downside. "What they, and I presume hundreds of others, are afraid of is that when they should arrive and should find things entirely unsuited to their way of thinking, then they would be just that much money out," the Nebraskan wrote, referring to the $160 membership fee, which was non-refundable unless an applicant was rejected.[13]

It's safe to say the Equality colonists' reasons for joining were as diverse as their backgrounds, as varied and in some cases as colorful as the scenery they encountered along the way. The most devoted socialists among them, including Halladay, believed the time was right for radical change regardless of the risks; they turned out to be bigger believers than achievers, and that partly explains why the Equality story unfolded as it did.

Like many Middle Western farmers of his generation, coming of age in the immediate aftermath of the Civil War, Halladay felt sure he knew what ailed the country: bankers. "Money gamblers," he called them. They were not to be trusted and certainly not to be thanked for greasing the wheels of capitalism. They were the main reason capitalism had cooked up a poisonous brew of extreme wealth and grinding poverty.

Halladay leaned toward conspiracy as his favored theory. Money men were to blame for "every financial panic that has cursed this country, broken up homes and robbed the masses of the proceeds of their toil," he puffed to a local newspaper editor who, at the depths of the mid-90s depression, triggered Halladay's anger by offering faint praise for bankers.

It was, however, not the individual bankers Halladay despised. It was the system they manipulated.

"There is not in all the United States a business conducted on more unjust, corrupt and rotten principles than the banking business," he wrote, not caring who might accuse him of exaggeration. He was sure he was right, even if his judgment might have been clouded by anger. At that moment lenders were maneuvering to force him off his farm for unpaid debts. He was among hundreds of northwest Kansas farmers facing the pain of foreclosure, the cost of which could not be counted in dollars and cents alone. Dignity was at stake.

Politicians also ranked low on Halladay's list of tolerable humans.

"The people have awakened to the fact that they have turned over the government of the United States to the men who ape the aristocrats of Europe," he wrote in a letter to an Oberlin, Kansas, newspaper editor in 1890. "The dear farmers have been gulled [deceived] by the old parties for many years, but they have been going to school lately and learning to read. So, look out ye noblemen, something is going to drop."

Ten years later, Halladay was declaring the socialist experiment at Equality a success, setting aside the plain fact that the revolutionary spirit had faded.

"We are creating wealth, and the beauty of it is, it belongs to us who created it," he wrote in September 1900. "The capitalistic parasite does not live in Equality. There are no lawyers, no police, no politicians or preachers; everybody [is] engaged in some useful labor."

Halladay's political views were influenced by the writings of a Chicago leader of the People's Party, Seymour F. Norton, often called the "Colonel" in a nod to his Civil War service.[14] He had been a member of the United States Sharpshooters, celebrated for their exceptional marksmanship and heroic achievements for the Union, including in the battles at Gettysburg and Antietam. After the war, Norton took aim at the American economic system, which he targeted in a speech he later developed into a pamphlet and book titled, *Ten Men of Money Island.*[15] The book is a parable illustrating his argument for overhauling the capitalist system. He advocated a version of the graduated income tax, an idea widely accepted now but considered recklessly radical at the time.

In the final decades of the 19th century, conventional wisdom held that a federal income tax was part of a socialist plot to permit the poor to plunder the rich—a kind of class warfare. Sen. John Sherman of Ohio famously called it "socialism, communism, devilism."[16] During floor debate in 1894 on legislation authorizing a flat 2 percent tax on annual incomes over $4,000, Sherman, a Republican, insisted the government had no need for this additional revenue source. He called it "a low and mean form of socialism." The legislation passed the Republican-led Congress, but the following year the Supreme Court ruled it unconstitutional. As in many areas of social and economic policy, the path of public opinion took a progressive turn in the early years of the 20th century, and adoption of the 16th Amendment in 1913 gave permanent sanction to a federal income tax.

In Norton's tale, and in the minds of many liberals of that era, the rich logically bore the heaviest tax burden, curtailing their ability to accumulate great wealth. The poor paid none, allowing them a better chance at a normal life.

"This proved a very successful means of bringing about that condition of affairs most essential to the well-being of a truly republican form of government—a state of comparative equality of wealth; at least a state where enormous wealth on the one hand and monstrous poverty on the other does not exist," Norton wrote.[17] By the mid-90s, Halladay was recommending the book to his critics, some of whom considered him tiresome and intolerant because of his uncompromising views.

Henry Woods Halladay was born in 1849 in northern Indiana to a poor farm couple, Stephen and Lydia Halladay.[18] They moved to western Illinois in the mid-1850s, and to southeastern Nebraska a decade later, where they homesteaded in Otoe County. This was a common path of westward migration as the West opened more widely to white settlement with the spread of railroads, the enactment of the Homestead Act, and the forced removal of native tribes.

Henry was an adolescent when the Civil War started, too young to join the fighting but old enough to feel its sting. An older brother, Isaac Newton Halladay, was mustered into service in the Illinois infantry in September 1862 and died of disease two months later at Camp Butler, his training base.[19] (Available records are silent on what illness took Isaac, but smallpox was a major killer at Camp Butler that year.) Another brother, Benjamin Franklin Halladay, moved with his wife Mary to a town called Needy in Oregon's Willamette Valley in 1877. Their enthusiastic letters home describing a mild climate, favorable conditions for farming and ranching, and a landscape of "grand evergreens" may have given Henry ideas about one day migrating to the Pacific Northwest.[20]

At twenty-five, Henry married Josephine H. Thummel, a 21-year-old Illinois native who would become his lifelong partner. After the birth of their third child, they moved from Nebraska to northwestern Kansas and settled in Decatur County, along the Nebraska border. This was still a raw frontier, no place for the coddled or the nervous. It was the kind of place where anyone could (and Halladay did) pocket extra cash by helping thin out a wolf population that menaced farmers' livestock. The county paid one dollar per wolf scalp.

In the early autumn of 1878, a few years before the Halladays' arrival in Decatur County, the last of the so-called Indian rampages, or raids, took nineteen settlers' lives. The "Dull Knife" massacre, as it came to be remembered, was one episode in a longer tragedy of conflict between the U.S. government and the Northern Cheyenne and other Native American tribes forced from their traditional lands. In Decatur County, the trauma of 1878 was real and long-lasting; a granite monument to the dead was built in 1911 and still stands in the Oberlin cemetery. Tourists can visit Oberlin's Last Indian Raid Museum.

The Halladay farm was situated along the south fork of Johnson's Creek, about five miles west of Oberlin, the county seat. This was the Wild West we associate with folk heroes like "Wild Bill" Hickok and with cowboy songs and other frontier ballads inspired by cattle drives on the Chisholm Trail. Three counties to the east lay the landscape that inspired Brewster Higley to write a poem that became the lyrics for "Home on the

Range." By the 1880s, when the Halladays put down roots, few buffalo still roamed, having been slaughtered to near extinction, but you could easily hear a discouraging word. Foul winds of economic distress were sweeping across the Plains.

Halladay, too, was in transition. He arrived in Kansas a traditional Republican and left a radical socialist. In between, he favored the People's Party, which began as a loose alliance of agrarian interests in the mid-1880s, several years before it became a national political party. Initially known in Kansas simply as the People's movement, its leaders argued for unprecedented intervention by the federal government to counter a depressed farm economy and to support working class interests in ways they believed Democrats and Republicans would not. In 1890 the People's Party gained control of the Kansas House of Representatives and got a newspaper editor, William Peffer, elected to the U.S. Senate. Two years later they won the Kansas governorship.

The People's Party was on the march.

Halladay had no appetite for politicking, but a few years after arriving in Decatur County he was causing a stir in a small-town sort of way. A Republican-friendly newspaper, the *Oberlin Herald*, in 1883 counted him among eight lifelong Republicans who quit the county Republican Central Committee to join the People's movement. These eight, including the chairman of the county board of commissioners, were among "the best and staunchest men" in the county, the *Herald* wrote in befuddlement. Why had they bolted to become populists? What did these defections portend? The *Herald* had no answers.

Over the next several years, Halladay became deeply involved in the populist movement, serving as secretary of the Decatur County People's Party Central Committee. He also had a hand in many non-political civic duties, serving at various times as a county-appointed "viewer and surveyor" for road projects and as justice of the peace. He was a director of the Decatur County Exposition Society and helped establish the county's Agricultural, Horticultural and Stock-raising Society. He knew his way around a barnyard; his sheep and chickens regularly won top honors at the county fair.

Judging by his letters to editors of Decatur County's several newspapers, Halladay became more radical as time passed and the economy sank. By 1894 he was advocating "cooperation" — a socialist buzzword for an alternative to free-market competition. It was the intellectual foundation of Lermond's envisioned "cooperative commonwealth." Halladay likely had no awareness of Lermond at the time, but he echoed Lermond's argument that reform organizations—those seeking social as well as economic change—needed to band together or fall prey to "the most gigantic corporation on earth, the money corporation."

As Halladay saw it, most Americans were politically naïve. They would support laws against liquor sales, gambling dens, houses of prostitution and other "very common crimes." But when it came to "aristocratic crimes that are legally committed, such as gambling in stocks, bank failures, contraction of the currency," people were allowing themselves to be robbed "year after year by a few well-organized bandits and pirates."

The following year he wrote, "We farmers are aware that under the present system as it is controlled by the money gamblers, we have lost our commercial freedom." That kind of talk drew ridicule in some circles, even from people sympathetic to his disdain for bankers. A local newspaper editor whose political views were squarely in the populist camp, wrote, "The fact is, Brother Halladay, you have got 'cooperation and colony' on the brain until you take a gloomy view of all our institutions and instead of enjoying the blessings at hand you sigh continually for those utopian pleasures enjoyed only in the minds of cranky enthusiasts."

Halladay was an example of what conservatives in the late 19th century derisively called a "calamity howler"—a sky-is-falling liberal who would exaggerate the nation's problems for the sake of political gain. Liberals in one small town in Kansas had a little fun with this label by publishing a newspaper for several weeks in 1891 called the *Daily Calamity Howler,* which the local establishment paper denounced as "an ignorant, mean-spirited old wench." The town's leading liberal introduced the new paper: "We may well be proud of the name our enemies have given us in derision and scorn," since populism was destined to win the day.[21]

Howling Halladay was sounding the alarm, warning darkly of the consequences of delaying radical change.

"We are nearly all paupers out here," he wrote in the summer of 1895.[22] "It looks like northwest Kansas will have to be abandoned as a farming country, as we have not grown a crop for two years. The money gamblers have gobbled everything the people brought here."

By early 1897, Halladay had officially joined Lermond's bandwagon. He saw no redeeming value in the capitalist system, which he believed was based on the selfish principle of "the devil take the hindmost"—a variation on social Darwinism's "survival of the fittest." He and a local shoemaker formed a group that met each Saturday at the county courthouse in Oberlin to discuss Lermond's Brotherhood of the Cooperative Commonwealth, which Halladay believed would "aid in rescuing men, women and children from a life of slavery, degradation and crime."

Halladay, lean and handsome, at times wore a neatly trimmed toothbrush-style mustache that gave his angular face a distinguished look. He was known to talk politics with anyone who would listen, but he was not all business, all the time. He had a softer side. Recalling her childhood at Equality, one woman said Halladay nicknamed her "Cricket" because her "energetic bounce" reminded him of the crickets of western Kansas.[23] He had a sense of humor, too. In 1892 he wrote a short article for an Oberlin paper as an open letter to President Benjamin Harrison mocking his recent claim that cereal grain prices had risen 33 percent. "Many anxious Kansas wheat raisers are looking for that market. We desire to begin shipping at once." He signed off, "Your obedient servant, Henry W. Halladay."

He knew his views were outside the mainstream, and that bothered him not a whit. He believed too many people sleepwalked through life, blindly following the scent of money, the convenience of conformity, and the lure of social favor. "Woe to the individual who dares to think or act his true feelings or express his natural desire for a better social system," he wrote.[24]

Although Kansas is better known as a scene of Dust Bowl devastation during the early 1930s, hardship scorched the state a half-century earlier when the Halladays were still trying to grow a future in Decatur County. Drought had turned hope into a mirage on farm after farm, and homesteaders were abandoning their claims at an alarming rate. Henry and Josie Halladay, however, were not quitters. They used the Homestead Act and the Timber Culture Act to acquire two quarter-sections of land totaling 320 acres just west of Oberlin. They grew wheat and raised sheep, hogs and chickens, but times were tough and money was tight. By the end of 1889, the Halladays were struggling with a $1,300 mortgage held by the Lewis Investment Co. of Iowa. Tragedy of a more personal kind struck soon after.

Their daughter Alma, not yet ten, died of heart failure after falling ill with influenza.

The Halladays managed their sorrow but not their debt. In 1896, just as Henry was building up hope for Lermond's cooperative commonwealth, his world came crashing down. Lewis Investment foreclosed on the mortgage, and in June the farm was auctioned by the county sheriff.

The following spring, after selling what remained of their livestock, the Halladays were on their way west, but not before "scattering the socialistic seed" in Oklahoma and elsewhere along the trail. They arrived at Equality about two weeks after the colony's November 1 birth.

The *Oberlin Herald* offered the Halladays a sort-of-fond farewell: "We wish them the greatest success and prosperity but fear that Utopia is a long way off."

Chapter 7

Boomer's 'Unremitting War'

The Halladays were outliers among the discontented of the 1890s. Most did not turn to socialism or venture to the Pacific Northwest for a fresh start. They stayed put with their complaints about capitalism—perhaps curious about socialism but not inclined to make a radical move.

Westward migration had entered a new phase, as shown by a remarkable statement tucked into the federal census of 1890. It said the American frontier line, the forward edge of white settlement that had been advancing steadily westward since the nation's earliest years, had officially disappeared. Unsettled areas of the West had been penetrated so extensively by new arrivals, the census director wrote, "that there can hardly be said to be a frontier line." That forward edge of settlement had edged right off the map.

In the popular view, this seemed like a good thing, even a triumphant one. The West had finally been settled. In important ways, however, the United States had rarely been more *unsettled*. As historian and author John D. Hicks wrote, looking back at the dispiriting decade of the 1890s: "The frontier was turned back upon itself. The restless and discontented voiced their sentiments more and fled from them less."[1]

The Far West was by no means unalluring or lacking in possibilities, but a once-endless frontier was now seen to have limits. Considered from east of the Rockies, the West appeared a bit tamer and smaller than it had a decade earlier. Opportunity looked less robust, the horizon less entrancing, particularly in a depressed economy. Western migration as an outlet for social and economic frustration was no longer the obviously easier choice.

In his autobiography, *A Son of the Middle Border*, novelist Hamlin Garland told of his father's struggle and ultimate failure to make a decent living as a wheat farmer in Dakota Territory in the 1880s.[2] The elder Garland believed deeply that his and the nation's future lay in the West—not necessarily the West Coast, but in untamed lands west of the Dakotas. But after years of crop failures, savage Dakota winters, and an acknowledgement that his own uncomplaining wife had been worked nearly to death in this hard life, he gave up his ambition to go west and start over again. He retreated to his brother's homestead in Wisconsin—a path of deeper meaning. "It meant a certain phase of American pioneering had ended," the younger Garland wrote.

Others never intended to go out West but ended up there anyway. George Boomer, for example, probably would not have joined Lermond's solitary society in the Northwest wilderness had it not suddenly become an attractive alternative to the lynch mob in Kansas.

When Boomer reached Equality he confronted the colony's idle printing press, a contraption he knew as intimately as a dentist knows teeth. In his teen years he had learned the intricacies of typesetting—the art of arranging individual pieces of metal type to compose words for the printing press. He likely started out on the progressive-reformist *Greenback Labor-Chronicle* in the Maine mill town of Auburn, the older of the Auburn-Lewiston "twin cities" that stand on opposite sides of the Great Falls on the Androscoggin River. He learned the printer's trade from two uncles, George C. Boomer and William "Billy" H. Boomer.

Uncle Billy was an accomplished, even acclaimed, typesetter, humorist and family historian.[3] Billy's older brother George was a Civil War veteran whose combat record included Antietam and Gettysburg; later in the war he was shot in the right ankle at Morton's Ford on the Rapidan River in central Virginia.[4] He recovered and returned to duty, only to contract smallpox. After the war, back home in Maine, he re-entered the newspaper business. While editing and publishing *The Auburn Clipper* with Billy, he became known (and, in some quarters, despised) for freely swinging a verbal sword at Republicans on every level, including a sitting president, Ulysses S. Grant, whom he denounced in print as a drunkard, a hopeless buffoon, and an "indecent despot."[5]

Uncle George's spicy ways seemed to rub off on younger George, as did Uncle Billy's nomadic instinct. In recalling the era before Linotype machines revolutionized printing by making manual typesetting obsolete, Billy offered a simple explanation for the restlessness of an old-school newspaper printer. It was, he wrote, a "Bohemian love of a free-and-easy existence and desire for change" that compelled many like him to become what he called affectionately a "tramp printer," moving at will and on whim from one newspaper to the next.[6]

The younger George Boomer worked on more than half a dozen newspapers before he got to Equality. There his first challenge was a Hoe double-cylinder printing press that Lermond had hurriedly purchased from the *Tacoma Ledger* newspaper for $1,200. It was standing silent in Edison for lack of a steam engine and boiler. This was an urgent problem because Lermond knew a newspaper was crucial to communicating the Brotherhood's message and rallying support. The very act of publishing a socialist paper would be a point of colony pride and a morale boost. The paper's name, *Industrial Freedom,* was derived from a saying among socialists that American workers enjoyed political freedom but suffered industrial slavery.

Boomer made short work of the power problem. He figured a way to connect the Hoe to a gasoline-powered flywheel engine of the kind typically used on farms to run devices like threshing machines and water pumps. It worked. The press's two cast-iron cylinders—one carrying the metal type, the other the printing paper—came alive and soon 7,000 copies of *Industrial Freedom* rolled into nationwide circulation.

With that, Boomer picked up where he had left off in Girard—defying his critics and taking every opportunity to poke authority in the eye. He started by revisiting the flag flap. Using his Uncle Sam pen name, he denied having disrespected the Stars and Stripes and tried to turn the tables on his accusers. He argued that if anyone deserved criticism it was politicians who printed campaign photos on images of the flag and businessmen who debased Old Glory by using it in advertisements "to attract attention to their sweatshop wares." He had a point, and it was shared even in some politically conservative quarters.

In a coincidence of timing, just weeks after Boomer fled Kansas a Wyoming newspaper of Republican loyalties used its editorial column to denounce "flag-inspired patriotism." It uncritically recalled Horace Greeley's New York Tribune having called the flag "hate's polluted rag," and it argued that while the flag deserved reverence as a symbol of national sovereignty, "it should not be debased into an idol or become a talismanic charm" for political opportunists. "Conditions and circumstances—not platitudes or worship of an emblem—make patriots."[7]

Boomer loved a good argument, but he did little to make a case for the Equality colony. He found fault at every turn and soon came to see it as a poor bet for those who favored revolution over mere reform.

During the final seventeen years of his life, all in Washington, he used his dogged and combative nature, his hard-edged pen, and his soapbox oratory to relentlessly argue the weaknesses of capitalism. Undeterred by a failed 1895 campaign for governor of Rhode Island, he tried his hand at politics in Washington, with equally poor results. He ran as the Socialist Party's candidate for secretary of state in 1904 and for governor four years later. In 1914, less than a year before he died, he ran for the U.S. House seat from Washington's second congressional district. He likely knew he would lose, but each campaign served as an outlet for his bombast, a release valve for his hell-raising impulses.

"The watchword of his life," a fellow socialist wrote, "was 'unremitting war upon the enemy at every point of contact.'"[8]

Boomer started his war in Providence, Rhode Island, where, after toiling as a typesetter in the 1880s, he became active in the local typographical union and the state labor council. In 1893 he began running the state's first socialist newspaper, *Justice,* as a voice for labor unions and a counterpoint to what he called the capitalist press.

When an East Coast affiliate of Coxey's "army" marched toward Washington, D.C., through gauntlets of ridicule by mainstream eastern newspapers, Boomer's *Justice* counterpunched: "They come in rags maybe, but they are the rags of the cast-off clothing of charity; they may 'shamble along' with unshaven faces and with hard lines on their countenances, but no human being can walk erect and proudly as God's creatures should walk when that human being has been reared and has existed in those pigsty tenements built by Capital and into which the worker has been forced by his wage slavery."[9]

Rants like that earned him few friends, but he didn't care. He stuck to his guns, critics be damned. Long after he had left Rhode Island, a Providence paper took note of his near lynching in Girard: "He was always regarded as something of a crank and eventually developed into a rabid socialist," it reported with a hint of disdain.[10] "So extreme were his notions that by those well acquainted with him he was called Anarchist Boomer."

As an agitator, Boomer was a legend in his own time. An associate, Bruce Rogers, recalled an 1896 episode in which Boomer deliberately sabotaged the Democrat-supported newspaper he was editing in Maryland. Unhappy that the national People's Party had endorsed William Jennings Bryan, the Democrats' presidential nominee, rather than nominate a candidate of its own, he put his creative typesetting skills to work "until he had killed the very paper he was running by printing Bryan's name with the letters inverted." Rogers didn't name the paper but it almost certainly was the *Eastern Shore*, which began publishing in Easton, Maryland, in May 1896 and folded several weeks before the November election.[11] Years later, Rogers and Boomer collaborated on a short-lived radical magazine in Seattle they called the *Barbarian* to reflect their view of the nature of capitalism.

Unlike some in radical circles who were never quite sure why they despised capitalism, Boomer had no doubt. Just four days after arriving at *The Appeal to Reason*, he spelled out the basis of his belief in socialism. He began by describing scenes of despair he claimed to have witnessed while traveling through West Virginia, Ohio, Indiana, Illinois and Missouri on his way to Girard to begin his new newspaper job in the summer of 1897.

"Hundreds of wage workers idle in every village, the small storekeeper on the verge of distraction, and nothing in sight that promises better times," he wrote, perhaps exaggerating for effect.[12] He foresaw his own generation being condemned one day for having tolerated an economic system that allowed the rich to manipulate the rest. "The idea that we should have hunger and poverty on earth while human beings are capable of producing five times as much as they can consume while all around lie untouched and inexhaustible resources," he wrote, was argument enough to kill capitalism.

"Therefore, I am a socialist."

And, therefore, he would stop at almost nothing to make his case, regardless of his opponent. In 1908, while campaigning for Washington governor, he traveled to North Yakima to challenge the mayor's promise that no socialist would be permitted to speak on his streets. Newspapers announced Boomer's arrival as a test of free speech, and when he mounted his soapbox, no one interfered.

For a man who rebelled so persistently against capitalism, Boomer's ancestry was steeped in Americana. His English forebears were among the first settlers of New England in the 1630s. From them, it seems, he inherited his contrariness. His paternal grandfather's uncle, Ephraim Boomer, served in George Washington's Continental Army during the Revolutionary War, against the wishes of his father, who did not favor fighting for independence from the British, not if it meant risking his son's life. A headstone inscription at Ephraim's grave in Fall River, Massachusetts, says, "in direct opposition to paternal views, he avowed himself a friend to the cause of American independence."

George E. Boomer was born in Lewiston in November 1862 to Joel and Eliza Boomer. Joel was a quiet man with little interest in politics. He worked in the textile mills that dotted Lewiston's riverfront in the latter half of the 19th century, the heyday for Maine as a powerhouse in cotton textile manufacturing.

Childhood was not carefree and cozy for George. He hardly knew his mother. She died at twenty-three, shortly after his second birthday. For a time, he and his widowed father lived with Joel's parents in Lewiston. Also in the household was George's Uncle Billy, the itinerant printer whose years at the Lewiston *Evening Journal* may have been George's inspiration to learn the newspaper business—that and his disgust with the dead-end life of a mill hand.

In 1884 he married a Providence native, Mary A. Vickery, and they started a family the following year. It was not an easy life for Mary. She and their two boys did not follow George on the socialist trail, but he seemed to hold out hope of reuniting. In May 1902, after he'd been living separately from Mary for several years, he told a Seattle newspaper that he was selling timber off a two-acre lot he had purchased on Bainbridge Island in Puget Sound "to make money quick and get his sick son and the rest of his family away from the effete East out into the home of Washington firs."[13] Three weeks later, the son, 17-year-old George L. Boomer, died of tuberculosis in Providence.[14]

The few surviving photos and newspaper sketches of

Boomer depict a bespectacled man wearing a stern expression and a modest mustache. He had a broad forehead, piercing eyes, and a look of impatience befitting an agitator in a hurry to change the world.

Boomer's political views were rigid, but he had a more relaxed side. He liked to fish, played a little baseball and was a member of at least two military-style brass bands—the Second Regiment of the Uniform Rank of Knights of Pythias, in Girard, Kansas, and later, the Tacoma Military Band. In each he played the piccolo, and he was secretary of the Tacoma Musicians Union. Indeed, rhythm escorted him to the afterlife; a brass band performed at his funeral on the Olympic Peninsula.

For all his bombast, Boomer was capable of an occasional accommodation with capitalism. In 1903 his personal testimonial was used in a national newspaper ad campaign by an Iowa drug company. "I have always wanted to know this company since 1891, when Chamberlain's Colic, Cholera and Diarrhea Remedy saved my life," he was quoted as saying.[15] He and a fellow printer at the Wheeling, West Virginia, *Register* had come down with an illness resembling cholera. "He went to the hospital and died. I went to a boarding house and after I got so weak I could hardly button my clothes I tried this remedy." Two days later Boomer was back at work, or so his story went.

Throughout his years of preaching the gospel of socialism, Boomer withstood torrents of insult and abuse. In 1897 he was publishing a radical weekly in the Potomac River town of Cumberland, Maryland, called *Uncle Sam*, his pen name, when a rival newspaper in nearby Frostburg[16] denounced him as an ill-tempered imbecile, a "skunk unworthy of confidence," a ghoul, a bully, and an "intellectually moral outcast." When the clergy of Frostburg urged the Postmaster General in Washington to deny Boomer further use of the mails on account of

Uncle Sam's "vileness," the rival paper labeled him a "martyred defamer." Sometimes the insults were more creative, as when the Frostburg *Mining Journal* mocked him as a "Haroun al-Rashid Bustid"—a flamboyant fraud, a pompous pretender.[17]

Even a former ally, Julius A. Wayland, turned on Boomer in 1902, insisting he was worse than incompetent as a spokesman for the newly created Socialist Party of America. Wayland, publisher of *The Appeal to Reason*, the socialist weekly where Boomer had created a furor four years earlier with his "rag on a stick" column, called him a "freak" who excelled only at dividing people and who should be forcibly retired or sent to "an imbecile asylum." Boomer responded in *The Socialist,* a Seattle weekly where he was a columnist and associate editor. He acknowledged that his methods sometimes irked fellow socialists, but with typical defiance he insisted the offended were lousy leftists—soft, foggy headed, and too willing to compromise their political principals.

Later, when Boomer ran the *Tribune Review* in Edmonds, just north of Seattle, the mayor—himself a socialist—publicly denounced the weekly for a "raving, maniacal, 'shoot-up-the-town'" editorial policy.[18]

In a final insult, fire in October 1915 destroyed the office and print shop of his last socialist newspaper venture, *The Peninsula Free Press* of Port Angeles, Washington, a small city on the Olympic Peninsula. Port Angeles happened to have been the site of the state's first experimental socialist community, predating Equality by a decade and lasting several years.[19] Six months before the fire on Front Street, Boomer died of intestinal paresis, or paralysis of the digestive tract. His second wife, Alice, whom he married in 1903, was running the newspaper and living in rooms at the rear of the print shop when it burned down. A local paper called it a "fire of mysterious origin." Alice survived and although she was a printer and

Linotype operator, she decided not to rebuild and restart the *Free Press.*

To his dying day, Boomer stayed true to his anti-war instincts and to his disdain for corporate exploitation of patriotic folly. In one of the last issues of the *Free Press* before he died, he editorialized against what he saw as America's mistaken march to war—this time in Europe—for the benefit of corporate chieftains and at the expense of ordinary people.

"It would be the supreme height of asinine folly for a single worker of this country to offer his services to the end that more wealth may be safely shipped out of the United States to the despoilation and increased suffering of those who have produced it," he wrote in February 1915. "But the capitalists of this country will demand war, if necessary, in order that they may continue their unholy traffic and make a few more blood-stained dollars."[20]

To magnify his scorn, Boomer reprinted above his editorial a newly published poem, "Illusions of War," by the English writer Richard Le Gallienne, calling war "dark butchery without a soul."

For others less militant than Boomer, the impulse to heed Lermond's call to lead a socialist revolution in Washington was generated by a mix of idealism, desperation and wanderlust. The motive they shared most commonly, however, was frustration rooted in a feeling that life had cruelly failed to deliver on the promises offered in the innocence of youth. The notion of equality, after all, is learned in childhood: share with others and treat them as your equal; everyone deserves a fair shake. School children are taught that the Declaration of Independence says it's a self-evident truth that "all men are created equal." If so, many of Boomer's generation asked, why is there such poverty in a land of great wealth? They did not share the view that the creed of equality does not grant equality but rather invites people to seek it.

Others turned to Equality for less philosophic reasons. They saw it as a chance to dig out of a money hole; they believed Lermond's forecasts of utopian peace, prosperity, and economic security. In April 1898, a few weeks after he'd arrived on the scene, Lermond wrote that his Brotherhood was "the safest and best insurance" against destitution in old age. "The BCC is a great cooperative mutual insurance company—the only insurance company that builds a home for you," he wrote.[21]

Still other arrivals at Equality knew little about socialism and cared even less; for them the colony was simply a way station on the road to nowhere. As one put it: "It promises a meal." Another, a true believer, claimed he had recognized the goldbrickers early on—people who were "of small ability and many wants—too indolent and incompetent to make a living on the outside."[22]

Hope for their children's future is what brought Jesse and Sarah Ann Pomeroy to Equality—that and plain poverty. They traveled for several months in a covered wagon from their coal company-owned home in what was called Indian Territory, roughly the eastern half of present-day Oklahoma. Stopping frequently along the way to work for their food and other necessities, the Pomeroys arrived at Equality in October 1898.

Frederick E. Smith,[23] who grew up in tiny Blanchard in the 1920s, barely a stone's throw from by-then-abandoned Equality, spent years researching the experiences of the Pomeroys and as many other of the colonists and their descendants as he could track down in the 1960s. He prepared a handwritten manuscript and partnered with his sister Florence in editing and typing it for publication, but he died before he could find a publisher. Equality, he wrote, was a phenomenon "colored with innocence, exuberance and tragedy."[24]

In Smith's telling,[25] Jesse Pomeroy and Sarah Ann Hines grew up on adjacent farms in Missouri in the 1860s. Although they moved away after marrying, they kept Missouri close by naming their first child Hannibal, the Mississippi River town of Mark Twain's youth and the setting for his most famous novels. The second child was named Minnie Missouri Pomeroy. Jesse worked in a coal mine in southern Missouri before the couple moved first to Texas and then, in the late 1880s, to Indian Territory, where they and their five children lived in grinding poverty in a mining camp called Liddle (now Coalgate) on Choctaw tribal lands just west of the Ouachita Mountains. This was fertile ground for radicalism among the disillusioned and the hopeless.

"Every night Ann drove the wagon to bring her husband home from the mine numb with fatigue," Smith wrote. "And in the morning, she would deliver him back to the mine still tired."

By comparison, life at Equality must have seemed like easy street. For many other newcomers, however, colony life was harder than they had imagined. The first challenge was coming up with the $160 membership fee, a significant sum that the Equality treasurer counted on to get the colony through its rocky first months. Cash payment was preferred, but some traded property or equipment for membership. Some paid in cash installments. Some worked off the fee over time. Indeed, a lack of start-up cash was among the colony's greatest shortcomings, reflecting the equally important flaw of inadequate planning by Lermond and Pelton, who failed to see, or simply ignored, the fact that socialists nationally were turning away from colonization as the preferred path to political relevance. They realized too late that national support was too weak.

In a note published in the BCC's initial mouthpiece, *The Coming Nation*, in mid-December 1897, Pelton insisted no one come to Equality who lacked either the membership fee or an appreciation for the scale of manual labor they would face. Stump-dotted former logging areas needed to be cleared for crop planting. Dikes required shoring up on reclaimed portions of the Samish tidal fats, and housing was in short supply. And that was just for starters. The village under construction was merely a first step; farther along the hill they would build the real Equality once resources were at hand. It would be a permanent city extending southeast from the temporary village, with a public square surrounded by wide streets, park-like gardens, and dozens of lots for homes.

"Our prospects are brightening daily, but we are not out of the woods yet," Pelton wrote, adding in capital letters, "THIS COLONY MUST NOT AND SHALL NOT FAIL."

In those early months before Lermond and other members of the BCC national board came on the scene, Pelton pinned his hopes on colonists' willingness to match his work ethic. Few could. None did. Nor were they equal to the challenges that would arrive with Lermond.

Norman W. Lermond, circa 1931. Oil portrait courtesy of American Malacological Society archives, Drexel University.

At Lermond's "Willows" estate in early 1898, left to right: Lermond, Eva Pelton, Helen Mason, Florence Pelton, Annie Pelton and an unidentified Lermond relative. Courtesy, Center for Pacific Northwest Studies, Western Libraries Archives and Special Collections, Western Washington University.

George Edwin "Ed" Pelton traveled from Maine in September 1897 as Lermond's "special agent," to buy land for colony No. 1. Courtesy, Center for Pacific Northwest Studies, Western Libraries Archives and Special Collections, Western Washington University.

Henry W. Halladay, a Republican-turned-Socialist, had little tolerance for bankers and politicians. Courtesy, Halladay family.

Henry and Josephine Halladay arrived at Equality in November 1897, having lost their Kansas farm to foreclosure. They remained longer than anyone — long after the colony collapsed in 1906-07. Both died in 1931 at the outset of the Great Depression. Courtesy, Center for Pacific Northwest Studies, Western Libraries Archives and Special Collections, Western Washington University.

William McDevitt, approximately 15, attended St. Charles pre-seminary school in Maryland. Courtesy of Bancroft Library, University of California, Berkeley.

McDevitt in his mid-20s in Washington, D.C., where he earned an advanced law degree. Photo by Barnett M. Clinedinst, White House photographer for presidents McKinley, Roosevelt and Taft. Courtesy of Bancroft Library, University of California, Berkeley.

Harry Ault came to Equality with his family from Kentucky as a teenager. Courtesy, Center for Pacific Northwest Studies, Western Libraries Archives and Special Collections, Western Washington University.

Equality colony cooks and kitchen help, 1900. Left to right: Susie Gifford, Grace Lewis, Eva Longberry, Virginia Hogan, Emma Huff (Halladay), Inza Joslyn. Photo and names courtesy of Skagit County Historical Museum.

Standing, center, at printing press is George E. Boomer, who arrived in 1898 after escaping a lynch mob in Kansas. Courtesy, Center for Pacific Northwest Studies, Western Libraries Archives and Special Collections, Western Washington University.

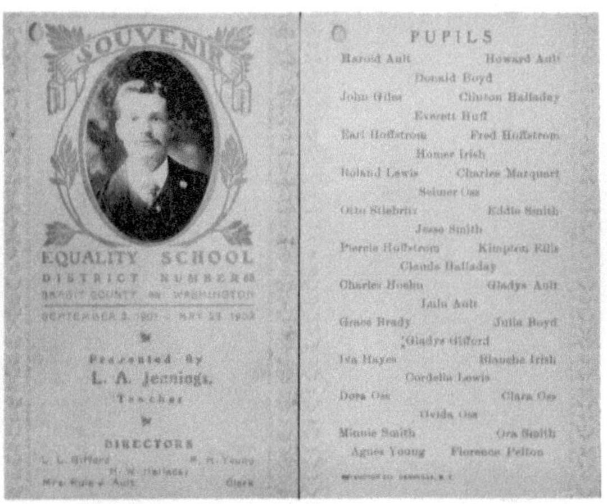

SOUVENIR

EQUALITY SCHOOL
DISTRICT NUMBER 68

Presented By
L. A. Jennings,
Teacher

DIRECTORS

PUPILS

Harold Ault — Howard Ault
Donald Boyd
John Giles — Clinton Halladay
Everett Huff
Earl Hoffstrom — Fred Hoffstrom
Homer Irish
Roland Lewis — Charles Marquart
Selmer Oss
Otto Stiebritz — Eddie Smith
Jesse Smith
Pierrie Hoffstrom — Kimpton Ellis
Claude Halladay
Charles Hoskin — Gladys Ault
Lulu Ault
Grace Brady — Julia Boyd
Gladys Gifford
Iva Hayes — Blanche Irish
Cordelia Lewis
Dora Oss — Clara Oss
Ovida Oss
Minnie Smith — Ora Smith
Agnes Young — Florence Pelton

Equality public school district No. 68, 1901-02 school year. Courtesy, Center for Pacific Northwest Studies, Western Libraries Archives and Special Collections, Western Washington University.

David Burgess, Equality school principal, (back row, left) and teacher Kate Halladay (back row, right) with 41 students. 1898. Courtesy, University of Washington Libraries, Special Collections. Photo origin unknown.

Burgess family, early 1890s. Left to right, back row: Edith, Emmor, Irene, Myrta. Front: David, Arthur, Anna. Photo by Sara Jessie Young, pioneering portrait photographer in Fayetteville, Arkansas. Courtesy, Lora Leschner.

David Burgess. Courtesy, Lora Leschner.

David and Anna Burgess were raised in Ohio as Quakers.
They came to Equality from Arkansas in August 1898.
Courtesy, Lora Leschner.

Margaret (Thompson) Joslyn grew up in upstate New York and in northern Illinois. Courtesy, Center for Pacific Northwest Studies, Western Libraries Archives and Special Collections, Western Washington University.

Margaret and John Joslyn, center and right, walked from Belfast train station to their new life at Equality with unidentified "stranger," July 1900. Courtesy, Center for Pacific Northwest Studies, Western Libraries Archives and Special Collections, Western Washington University.

Joe and Annie Billingsley in front of their Samish Island home, 1910. They came to Equality from Nebraska in 1898. Courtesy, Fred Miller, co-author of *Samish Island, a History*. Roger Fox collection.

Helen M. Mason left Equality in late 1898. She died of cancer in January 1901 and was buried in Mount Pleasant Cemetery on Seattle's Queen Anne hill. Author photo, 2025.

Chapter 8

Living a 'Glory-radiant' Dream

If ever a socialist came honestly by his grudge against capitalism it was William McDevitt, a member of Lermond's inner circle. His cradle days were a lesson in human suffering among the underclass of urban America, where the rich were revered and the poor were left to their miseries. And so, it was with pride and a dash of exaggeration that late in life McDevitt credited his generation with adding the vital missing ingredient in a recipe for social justice: a conscience.

"Willie," as the wee one was known in boyhood, was a foundling, a term of that era normally referring to a newborn or infant abandoned by his parents, although in McDevitt's case the circumstances are unclear. He once said, "I was not 'abandoned' by my mother but placed" with a Catholic nun who, in his birth year of 1869, established in Greenwich Village the New York Foundling Asylum of the Sisters of Charity.[1] This sanctuary was an effort to deal humanely with what had become a neglected social crisis in the nation's largest city. Abandoned infants and newborns were being found (thus the term "foundling") on stoops and streets, sometimes in trash cans, often sick or undernourished, never with an ordinary chance for a normal life. Many died, even those rescued by Samaritans.

For years, people had sneered at or outright opposed institutional support for foundlings, who were dismissed as illegitimate products of godless women—often European immigrants and the indigent. The stated wisdom was that it was morally wrong to "save" these women from their failure and poverty; rescuing their babies, some argued, legitimized foundling asylums, or sanctuaries, and made them "temptations to licentiousness," as a New York newspaper put it.[2] The implication: these mothers and their babies were subhuman.

The hard truth is that it was more convenient to ignore the problem or shrug it off as an unavoidable byproduct of survival-of-the-fittest capitalism than to consider the idea that this debasement of human life—and other disheartening consequences of economic inequality—was a problem that should be addressed by society, not just by a few "do-gooders."

Impatience with social injustice—not specifically the foundling problem but inequities more broadly—lay at the heart of the Equality project and partly explains its attractiveness to people like McDevitt. For some at Equality, delivering economic and social justice was the true meaning of socialism. That's why they called themselves a brotherhood. For others, such as McDevitt, correcting the ills of capitalism required something more. It called for revolution—the "unconditional surrender of capitalism," McDevitt once called it—although neither he nor any of his colleagues knew what that might mean or how it might happen. It's not even clear that revolution is what they truly wanted. There is no doubt, however, that they wanted radical change, and McDevitt pushed it as far as any—rhetorically, at least.

In old age, McDevitt seemed to concede that he had overreached. He wrote that he had arrived on Samish Bay with "my pristine enthusiasm" and indulged in the "glory-radiant dream"[3] of creating a successful socialist community, only awaken to a more practical reality. Yet, he remained a life-long socialist committed to resisting what novelist Jack London called the "Iron Heel" in his tale of an oligarchic force that crushed the working class under foot.

In infancy, McDevitt was among the lucky foundlings; he survived an ordeal that many did not. The story of how he happened to have been "placed in the arms" of the Sisters of Charity, as he put it decades later, seems lost to history, buried in tiers of time and shielded by privacy laws. When contacted about McDevitt's case in 2022 and again in 2025, the New York Foundling, as it is now called, said state law prohibited it from disclosing any information to a non-relative—even a confirmation that this man, who never married and had no known siblings or offspring, was taken in more than a century and a half ago.[4]

William James McDevitt was born in Brooklyn on February 21, 1869, and baptized seven days later at St. Vincent de Paul Catholic Church in the city's Williamsburg neighborhood, home to many European immigrants.[5] By fate's grim symmetry, this baby christened under the protection of Saint Vincent de Paul, coincidentally renowned among Catholics as a 17th century champion of foundlings, would soon become one himself. In the years ahead, Catholicism would take a darker place in McDevitt's life, weighing so heavily that it broke his tenderest ties.

Available church records reveal nothing about his parents except their Irish-sounding names: William McDevitt and Ellen O'Donald. It is unclear how much the young McDevitt ever learned—or wished to learn—about his family history.

Among his surviving papers is a handwritten note dated June 11, 1888, when he was nineteen, from the rector at St. Vincent de Paul. In sparse language, it certified the place and dates of McDevitt's birth and baptism and identified his parents and godparents.

McDevitt himself said on at least two occasions late in life that he had been among the first infants to enter the New York Foundling Asylum. Witty by nature, he told a San Francisco newspaper in 1953 that he likely was the "sole survivor of the 'class' of 1869 at the New York Foundling Asylum."[6] By coincidence, the topic came up a year later when H.L. Mencken, the renowned Baltimore journalist and social critic, contacted McDevitt to ask his birthdate. Mencken wanted to add that detail to his collection of their written correspondence, which dated to the 1920s. In his letter of reply, McDevitt repeated his line about being a member of the asylum's Class of '69. "It is rather likely," he added, "that I am the last of Sister Irene's children of that year,"[7] referring to Sister Mary Irene FitzGibbon, the nun credited with starting the New York Foundling Asylum with an assist from two other nuns and sympathetic neighbors.[8]

(In the 21st century, the term "foundling" has disappeared, but the problem has not. Mothers still abandon newborns, but "safe haven" laws in all fifty states designate places like police stations and hospitals where a parent can leave a child without risk of prosecution for abandonment. Child welfare services have replaced institutional solutions like foundling asylums.)

In boyhood McDevitt was sickly, and the attendant emotional scars seem to have lasted a lifetime. Clear in his mind decades later was the memory of a "humorless and tactless" school instructor telling his classmates, "We must make allowances for Willie. He will not be with us long."

McDevitt also suffered from the emotional homelessness of

orphanhood. That changed when, in his teens, he spent summers with a southern Virginia family. "For the first time in my life," he wrote years later, "I was enjoying the deep satisfaction of 'coming home': the assurance that I was no long *sans famille* but definitely *en famille* with the sense of belonging, that supreme yearning of nearly every orphan, the sense of being a full member of the society of humans."

At the age of about ten, McDevitt was taken from the care of Sister Irene's New York sanctuary to be placed in the home of a widowed dressmaker, Mary A. Riordan, and her three nieces in Frederick, Maryland.[9] In about 1880, he was resettled at St. Patrick's Orphans Home in Baltimore. His legal guardian was the Rev. John T. Gaitley, an Irish immigrant who ran the orphanage on South Broadway at Bank Street as pastor of the adjoining St. Patrick's Catholic Church.[10] Gaitley likely had a hand three years later in getting McDevitt admitted to St. Charles College, a Catholic prep school for young men aspiring to the priesthood.[11] There, near Ellicott City, Maryland, on Baltimore's doorstep, McDevitt encountered the "humorless and tactless" Sulpician padre. More importantly, he was befriended by, and soon afterward informally adopted by, an English literature teacher and poet, the Rev. John Banister Tabb, who adored the boy and would become the most influential man in his life.

Tabb was a Virginian and an unreconstructed Southern rebel; in his own words: a "Rebel unredeemed and unredeemable."[12] As a teenager he served in the Confederate navy as a civilian aboard blockade-running ships in the Caribbean and along the Atlantic seaboard, dodging a Union blockade that ran from the Virginia Capes south around Florida and across the Gulf of Mexico to Texas. In McDevitt's telling, Tabb was his touchstone, a devoted stand-in for the father he never knew. Tabb's sister, Harriet, saw so much of her brother in

Willie's character that she once told Tabb the boy was "your personal production."[13]

Though born in the Yankee north and a West Coaster for the final six decades of his life, McDevitt concluded in old age that his nature "sloped to the Southern side" —a measure of Tabb's enduring influence. During his six years at St. Charles College, McDevitt spent each summer at Tabb's birthplace and ancestral estate, *The Forest*, one of about a dozen homesteads of the extended Tabb family, wealthy owners of a vast network of tobacco and corn plantations amid ancient oaks and loblolly pines in Amelia County, Virginia. *The Forest,* about thirty miles west of Richmond and seven miles north of Amelia Court House, offered young McDevitt a taste of undiluted Dixie culture. If there was a motherly presence in his life it may have been a Tabb cousin, whom McDevitt identified only as Mrs. Barksdale, who lived on a nearby Tabb ancestral estate called *Clay Hill.*[14] McDevitt suspected Tabb and Barksdale had been childhood sweethearts, "which is possibly the reason she treated me as if I were her own son."[15]

When he entered St. Charles College at age fourteen, McDevitt was the youngest and smallest first-year student.

"My comparative invisibility was what perhaps prompted Tabb to adopt me, almost from the start, as his son, and he remained my 'father' until his death in 1909," he wrote.[16]

After six years at St. Charles, completing four years of high school and two years of college-level course work, McDevitt graduated with honors and as president of his senior class in the spring of 1889.[17] He then let loose his rebelliousness by refusing the expected next step of entering Baltimore's prestigious St. Mary's Seminary. This decision to abandon the path to priesthood was looked on as something like heresy. It cost him his relationship with his guardian, the Rev. Gaitley, a St. Mary's graduate of great distinction. McDevitt was reported to have said the disappointed priest disowned him and "chucked [him] out on his head."[18] McDevitt's adoptive father, Father Tabb, took his side. It was "all for the best," Tabb told McDevitt, that the seminary plan "did not succeed."[19]

The following year McDevitt moved to Detroit to make profitable use of shorthand skills he'd picked up at St. Charles. He worked first at Pernin's Shorthand Institute, where his duties included teaching typing and taking dictation from the proprietor, Helen M. Pernin, and then as a stenographer at the Detroit law firm of Sloman, Berry and Duffie.[20] His ambition burned bright even as the religious flame flickered, and in 1892 he returned to the East Coast and enrolled at Georgetown Law School in Washington, D.C. He paid the bills by working as a clerk at the United States Geological Survey, later doing similar work at the Smithsonian Institution. The Geological Survey job paid $720 a year[21] and enabled him to further hone his remarkable skills in shorthand and stenography. Shorthand became his calling card. In the mid-90s, he wrote, published and sold shorthand instruction booklets for his proprietary system, which he called "Rite-it-Rite."[22]

At Georgetown he earned a Bachelor of Laws degree, finishing fourth in his class of sixty-four.[23] He also won honorable mention in an essay contest for his entry, "Moral Insanity as a Legal Defense."[24] (He was a lifelong opponent of capital punishment, which he called "legal lynching.") The following year, 1895, he was awarded a Master of Laws degree and was among a handful of graduates invited to make a banquet toast.[25] Educated and well connected in the nation's capital, he seemed on his way to prospering in mainstream America.

McDevitt loved an intellectual challenge. He served as president of Georgetown's debating society and was the sort of tireless talker who would spend an evening with neighbors debating such obscure topics as the merits of English poet Matthew Arnold's critique of Leo Tolstoy. His taste in literature ran to the classics; his favorite writer was Britain's Walter Savage Landor, a rambunctious writer and poet of the early 1800s perhaps best known for his line about living life to its fullest: "I warmed both hands before the fire of life."

McDevitt also liked sports, having outgrown his childhood frailty. Baseball was his game at St. Charles, and later he played tennis for the Riverdale Athletic Club in Maryland and competed in long-range bicycle races as a member of the Hyattsville Cycle Club. He hung out with fellow Georgetown students at Stegmaier's, a roadside tavern near the Anacostia River town of Bladensburg, just beyond the District of Columbia line. There he indulged in home-cooked chicken dinners and a plentiful supply of Gin Rickeys and other popular potations.

It was at Stegmaier's that McDevitt got his first serving of radicalism, dished up in the summer of 1894 by leftover protesters from the Coxey "army" that had marched on Washington a few months earlier. After being evicted from the capital, Coxey and a few hundred of his fellow "commonwealers" set up temporary tent headquarters on a property owned by George W. Stegmaier, the tavern owner, at or near present-day North Brentwood, Maryland. Among the populist and socialist literature they shared with McDevitt was *The Dogs and the Fleas, By One of the Dogs.* This newly published book was intended by its author, who used the pseudonym Frederic Scrimshaw,[26] as a warning that greedy "fleas" among American capitalists were sucking the blood out of passive worker "dogs." Industrial Age capitalism was so corrupt, he wrote, that "no one can come to great wealth except by some of the many forms of legal stealing."

This struck a chord in McDevitt. He would count May 1, 1894, the day he watched Coxey's marchers enter the capital city, as "my birthday as a socialist." He was twenty-five. Not by coincidence, this also was the year of a wrenching break in his relationship with Tabb, the poet-priest who once told McDevitt that he kept a picture of him over his private altar, "so you never get farther from my sight than from my heart, where God put you forever."[27]

In private letters to McDevitt that year, Tabb made clear he wanted never to see him again, although they continued to write to each other. Tabb believed McDevitt had gone astray, wasting his intellect and education by adopting the "worldly life" in Washington at the expense of his Catholic faith.[28] The priest's stern tone was unmistakable. McDevitt, Tabb said, had abandoned his "religious duty." Tabb went so far as to suggest that in turning from Catholicism, the young man had disrespected the memory of a mother he never knew:

> I was sure, son, you did not quite realize the change that our last meeting manifested. It was your birthday — a time when, till then, you had piously thought of your mother and gone to communion for her, as you and I only, in all the wide world, had for many years done. That morning I went to the altar alone, and knowing that you were not even at mass, could but feel that our tenderest tie was no more.[29]

McDevitt asked Tabb to visit him at Georgetown, but the priest refused.[30] In October, Tabb once more invoked the memory of McDevitt's mother in explaining why he deplored the change he had seen in the young man:

> If it seems to you strange that I deprecate, son, ... believe me it is only as your mother might have felt had she seen you so changed — were it even for the better — from the baby she loved.[31]

Tabb accused McDevitt of having "dissolved your old sonship with me,"[32] although in public McDevitt never stopped referring to him as his father. In Tabb's view, the relationship was lost irretrievably; McDevitt was a casualty of a "malaria of skepticism" —a diseased spirit. "To take up our broken thread now," he wrote in 1895, as McDevitt was finishing up at Georgetown, "would be painful to you as to me; so, till you need your old father again, suffer him to be, as he is, ever yours."[33]

McDevitt was an idealist in a morally earnest but impractical way. Money didn't motivate him. If it had, he would not have wriggled his way into Lermond's inner circle and chased the Equality dream. Like many others drawn to the Brotherhood, McDevitt imagined finding the key to a brighter future—for society more than for himself.[34] It's not possible to say for sure where or when he acquired this brotherly impulse. Could it have been a product of his Catholic upbringing? His encounter with the Coxey protesters? Or might it simply have been in his blood? As a foundling, he never knew his kin, never was secured by the emotional anchor that only parents provide.

The Equality colony experience did not reward McDevitt's idealism, but it pushed him to broaden his horizons. He decided he needed what he called "some practical experience in manual labor." He had been an industrious student but had never done a lick of non-office work in thirty years of living. So, shortly after giving up on Equality, and rather than settle for a small challenge close to home, he went big and far.

He made his way to Alaska Territory to work on the White Pass and Yukon railroad, which climbed 3,000 feet on a treacherous path from the port town of Skagway, at the northernmost point of the Inside Passage, to the summit of White Pass and on to Whitehorse in Canada's Yukon Territory.[35] This experience in the Far North may have boosted McDevitt's spirit and satisfied his thirst for manual labor, but it did little for his pocketbook. Afterward he would refer to "my costly trip to Alaska," lamenting that it had left him "very straitened financially."[36]

He solved his money trouble by re-entering his comfort zone: government and academia. He took a job as stenographer for the Washington state superintendent of public schools in Olympia and taught high school English in the logging town of Chehalis, south of Olympia. In 1901 he became the assistant registrar at the University of Washington in Seattle and was promoted the following year to registrar. Late in life, McDevitt claimed cryptically that he was removed as registrar "for political reasons."[37] In Seattle his worlds were colliding. In August 1902 he resigned as secretary-treasurer of the state Socialist Party, citing party rules that said no one could hold office who had not severed "all relations whatsoever with the capitalist parties." He decided (or, more likely, it was decided for him) that this was a problem because he had been appointed registrar by the state university's board of regents, capitalists one and all. So he resigned his party position to keep the university job, only to lose that, too, the following year.

Over the years, McDevitt earned just enough to enable his proselytizing for socialism. In the early 1900s he traveled up and down the West Coast delivering lectures on what he foresaw as the golden age of socialism. "Today's Greatest Gospel: Socialism. A Red-Hot Lecture by Wm. McDevitt," blared a newspaper announcement of his appearance in Medford, Oregon. "The War in Goldfield," was his topic on a winter evening in Portland in 1907—a chance to defend labor's stand in a series of strikes and lockouts of gold miners in Nevada.

Although he was admitted to the Washington state bar in 1899, he was never a practicing attorney. (He cared more about being a linguist than a lawyer, although he routinely added the "LL.M." designation after his name, indicating advanced legal training.) He had a contentious relationship with the law. He claimed with apparent pride, as if it were a compelling credential, that he was arrested by police twenty-one times in three states during his lifetime—in most cases as part of a 1905 free-speech campaign in Oakland, California, to test the constitutionality of city ordinances restricting street-corner oratory.

McDevitt was a romantic at heart, and literature was his first love. In the San Francisco Bay area he seemed finally at home. He rubbed elbows with all manner of socialists and men whose literary chops far exceeded his own. They included Jack London, a revolutionary socialist whose novel, *The Call of the Wild,* had recently lit the fuse of his skyrocketing fame.[38] Among others: London's close friend George Sterling, the acclaimed poet and playwright who helped establish California's famous artist colony, Carmel-by-the-Sea; and *The Jungle* author Upton Sinclair, crusader for social justice. In one of his many notes to McDevitt, Sinclair signed off, "Yours in Revolution."[39]

Sterling and McDevitt were the same age and had been classmates for three years at St. Charles College. New Yorkers by birth, McDevitt said he and Sterling were San Franciscans "by re-birth." Their last conversation, in which they reminisced about St. Charles, was several months before Sterling killed himself by cyanide poisoning in 1926.[40]

"George wound up by being the admired Prince of Bohemia, while I got 'mired' closer to Hobohemia—as a soap-boxer among the proletarians and, thereafter, an 'orator' among the radical politicians," he wrote.[41] His speaking style impressed some. A San Francisco newspaper columnist credited him with "a kind of bull-tongued delivery that rattled the rafters over men's heads."[42]

McDevitt had a thing for the bohemian theme. Then, as now, it connoted a free spirt, a counter-culture chic, a rejection of social or political orthodoxy. While at Georgetown, he was a member of the Capital Bohemians, likely styled after the grander Bohemian Club started two decades earlier in San Francisco as a gathering place for artists, musicians and writers —urban bohemians like London and Sterling.

McDevitt had a remarkable knack for connecting with people. During his San Francisco years, he came to count Mencken, the Baltimore essayist and journalist, as a friend, although they may have been more like pen pals than actual friends.[43] Mencken shared the Bohemians' disdain for cultural provincialism, but he was no rebel and McDevitt was hardly his natural ally. Mencken thoroughly despised socialism. And yet, he and McDevitt had a lot in common even beyond an affinity for Baltimore. Both men opposed America's entry into the First World War, regretted the government's wartime abuse of free speech rights and 1920s crackdown on radicalism, and expressed a lifelong fascination with the oddities and intricacies of the English language.

McDevitt fancied himself a great writer, but the opinion was not shared widely.[44] He loved a good yarn, particularly if it featured an underdog. And so it was that, in his final years, he kept close at hand a copy of *Ben Hardy's Flying Machine*, a classic of boyish dreams and heroic deeds.[45]

A born bookworm, the publication McDevitt pointed to as the biggest influence on his thinking about socialism came to his attention by accident at age twenty-six. He stumbled upon it in a library at the Smithsonian's Bureau of American Ethnology, where he worked at the time. It was called *Icaria: A Chapter in the History of Communism*, published in 1884 as an assessment of a radical movement in France inspired by an 1840 utopian novel. The Icarians, as they were known, established a series of communes in the United States, the last of which disbanded in Iowa in 1898. Albert Shaw, author of the book that caught McDevitt's eye, was not an advocate of communism or socialism, but he credited the Icarians with trying to "realize the rational, democratic communism of the Utopian philosophers."

As it turned out, the Icarians' burdens as described by Shaw were remarkably similar to those of the Equality colonists McDevitt was about to join on Puget Sound: "hardships, dissensions, and disappointments."

A short time later, the Smithsonian figured again in McDevitt's awaking to radicalism and his urge to make a clean break with ordinary society. One day in 1896 he spotted a socialist newspaper in a waste basket in the office of his Smithsonian boss, William J. McGee. It was *The Appeal to Reason*, the paper that Boomer would join the following year. It's hard to tell whether his allowing a copy of the *Appeal* in his office meant McGee was a closet radical or whether its presence in the waste basket meant he was not. Either way, it added momentum to McDevitt's political transformation.

The following year, McDevitt thought seriously of joining the socialist Ruskin colony in eastern Tennessee, perhaps feeling a tug to the "Southern side." Instead, he opted for a newer, less well-known project—Lermond's plan to launch a socialist colony in the timberlands of Washington.

"I preferred to be in at the start of my dream newfoundland," he wrote later.

Chasing the dream meant giving up steady, if not terribly stimulating, clerical work at the Smithsonian, paying an even $100 a month,[46] and leaving behind a network of friends in Washington D.C., and in the eastern suburbs of Maryland where he had lived for seven years. McDevitt seemed, however, to have been born with a streak of vagabondage; the idea of starting from scratch a faraway socialist colony was irresistible. He saw Equality as a can't-miss chance to reach for the stars. "In a word, it hypnotized me," he wrote.

Off he went on a week-long train journey from Washington city to Washington state by way of Chicago. Before departing on February 28, he sent a letter to *The Coming Nation*, the socialist newspaper still serving as the voice of Lermond's BCC. His words hinted at worry for the future. "Continuous harmony," he wrote, was essential to developing a utopian or socialist community; the noblest of intentions could be destroyed in internecine backbiting. He added:

> This is my only fear—the fear that disunion, or exclusiveness, will develop with our growth, and we may forget to profit from the lessons of the past furnished by the earlier history of applied socialism.

McDevitt was wrong about a lot of things, but he was right to worry about that one. His fear may have been rooted not only in the example of the Icarians but also in lessons from the collapse of a utopian commune in southern Indiana in the 1820s. Known as New Harmony and bankrolled by a prosperous Welshman, Robert Owen, its members discovered that harmony was too hard. One wrote after the collapse, "The more we desired and called for 'union,' the more this diversity seemed to be developed, and instead of that harmonious cooperative we had expected, we found more antagonisms than we had been accustomed to in common life." [47]Another put it more simply: New Harmony suffered from "too many heads and not enough arms,"[48] an imbalance that would topple Equality, too.

Chapter 9

Lermond Arrives, Trouble Follows

When McDevitt's train reached Chicago, he linked up with the Lermond party, which had arrived on the Chicago & Grand Trunk line from Maine by way of Montreal, Quebec; Sarnia, Ontario; southern Michigan, and South Bend, Indiana. Along the way, Lermond picked up Brotherhood colleagues and perhaps a few new converts.

At South Bend a most unusual man joined the travel party. His name was Robert Barton. A lifelong resident of Battle Creek, Michigan, his blacksmithing skills earned him a seat aboard the Lermond bandwagon. What Lermond probably did not know was that Barton had a history of mental instability. The truth of his condition, whether illness or simple eccentricity, is impossible to know from available public records.[1] The previous July, local newspaper reports in Battle Creek said, improbably, that Barton was "taken suddenly insane." He was placed in what was known at the time as the state insane asylum at Kalamazoo, now the Kalamazoo Psychiatric Hospital. This was his second confinement there—and not the last time he would suffer the indignity of being publicly declared insane. The first time, in 1879, he was just twenty-eight years old; a local newspaper called it a case of "overwork and excessive heat" from which he could quickly recover. These episodes, in an age of limited medical privacy, were reported by area newspapers whose diligence in verifying facts is impossible to judge decades later.

News reports about Barton's condition asserted with certainty that his insanity was caused by physical exhaustion, although diagnosis and treatment of mental illness in that era was at a relatively primitive stage. He was a family man and a respected member of the Battle Creek community. Still, his attraction to the Brotherhood and his decision to leave his family for the Equality colony were chalked up in local news accounts to an "excessive enthusiasm" for the labor movement and his outspoken support for "radical" politics.

"He is an honest, industrious man and a first-class blacksmith," the *Battle Creek Moon* newspaper reported the day after he left for South Bend to visit his two daughters and to link up with the Lermond party. "Mr. Barton has many friends here and all hope that he will have that success and peace and happiness in his new home under the new industrial system that he has always so earnestly advocated."

Barton made the cross-country trip with Lermond and several of the BCC leader's closest associates, including Helen Mason, the temperance activist and schoolteacher from St. Louis who had moved to Maine a year earlier to work for Lermond. She joined his Puget Sound-bound travel party in Montreal after making a side trip to her hometown of Glens Falls in upstate New York to say farewell to a younger sister, Harriet. Never married, Mason was now fifty-eight years old. The previous year, just two days before leaving St. Louis for Maine, she recorded her last will and testament. It's unclear whether she was aware then of the cancer that would soon ravish her body.

Also joining Lermond were Ed Pelton's wife, Annie, and their two daughters, 6-year-old Florence and 13-year-old Eva, the latter a product of Annie's earlier marriage to Ed's brother Ernest, killed in Minnesota in 1885. To mark the occasion of this life-altering move from the Atlantic Northeast to the Pacific Northwest, Annie and the girls posed for a photograph with Mason and Lermond and his livestock before they departed his *Willows* farm. For Annie, the move would bring a welcome but bittersweet reunion with Ed, whose obsession with Equality would create family friction and set the scene for his tragic end.

At St. Paul, Minnesota, the travelers switched to the Great Northern line and welcomed aboard the Rev. C.E. Walker and his wife, Minnie, of Sherburn, Minnesota, for the long run to Seattle.

In a travelog written on March 5, as they rolled westward from St. Paul in a Wagner sleeping car, the Lermond group claimed to have converted several fellow passengers to the socialist cause.

Spirits ran high.

"Miss Mason entertained us with reading the beautiful reform poem, 'A Vision of the Future,'" they wrote. McDevitt recalled Klondike-bound passengers getting off to practice panning for nuggets with their new washbasins each time the train stopped near a stream. These basins, he said, held a "miraculous magic of hope" for the gold rushers, not unlike the magic he believed would produce the perfect society at BCC colony No. 1.

The train trip to Washington came five months into the young life of Equality. Lermond had decided the time was right to move the BCC staff closer to the action and to accelerate the process of developing not just a starter colony but a statewide network. He seemed to suspect, correctly, that his recruits at Equality had misgivings about branching out so soon.

At Everett, one of the final stops on Puget Sound before reaching Skagit County, Lermond slipped word to a newspaper reporter that the colony was "flourishing," and its success was "already assured." The reporter seemed impressed with these easterners. "They were an intelligent, thrifty-looking company, and appeared not to be afraid of toil," he wrote.[2]

Stepping off the train at the Belfast station on March 9, McDevitt, Lermond and the others made their way to their new headquarters in Edison, about five miles west. Years later, McDevitt recalled riding with his party in a stage coach from Belfast over wood-plank trails, sometimes called puncheon roads, which he said were "as primitive as they were picturesque." Lermond remembered that leg of the journey a bit differently; he said he walked it, inspired by wonders of the woods— "the huge Douglas fir and on a road lined with mammoth ferns. How we enjoyed that walk, all singing, talking and laughing!"

They might also have chuckled at how far the news of their arrival had spread. Newspapers as distant as New York published stories, although it seems the news value was based on a mistaken impression that this was a "Debs colony," referring to the widely reported but not-yet initiated Eugene Debs plan to build socialist colonies in Washington.

In Edison, the BCC officers settled into a workspace on the second floor of a wood-framed building leased from the Independent Order of Odd Fellows, an international fraternal group whose social aid programs and philosophy aligned somewhat with that of the BCC, although it had no affiliation.[3] In fact, almost nothing about Edison suggested it as a logical host for left-wing radicals. The town was named for the great thinker and tinkerer, Thomas Edison, but that did not mean Lermond could flip a switch and expect the locals to see the socialist light.

Edison was, nonetheless, a convenient spot. Situated about two miles from the colony, it offered the small luxuries of ordinary life on the "outside"—livery stables, a drug store, meat market, hotel, candy story and barber shop, for example. That might explain, at least in part, why none of the initial eight members of the BCC's national board chose to live at Equality. Lermond and four others rented hotel rooms in Edison, and the rest were not even in Washington state. Myron Reed, the BCC's figurehead president, remained in Denver, where he preached on behalf of the Lord and socialism for many years. The BCC's new organizer, or chief recruiter, George Candee, lived in Toledo, Ohio. Frank Parsons, the "dean" in charge of educating the wider public on the merits of Equality-style socialism, split his time between Boston and Manhattan, Kansas.

While the colonists scraped and scratched for survival, Lermond and other board members were focused on broader goals—strengthening the BCC's lifeline of financial support and planning next steps for a broad network of colonies. The goal, after all, was not just to make a success of Equality but to do it so quickly that many more colonies would spring up in support, strengthening the Brotherhood's economic clout and capturing the state for socialism. It was this basic feature of the Lermond plan—to build a federation of colonies rather than autonomous, individual ones—that had sold McDevitt on leaving Washington, D.C. and joining the Equality bandwagon sight unseen. His first impression of Equality was positive, but just barely. As a group, the colonists struck him as "seemingly solid, stalwart." They were not the "neurotic or freakish or over-brow" types he feared he would find. What he could not immediately appreciate, however, were the hardships they had already endured.

THAT FIRST WINTER exposed Equality's weaknesses. These might have been offset, at least partially, with the right combination of resources and leadership, but Equality had too little of either. BCC membership dues and private donations proved inadequate, as early doubters had predicted, and although Lermond was the leading intellectual force and Pelton the hardest worker, the colony suffered from a surplus of ideas and a deficit of decisiveness. These earnest but quarrelsome people had no true leader, and in the opinion of one early visitor, "they would not submit to one if they had. They were not built that way."[4]

Among the few talented and technically trained leaders at Equality during its infancy was Charles H. Swigart, an Ohio native who was civic minded long before the term entered common usage.[5] He was trained as a civil engineer and later built a distinguished career in Everett and Seattle with the Great Northern Railway, whose president, James J. Hill, the "Empire Builder," was one of the more consequential capitalists of the late 19th and early 20th centuries.

Swigart embraced Equality and its socialist aims, but in time he would drift to the right, finding the colony too radical. His first post-Equality job was as engineer in charge of building two huge docks at Smith's Cove on Seattle's Elliott Bay to serve as Great Northern's western terminus and as a shipping pier. Smith's Cove was among the first harbor facilities built by the Port of Seattle, a local government agency created in 1911 in a push for public ownership of Seattle's waterfront, which had been controlled largely by railroad companies.

Swigart later worked for the U.S. Reclamation Service (now the Bureau of Reclamation). He became the supervising engineer for its Washington division, where he played a key role in some of the most important irrigation works of the early 20th century, including the Yakima Project in south-central Washington. In that role he also showed flashes of the liberal instincts that had drawn him to Lermond's Brotherhood. For example, he decried the injustice of holding a Reclamation Service employee responsible for years of bills for treatment of a severe injury sustained in an accident on the job in 1907, just months before Congress passed legislation requiring the federal government to compensate its workers for on-the-job injuries. "I have always believed that this was entirely unjust," Swigart wrote in support of a Washington congressional delegation push in 1916 to approve $900 for the injured man.[6]

The origin of Swigart's interest in civil engineering is unclear, but it was a profession of growing popularity in the 1880s, linked to western expansion and to the idea that engineers had a social mission—to open pathways that would enable more people to benefit from the power in nature. As this applied to the work of the Reclamation Service, Frederick H. Newell, the agency's first chief engineer, saw the mission as "a duty of the highest citizenship." Irrigation networks, he wrote, are a matter of concern to all citizens, not just the rich and powerful.

"It is their duty as citizens to guard the public lands, the heritage of their children, and prevent their falling into the hands of persons who will treat them as speculative commodities," he wrote.[7]

President Theodore Roosevelt's creation of the Reclamation Service in 1902 marked a noteworthy moment of recognition that the public good can be served by leveraging the government's deep pockets and national reach, even if some critics would call this creeping socialism.

Swigart was the most important, but not the only, civil engineer to join the Equality cause. Another was a Pennsylvania native named Horace Greeley Cupples, who had heeded the advice of his namesake and gone west as a young man. He had been living in Whatcom County for more than a decade when he became a late joiner at Equality, just as it was disintegrating.

During the First World War, after Cupples left Equality and resettled in St. Louis, he came under government suspicion for promoting a radical idea—to build an "Arcadian Highway" from the Great Lakes to the Gulf of Mexico. He envisioned the start of a national highway network to accommodate America's future defense needs and its emerging lust for the open road, just eight years after Henry Ford introduced the Model "T". Cupples proposed that the federal government foot the bill, and, in a nod to the "Coxey's army" theme of a generation earlier, he suggested hiring the unemployed to do the road work.[8]

As a known socialist during a period of national hysteria over political radicalism, Cupples was arrested in St. Louis in 1920 and questioned for two days by government agents about his highway plan, his loyalties, and his incidental association with two bigger-name socialists—Eugene Debs and Kate O'Hare[9], both of whom had been imprisoned for speaking out against the war in Europe. Like other radical ideas that were ahead of their time, the Cupples plan for a national highway hit a dead end. Four decades later, in the early years of the Cold War, it was resurrected by President Dwight D. Eisenhower with his push to create today's interstate highway system.[10] In an echo of Cupples' logic, the president said this was a public enterprise of benefit to the nation's economy as well as its defense, so the government paid 90 percent of the cost. Construction began near St. Louis.

SWIGART CAME to Equality in the spring of 1898, shortly after Lermond and almost certainly in coordination with him. In fact, Lermond may have done a little arm twisting to persuade Swigart to leave Bucyrus, Ohio, the small city southwest of Cleveland where he lived with his young family. Swigart told a newspaper reporter in January that although the socialist colony interested him, he had no intention of moving until Equality had established "a sufficient number of factories to demand his personal attention."[11] Two months later, Equality had acquired Swigart but no factories. He attended instead to farmland and infrastructure.

Swigart held the title of master workman—essentially the colony's foreman or chief engineer—and a place on the BCC board of trustees. [12]

The son of an Ohio farmer, Charles Henry Swigart attended a preparatory academy at Heidelberg College in his hometown of Tiffin during the 1882-83 school year but seems not to have gone on to enroll in the college itself, which was a religious-oriented school established by the German Reformed Church. Instead, he moved to Columbus to attend Ohio State University, which at the time specialized in civil, mechanical and mining engineering. He also was a member of the university's military cadet training battalion.

In the late 1880s he worked on railroad survey crews in Michigan and Nebraska, and before giving up rail engineering to become a socialist trailblazer, he was an assistant road master for the Toledo & Ohio Central Railway. These had not been easy times for him; in 1891 his wife Minnie died at age twenty-four, one month after giving birth to a daughter, also named Minnie. Four years later he married another Ohio native, Pearl Battenfield, and on March 28, 1898, they arrived at Equality from Bucyrus with 1-year-old daughter Lucille. (The older daughter, Minnie, stayed in Ohio with her maternal grandparents.)

Writing for the colony newspaper, Swigart played up the area's agricultural potential, particularly for wheat and oats. He called himself a man who "knows grain when he sees it," having grown up on a farm. After Equality's first threshing season, he wrote of astonishing results: "Oats yielding from 75 to 110 bushels to the acre was a new experience, and this was not from selected patches but whole farms of from 40 to 160 acres; and then the ranchers said it was an off year, at that."

The soil also was well suited for a fruit orchard and a wide range of vegetables. The colony grew cabbage, potatoes, cauliflower, beets, rutabagas, onions, carrots, turnips, and peas. Apple and cherry trees flourished, and adults and children alike learned to peel and eat wild blackcap and salmonberry shoots. A nursery was established to cultivate tree, fruit and vegetable seedlings. "Equality Nurseries" claimed to offer "the best of everything," and a five-dollar order came with a year's subscription to *Industrial Freedom*.

In his periodic reports on Equality's land-clearing and other operations, Swigart offered few clues to his motives for joining the socialist cause. He may have seen the colony and its considerable civil engineering challenges as a personal proving ground and a springboard to bigger job opportunities in a rapidly growing state. At first, he talked the socialist talk, referring (at least in print) to his colony colleagues as "comrades," and he embraced Lermond's broad goal of creating a "cooperative commonwealth." But soon his tone changed, suggesting he saw Equality as too radical and fatally flawed.

Writing four months into his tenure, Swigart said his "pet theory" about socialism had been disproven by actual experience at Equality. He offered no detailed explanation but said he had come to realize that it was not possible to move swiftly from capitalist competition to "orderly and scientific operations of socialism" on a community-wide scale. People were cooperating on an individual basis, "but the next step on colony cooperation is much greater and will require a much broader view than most of us have attained," he wrote in July, suggesting few at Equality were up to the task.

Swigart apparently had begun considering an alternative to Equality, one that could hardly be called socialist. That summer he visited a slightly older "cooperative" colony on the Kitsap Peninsula, in south Puget Sound, west of Tacoma. From conversations with colony residents there he concluded that they "know what they want, and, from what I saw, know how to get it." The implication was that this group, the Mutual Home Association, whose colony was known simply as Home, had found a superior approach—letting members work collectively or individually, whichever suited them. The group had no political policy ambitions; its only stated purpose was to help colony members obtain and build homes for themselves and to establish "better moral conditions." This was not socialism, in name or in practice. In fact, this colony's guiding philosophy was anarchism. (The editor of its aptly named newspaper, *Discontent*, was an anarchist, James F. Morton, Jr., who paradoxically was a grandson of the man who wrote the patriotic hymn "America," better known as "My Country, 'Tis of Thee." The hymn served as the de facto national anthem for nearly 100 years, until "The Star-Spangled Banner" was officially adopted in 1931.)

Home's embrace of anarchism attracted notice by Emma Goldman. On a June 1898 visit, she lectured on three consecutive nights, addressing "The Woman Question," "Authority Versus Liberty," and "Patriotism." Her presentations prompted *Discontent* to comment approvingly, "There is no conservatism about her, she is as radical as anyone in the West."[13]

It's hard to imagine that Swigart favored anarchy. His focus was on attracting larger numbers of reform-minded migrants to Washington, even if they preferred not to join Equality.

Swigart was a stalwart, but there were not many like him at Equality.

"Able, willing, and practical workers were never present in enough proportion to outbalance the unproductive, the hangers-on, the dissidents, and the disgruntled," Charles P. LeWarne, a scholar of Washington state history, wrote in *Utopias on Puget Sound, 1885-1915*, his authoritative 1975 account of Equality and other socialist or utopian communities.

Swigart's concern about the thin stream of higher-quality recruits was a subtle acknowledgment that things had gone poorly in the first months after his arrival. Although fresh faces were showing up regularly, too few were suited for success. In late 1898 Swigart gave it up and moved to Everett to work for Hill's Great Northern Railway.

Chapter 10

A Teenage Rebel

Of the many newcomers that first spring, Harry Ault was an exception to the mediocrity that troubled Swigart. Ault was a nearly perfect fit for Equality. An idealist with a practical side, ambitious but collegial, he was more a rebel than a revolutionary. From a surprisingly early age, he was a devoted but not doctrinaire socialist. The colony could have used more like him. Instead, it tended to attract more quarrelsome types.[1]

"Venturesome" was a word Ault used to describe himself when, late in life, he looked back on his upbringing in Kentucky, his family's cross-country journey to Washington, his experiences at Equality, and the people who shaped his road to radicalism. He wrote unpublished sketches of colony life, brief profiles of its more colorful characters, and a draft of a memoir that remained unfinished when he died in a Seattle suburb in 1961 at the dawn of a new era of American radicalism.

Ault epitomized the young socialist of the 1890s and the early 20th century whose efforts, along with less radical progressives, foretold one of the most consequential social-political movements in United States history—the push to establish a social safety net and make it the federal government's business. That shift toward activist government remained a divisive topic for another century and beyond, as seen in the fights over access to affordable health care during President Bill Clinton's first term and two decades later in the administration of President Barack Obama.

A century earlier at Equality, where health care costs were shared within the community, it was Harry Ault's mother, Ruhama "Ruie" J. Ault, who made a statement that still resonates: "We are not obliged to be half dead before we call a doctor, for fear of the bills."[2] In her view, this made Equality more civilized than the outside world, where medical costs even then were frightful. The colony had its own doctor at times, but when patients required special care in nearby Edison or at a New Whatcom hospital, colony funds covered the cost.

Like many Americans of that era, the colonists relied on home remedies and health tips offered in a widely circulated publication, *The White House Cook Book*, which was much more than a recipe collection. The book, whose co-author was a former White House steward, had no direct connection to occupants of the presidential residence at 1600 Pennsylvania Avenue, but it was a trusted source of meal tips as well as suggestions for avoiding sickness ("Don't go to bed with cold feet") and treating a wide range of common injuries and illnesses, including colds, diphtheria, lockjaw, nose bleeds, and burns. The colony's well-worn copy, a distinctive 1894 edition with silver-stamped lettering on the cloth cover, was signed by J.B. Beel, a blacksmith who came to Equality from Chicago in April 1898.[3]

Harry Ault's non-conformist ways were set early. He was born in 1883, in the second year of a severe national economic recession, in the working-class city of Newport, Kentucky, across the Ohio River from Cincinnati. Always small for his age, he topped out in adulthood at five feet, four inches—thickset and filled with nervous energy. He grew up in a family with no shortage of offbeat thinking. His father, James B. Ault, was an unapologetic socialist, distrustful of what he called capitalist "sharpers," especially bankers, out to cheat the average guy. He had so little faith in capitalism that he advised Harry to spend rather than save the dimes he earned from his newspaper route because any savings would inevitably disappear through bank trickery.[4]

The elder Ault was an atheist and a devoted family man who lurched from one line of work to another, hopeful of bigger and better things for his children. Harry watched his father struggle to make ends meet; for several years he made wool dusters, operating out of their home in partnership with his half-brother, but that venture collapsed in a family dispute. Later he worked for Prudential insurance as a bill collector. Among Harry's memories of their Newport years was the period when his father routinely walked to and from Cincinnati—four miles each way—to spend ten hours a day behind a grinding wheel as a metal polisher. He walked, paying a bridge toll of four cents round trip, instead of taking a horse-drawn streetcar for ten cents because, in Harry's recollection, saving six cents a day was worth the trouble in a depressed economy in which eight pennies could buy a dozen eggs.

Harry's mother shared her husband's socialist beliefs and was a full partner with him in trying to make the Equality experiment work. After nearly a year at the colony, she enthused over its progress and the willingness of the women to chip in at dirty work like pulling tree stumps. "We still have our ups and downs, little differences and some petty jealousies, for we are not angels!" she wrote. "But I must say I enjoy living here. The wild free life just suits me. I like the novelty, variety and strange faces."[5]

She became a card-carrying "Red," joining the Socialist Party of Washington in September 1901, shortly after it was chartered by the new Socialist Party of America.

The Aults traced their roots to the colonial era of early 18th century America. Harry's paternal grandfather, Daniel Webster Ault, was descended from German immigrants who settled in eastern Pennsylvania three decades before the Revolutionary War, with later generations moving west to Ohio as pioneer farmers. Present-day Bratton Township in Mifflin County, Pennsylvania, was named for the many Bratton families who helped settle that area, south of the Juniata River, including ancestors of Harry's paternal grandmother, Rebecca J. Bratton.[6]

It's doubtful Harry had detailed knowledge of his ancestors' politics, but he was fond of claiming he was the first native-born American socialist born to a native-born socialist. His father voted for the Socialist Labor Party presidential ticket—Charles Matchett and Matthew Maguire—in 1896 and, four years later, for Eugene Debs and his Socialist running mate, Job Harriman. By then socialism was in Harry's bloodstream, as was newspaper work. Barely a month after arriving at Equality at age fourteen, he helped start a Junior BCC, a kids' version of Lermond's Brotherhood. The following year he began publishing what he called an amateur magazine, the *Young Socialist.*[7] This led to a long career in newspapering, mostly in Seattle, including a stint as managing editor of *The Socialist* and a longer run as editor of the daily *Seattle Union Record,* the official voice of Seattle labor.

He eventually veered from radicalism to mainstream liberal politics. He ran for Congress as a Democrat in 1936, losing in the primary to a Seattle lawyer who would become a giant of

20th century Washington politics, Warren G. Magnuson. Two years later Ault became what you might call the opposite of radical; he was named Deputy U.S. Marshal for the western district of Washington, and he held that federal law enforcement position in Tacoma for fifteen years. So distant had his radical days become that in 1952 he was named U.S. Western region president of the National Association of Deputy U.S. Marshals.[8]

THE ELDEST OF seven Ault children, Harry was born Erwin Bratton Ault, in honor of his grandmothers—Erwin being the maiden name of his mother's mother and Bratton the maiden name of his father's mother. Erwin preferred his given name but acquiesced to his parents' quirky wish that he go by "Harry." (When he started the *Young Socialist,* he struck a blow for independence by listing himself on the title page as "Erwin B. Ault.")

Names were a kind of plaything in the Ault family. Harry's father had a closet full of nicknames for the kids. Harry was sometimes "Haddy." If he was in trouble, he was summoned as "Harvey." Sister Lulu, born Ruie Dell Lulu, was "Deetee." Brothers Harold and Herschell were "Spud" and "Curly." Sister Gladys was "Toots," and the youngest, Miskel, was "Mickey."

"Hardly ever were any of the children called by his or her real name," Harry recalled.

Harry's father used his imagination for more than nicknames. Like other early converts to the Equality experiment, he pictured a United States in which ordinary people were not beholden to the rich and in which freedom meant economic security for all. In Harry's recollection, his father tended toward a dystopian view of America and its future. This was evident in his willingness to let Harry join the Boys Brigade of Newport, a military-oriented precursor of the Boy Scouts.

"Yes, go ahead and join," Harry recalled his father saying. "There's going to be a revolution in this country sometime, and the more you know about military tactics the better you will be able to take your part in it."

At age twelve, Harry opted out of high school with his father's blessing. A quick learner, he had started first grade a year early and soon skipped ahead yet another year. His family agreed high school was a waste of time for a kid with loads of talent but no chance of affording college.

"Papa," as Harry called him, wanted his son to become a lawyer, and since it was not necessary in those days to have a college degree to pass the Kentucky bar, it seemed like a no-brainer to start his legal training immediately. And so, at age thirteen, it was agreed that a local lawyer would take Harry under his wing. The boy was hired to tend to the office fireplace, sweep and dust, deliver legal papers and learn to write letters on a typewriter so clunky that it had what he recalled as "an action like a threshing machine." He also began boning up on English common law, which he found interesting. Studying case law, however, he found distinctly uninteresting—so uninteresting, he recalled, that had his family not moved west the following year, he likely would have given up his law ambition in favor of making a living setting pins in the local bowling alley.

Instead, Harry found himself rolling toward radicalism. It was a path he would recall fondly in a collection of writings for his never-completed memoir, which he intended to call, cheekily, "*Thirty Years of 'Saving the World,'*" explaining his quest for social justice. As he pondered his past, however, he felt conflicted. "I wonder at times if the struggle was worthwhile," he wrote, then added: "If I do nothing more in my remaining years than merely exist, I have helped in no small measure to make this a better world for all, and I am happy."

Only later, in a private moment, did he reveal regret at having retreated from the radical cause in the 1930s. He confided to a friend that his decision to start a career with the U.S. Marshals Service was expedient but not honorable. "Damned cowardice," he wrote,[9] made him abandon radicalism to make a living in the same law enforcement arena that had, during the Red Scare of 1919-1920, trampled his rights by arresting him and others at the *Seattle Union Record*, a labor newspaper, on a trumped-up charge of seeking to incite rebellion.[10]

Several years before he died, ever hopeful and still mindful of the ideals that had fueled his search for social justice, Ault offered a friend a little advice on raising children: "Let them learn to be good rebels."[11]

Harry Ault's radical quest began in earnest at Equality, where his parents hoped to realize their socialist dream. In the spring of 1898, they committed to the rebel cause, and with their six children, including a four-month-old, left Kentucky for Seattle by way of Chicago and St. Paul. Accompanying them was a pal of Harry's parents, Julius Monnich, a bicycle repairman, paper hanger, all-round handyman and socialist agitator who would later become more than a family friend.

The morning skies over Puget Sound shed a fine drizzle as the Aults stepped from a Northern Pacific railcar at a red wood-frame station house near the foot of Columbia Street on the Seattle waterfront. It was April 18, 1898. The family had arrived in a city abuzz over two momentous events—the

Klondike gold rush in Canada's Yukon Territory, which was transforming sleepy Seattle into a boomtown, and the Cuba crisis, which was about to erupt into war against Spain.

Only a month earlier, the beat of war drums had grown especially loud on Puget Sound; the newly commissioned battleship *USS Oregon* had been ordered out of port at nearby Bremerton for an epic 66-day voyage around the southern tip of South America to join what would be a decisive defeat of the Spanish fleet outside the harbor at Santiago de Cuba.

The Aults may not have followed the progress of the *Oregon*, but they likely sensed that war was coming. In the men's washroom at the Columbia Street station, Harry spotted a penciled verse:

Remember the Maine,
To Hell with Spain.

The front pages of newspapers from coast to coast were puffed up with patriotism, boosted further on May 1 by the U.S. Navy's victory in the Spanish-ruled Philippines and an embrace of empire-building by the McKinley administration. War fever, combined with fantasies of finding instant wealth in the Yukon's Bonanza Creek, offered the beginnings of new hope among Americans willing to accept the idea that foreign conquests opened a path to domestic prosperity.

The Aults, however, were troopers of a different kind. They were looking to do their part in fighting for a more equitable society. Harry put it this way:

> We were part of the vanguard of the army that was to cover the thinly populated state of Washington with a network of cooperative settlements and quietly and peaceably—and

> quite legally—transform it into a cooperative commonwealth.[12]

To most of the aspiring colonists this was serious business. To some it was a lark. Harry recalled an exchange between William H. Kaufman, a country preacher and Minnesota newspaper editor, and his wife, Maude, who had joined the Aults in St. Paul for the train trip to Puget Sound. After reaching Seattle and heading north on their journey's final leg to Equality colony, Maude imagined the culinary treats awaiting —especially clam chowder and baked salmon. Harry overheard her ask her husband: "That's what we came here for, isn't it?" He replied: "No. We came here to make this a better world for people and not merely for our own enjoyment." For his principled devotion, which evolved to a defiant, almost fanatical, radicalism, Kaufman years later would nearly wind up in a federal penitentiary.

After changing trains in Seattle, the Aults and Kaufmans quickly covered the final seventy-eight miles of their cross-country journey to the Belfast station. The men walked the final five miles to the colony, past wild elderberry bushes, skunk cabbage and tangles of blackberry vines. The women and children rode with the luggage aboard a horse-drawn wagon that rumbled over a wood-plank road built in the shadow of towering evergreens.

And thus began the Ault family's adventure, which would end in a remarkable mix of tragedy and personal transformation.

Arriving not far behind the Aults were Boomer, the rambunctious socialist who had fled Kansas under threat of lynching, and his accidental acquaintance Lewis Ayer, the populist from Minneapolis who needed only a single encounter with Boomer and a two-day visit at Equality to conclude that the experiment in socialist living was on a fast track to failure.

Ayer saw two main flaws. First, too little of the colony's land was suited for farming, made worse by inadequate maritime access to commercial markets. Second, the approximately 3,500 nonresident "reserve" BCC members whose monthly dues were a key source of colony funds, were unreliable. "The class of people making up the brotherhood of 'reserves' are the most suspicious people on earth," Ayer wrote in a lengthy critique published in Seattle and Minneapolis newspapers. He was less harsh in his assessment of Lermond and the other BCC leaders he met. Though intelligent, he wrote, they "seem to me to be dreamers." (Lermond pushed back, writing weeks later that Ayers' article was a "mesh of malice and misrepresentation" meant to cripple the BCC.)

As for the colony's choice to build in a woodland and to farm on an inadequately diked tideland, Ayer saw nothing but incompetence.

"If they had searched the United States over for an inaccessible place out of reach of markets and a place expensive to get provisions into, and one that would require the greatest amount of labor with the least results toward self-sustenance, they could hardly have chosen better," he wrote. He blamed Ed Pelton, the Lermond agent who chose and purchased the land, and he suggested the rest at Equality were suckers.

"Poor deluded people! Their ideas of social equality will receive a rude shock when their stomachs get hungry."

That first year at Equality was, indeed, a lean one. Surely, at times there were low spirits and empty stomachs. The community's coffers needed filling, too. In January, barely two months into the colony's life, fourteen members signed a pledge to forego any compensation until their individual membership fees had been paid in full.

Despite these stresses, the colonists wore a remarkably brave face, which they began to present to the outside world on the pages of *Industrial Freedom* on May 7. The inaugural edition, originally planned for May 1 to mark International Workers' Day but delayed by that balky printing press, offered a mix of cheer and caution. Lermond gave an update on his "cooperative commonwealth" vision, acknowledging that it faced an uphill battle. "Americans are practical and skeptical. They do not accept a theory until it is proved a fact."

McDevitt, a master of Latin, a student of the mechanics of English usage, and a prodigious writer in any language, helped edit the paper. His contribution to the first issue was an uncharacteristically crisp argument for why socialism was inherently superior to capitalism.

"Competition makes for the artificial increase of the natural inequality of man with man, and for the consequent diminution of human justice and human helpfulness; cooperation minimizes inequality and magnifies the scope and capacity of justice and love," he wrote.

The paper's Olympia-based columnist, Bige Eddy, who had not set foot on colony grounds but would become a member the following year, predicted success at Equality but also saw potential for trouble.

"Internal dissension and jealousy are most to be feared in enterprises of this kind," he wrote.

In a similar vein, a supporter in California warned of the dangers of quarrelsomeness. "If there should be a disposition on the part of individuals to insist on having their own way the conflict thus caused might be strong enough to destroy the Brotherhood," he wrote prophetically.

Annie Billingsley, who came to Equality from Buffalo County, Nebraska, with her husband Joe and would become a quiet but influential voice in colony affairs, used the newspaper's debut to predict that "love and pride of independence" would carry the colonists through inevitable obstacles on the road to revolution. "They are pebbles in the way of a mighty army," she wrote.

One obstacle, more threatening than any pebble, was already impeding progress, and a second would soon mark the beginning of the end of Lermond's dream. Both problems might have been anticipated. They were of the kind feared and perhaps foreseen by columnist Eddy.

The first was a dispute over sharing the workload. This was more than an argument about schedules and balance; it was a fundamental disagreement over the proper practice of socialism. The gist of the debate was this: Should individuals be assigned tasks based on the community's needs, or should they be free to choose their work and do it only when and how they saw fit? This was, after all, a "cooperative" society. So, should individuals be at liberty to cooperate on their own terms? Some feared that voluntary socialism, as it was called, was incompatible with productive work and sustainable democratic practices, and that it would create instead what one called an "anarcho-democratic" society.

Who would decide these important questions about work-sharing? The colony was committed to democratic methods, so no individual had authority to dictate the way forward. As it turned out, leadership was so diffuse and opinions so divided that this issue was never satisfactorily settled. Left to fester, it led to rivalries and suspicions about who among them were freeloaders.

George Savage was one who argued for volunteerism. He was a local surveyor, millwright and woodsman who spent several months at the colony in 1898 running a portable sawmill made from a steam-powered threshing machine.[13] The mill produced lumber and shakes to construct some of Equality's first buildings, including its first apartment-dormitory. He owned the saw and other equipment and ran it with volunteer help; in his view this was "voluntary socialism," allowing for the greatest degree of individual freedom, and should be a model for the entire colony. In hindsight, this notion of socialism sounded more like free enterprise. "It seems to me," he wrote in the spring of 1898, "that if a person is free and untrammeled and is working for himself he will naturally place his labor, skill or knowledge where he really believes it will do the most good." This volunteerism, he argued, allowed colony work to be managed, "individually or as a body, without a tangible leader and forcible directions."[14] His argument swayed some, but in the view of a large and more influential number, the colony's survival and eventual success depended on individuals' willingness to put community needs ahead of personal desires.

More than a mere stumble on the road to Utopia, this episode revealed fundamentally divergent views of what the ideal society looked like and what kind of "cooperative commonwealth" was achievable in a democracy.

"Voluntary cooperation is an ideal relation for ideal people —very well for angels but rather risky for flesh-and-blood mortals," an unsigned editorial in the second published issue of *Industrial Freedom* said, apparently reflecting the majority view of the colony's leaders.

"Voluntary cooperation is excellent for ten hours at a picnic, for each member may go home when he sees fit; but it is not conducive to large production for a foreman to go to the field and find that three of his force have chosen to work in the construction department. Neither is it conducive to harmony for twenty people to go to the dining hall to find that the cook has volunteered to go visiting, or for the foreman of the printing department to find that during a press of work one of his force has gone hunting!"

Most believed the work arrangements had to be more like marriage: "You may go in or stay out as you choose, but once the agreement is made you can't 'volunteer' to back out," as one put it.

That debate in the spring of 1898 was papered over by resorting to what some called "business methods" of socialism in which elected work supervisors would draft individuals for job assignments whenever volunteerism left unacceptable gaps. In practice, this often meant the ablest and most devoted carried the heaviest workload and did the dirtiest of the dirty work.

Even a summer visitor could sense the tension. Helen J. Wescott, a lawyer who traveled from her home in Kansas to observe Equality for five weeks, wrote, "If cooperators cannot cooperate, how shall they demonstrate to the world the beauty and practicability of cooperation?"[15] William E. Giles, who came to Equality from Kansas as a teenager, later offered a brilliantly simple explanation of what lay at the root of Wescott's doubt. In his view, it was human nature that marred the beauty of cooperation, and so doomed Equality. "They got to know each other too well," Giles said of the colonists. "Then they quarreled."[16]

A second, related controversy added to the conflict. Initially, in keeping with the notion of equality, colony members rotated work assignments. Men trained in a skill like carpentry, tailoring or blacksmithing, would take a turn at unskilled jobs like ditch digging, driving a team of mules, or peeling potatoes. When that approach to sharing was shown to put a crimp in productivity—and perhaps elicited a few extra complaints about the food—skilled workers were excused from the rotation. This fed a suspicion that they considered themselves privileged.

"This suspicion was not easily dispelled, and the skilled

people, who as a group had early shown themselves to be most willing to sacrifice for the common welfare, later were the most ready to leave the colony when opportunities improved on the outside," Frederick Smith, the local author, wrote in his mostly sympathetic account of Equality history.

For the unskilled, opportunities in the spring and summer of 1899 included hiring out to farmers beyond Equality's borders. The *Argus* newspaper in Mount Vernon took note of this seemingly un-socialist-like behavior among men who professed to despise capitalism and who embraced the Lermond idea that commercial competition was the root of evil.

"Quite a number of the Colony men are working in the hayfields about Edison," it reported in July. "It would seem that the competitive world is not so bad after all, eh, brothers?"

The newspaper's insinuation that some colonists had come to see the error of their ways was not wrong. They were answering an irresistible urge to make money—cooperation be damned. On the other hand, some—certainly not all—adhered to the Equality rule that money earned from outside employment was to be turned over to the colony in exchange for scrip. In fact, this was openly stated from the get-go as an acceptable practice, and at times it proved useful. The colony reported, for example, that for the first two weeks of August 1898, its main source of income was "our boys in the hayfields." That same summer, the colonists worked out a deal to help harvest the oats of a local farmer known to be staunchly anti-socialist. The crop was split 50-50 between the farmer and the colony. "When folks get a close view of the [socialist] 'critter,' they are surprised to find that he is not the monster they imagined him to be," *Industrial Freedom* reported, describing the work as an example of practical socialism.

Still, everyone at Equality knew that each hour spent

laboring on the "outside" meant a bigger work burden on those remaining inside.

Those labor issues, while sometimes damaging to colony cohesion, were minor compared to a more profound dispute that developed in parallel. It was settled by a vote, but not before relations between the colonists and the BCC directors (officially the BCC national board of trustees) had been irreparably harmed.

This deeper rift reflected a practical as well as a philosophical divide. It burst into the open at a meeting Lermond convened in early April to bring together the colonists and the newly arrived directors, according to an account offered many years later by McDevitt, who was one of Lermond's closest assistants. The rupture revealed what Pelton described with characteristic understatement as "our first serious trouble."

The meeting was convened on Good Friday, but the colonists were not in a reflective mood. They raised holy hell when Lermond announced that a second colony was being established; it was to be situated at Edison and would consist mainly of him and the other BCC directors.[17] If McDevitt's account of the proceedings is to be believed, Pelton denounced the decision in no uncertain terms. Without quoting Pelton directly, McDevitt—himself a BCC director—wrote that Pelton saw the move as "fantastic and premature and ruinous," all of which, McDevitt added, was "unfortunately, only too true." He recalled the usually restrained Pelton unleashing a verbal assault on Lermond, leaving Helen Mason, the steadiest and most faithful of Lermond's aides, "discouraged and disturbed."

"Good Friday, yes, they also crucified Christ on Good Friday," McDevitt quoted Mason as saying.

The meeting voted down the proposed second colony, a blow from which Lermond would not recover.

McDevitt, whose role was unexpectedly transformed by

this crisis, attributed the disagreement to a "dangerous lack of unity" between the directors and the colonists. As McDevitt saw the situation, some directors were practically strangers at Equality; they (McDevitt included) lived and worked in Edison with the conveniences of an established town and few of the hardships of colony life. Though separated by only a couple of miles, the colonists and the directors suffered from a culture and trust gap that fed suspicion about each other's motives.

In Lermond's view, the logic of immediately establishing a second colony was ironclad and obvious. The BCC's main purpose, after all, was to build a statewide network of colonies, giving socialists the influence needed to win political control of state government. Why wait? Time was of the essence. To Pelton and most of the others at Equality, it was equally obvious that early expansion would be a grave and irreversible mistake. Equality's survival was still in doubt. To spend money, time and effort on expansion at this early stage risked failure at colony No. 1 and collapse of the entire enterprise.

After the proposal was voted down, an air of hostility lingered, and yet Lermond seemed to think that his persuasiveness would eventually prevail. He was wrong. This episode suggests that Lermond lacked an understanding of—and, perhaps, regard for—the colonists' view of the proper path to the socialist revolution they had signed up for.

Publicly, Lermond pretended the disagreement over starting new colonies was minor.

"Some of us are singing exuberantly, 'The more the merrier,' and some of us are chanting in our caution, 'We'd better bide a wee,'" Lermond wrote in a June 11 letter to *The Coming Nation*, the socialist newspaper that had been helping promote his BCC dream. He seemed not to have lost focus on the broader goal of magnifying the socialist message. In early July he pushed plans for what he called a BCC hotel wagon to set out from Columbus, Ohio, as a "socialist hotel, bookstore, and rostrum, all in one." Its operators would offer lectures, sign up new BCC members, and raise money across the state. "The Brotherhood proposes to operate one or more of these Socialistic caravansaries in each state in the Union," he wrote.[18] The plan fizzled, and soon Lermond's commitment lost steam.

Increasingly unhappy with Lermond and his fellow directors after the April fracas, the colonists proposed a formal break with the BCC. "Autonomy," they called it. They wanted control over their affairs and their future, but they weren't angling to leave the BCC. Instead, they wanted to adjust the relationship so that vital decisions would be in their own hands —and to give themselves more control of BCC income from monthly membership dues. It amounted to an admission that the colonists had lost faith in their leader.

Without mentioning Lermond by name, Swigart, the civil engineer, argued that autonomy was a natural evolution of the Equality pioneers' thinking, and that it should be welcomed.

"I have found by observation that most people will not trust the superintendence of the operations of the colony business in the hands of anyone not elected by themselves alone," he wrote. "It is an experiment, and they wish to work out the success or failure of it themselves."[19]

By late June, the directors and the colonists had agreed on a way to end the autonomy debate: hold a referendum. Let the full BCC membership, now totaling about 3,500 people nationwide, vote on a proposed amendment to the BCC constitution. The vote would settle this yes-or-no question: Should each colony—Equality now, others later—be allowed to unilaterally amend its relationship with the BCC national board? If so, colonies wishing to reject BCC supervision could declare full autonomy. This meant they could govern themselves, with the BCC continuing to hold in trust all land titles, recruit new members, publish *Industrial Freedom*, and receive monthly dues.

For all practical purposes, the Equality colonists won their fight even before the votes were counted. Ahead of the balloting, the colony was granted provisional autonomy, pending the vote's outcome. Surely all realized this "provisional" status was temporary in name only.

Henry Halladay, the former Kansas farmer who was now president of the colony, believed that the heavily eastern makeup of the national board was a hindrance to harmonious and efficient management of Equality. Better to leave colony business to men who have "grown up in the forests and mines." Halladay could be persuasive, but his title of colony president conveyed no actual power; it offered a bit of prestige and meant he presided at meetings of the General Assembly.

"It is more practical and nearer in line with what we know of the average human nature to have home rule or self-government, when possible," Halladay wrote.[20] To be governed by absentee officers, even if they were in nearby Edison, was a recipe for confusion and misunderstanding, he added. "It is only natural that jealousies and suspicions should thus arise."

Arise they did.

"Some of the Equality folks resented the sparse elegance at Edison, and most especially, they resented the colonization funds that never got as far as Equality," author Smith wrote.

The easier living at Edison hardly went unnoticed by those still enduring pioneer conditions at Equality, such as dirt paths that turned to mud when it rained. As Harry Ault, the boy editor from Kentucky, put it years later in describing the uneven living conditions, "Since it was a primal principle of the Brotherhood that every man was as good as the next, this was a most serious basis for dissension."

To Lermond's great regret, the referendum on autonomy

passed easily, although participation was ominously sparse. Of the approximately 3,500 eligible BCC members, fewer than 500 bothered to vote. This was likely due in part to the BCC leaders' weak effort to explain the proposed amendment, which left some non-resident members confused about its purpose and implications. More importantly, it reflected the reality that on a national scale the fractured socialist movement had lost interest in colonizing in general and in Lermond and Equality in particular. Socialists were again focusing on state and national party politics.

Equality was not yet a year old, but as Smith put it, "The colonization movement was a spent force."

Swigart, with his engineer's instinct for problem-solving, was not giving up on colonization, but he realized that many socialists already had. He announced creation of a Society for Socialistic Immigration, a kind of information agency of the BCC. Its purpose was to attract socialists to Washington even if they did not want to join a colony. He reasoned that more motivated socialists would come if given detailed information about local conditions in the capitalist economy—job possibilities, investment prospects, and property and housing costs. For a fee of fifty cents a year, his Society would provide a monthly or quarterly bulletin of information not available from state or federal government offices.

"Let us all work toward this one end of making this state the first to fall in line for the great cause of humanity and use all the means in our possession to accomplish this," he wrote. His information agency might have been a bright idea, but it went dark quickly.

By August, Lermond was fed up. After spending the better part of three years conceiving and nurturing a dream and moving three thousand miles from Maine to Washington in hope of seeing it come true, he was finished. He resigned and returned home, where he helped form Maine's Socialist Party and was its unsuccessful candidate for governor in 1900.

The Equality colony newspaper tried to put the best spin on Lermond's abrupt departure. A brief article reported that an unspecified illness had sidelined the BCC leader, perhaps only temporarily.

"Through the sad fact of our Secretary's impaired health from overwork and care, we are deprived for the time being of his invaluable presence in counsel and work," it said.[21] "Mr. Lermond has returned to his home in Maine to secure the rest which has become so essential." At Lermond's suggestion, it added, McDevitt would succeed him.

McDevitt repeated the fiction of Lermond simply needing a rest break. He told readers of *The Coming Nation* that Lermond had been forced to "retire temporarily from the active duties of his office and to take a much-needed relaxation from the work and the worry." As successor, McDevitt was looking for ways to buck up the colonists. He saw an opportunity when the *Seattle Times* reported on Equality's plans to build a fruit-drying and canning plant, which, incidentally, never came to fruition. "Our neighbors, you see, are beginning to take us very seriously," he wrote on August 27.

Years later, McDevitt recalled Lermond's exit in less charitable terms. Lermond had "clandestinely disappeared" without explanation, he wrote. "The end of the Lermond leadership marked the turning point in the history of Equality. Its age of innocence, its sanguine spring of hope and unlimited faith, its lovely vision of inevitable success, began to fade."[22]

Lermond's version of these events evolved over time. In 1900 he was sticking to his story about leaving to recover from illness. "I was taken sick and was obliged to retire for needed rest and change," he told *The Appeal to Reason* newspaper. He offered that explanation as a way of rebutting a fellow socialist's accusation that he had "deserted" the colony "in a most inexcusable manner." The accuser, journalist Herbert N. Casson, singled out Lermond while condemning the entire history of socialist colonies in America. Though well-intentioned, these colonies were unmitigated failures, he wrote, and having lived at the Ruskin Colony in Tennessee for several months in 1899 and served as editor of its newspaper, Casson believed he knew what he was talking about.

Lermond dismissed Casson as uninformed, although a new version of the story of his abandonment of Equality came to light nearly a century later with the discovery of his unfinished autobiography. In it he made no mention of physical illness. Nor had he quit because of disputes over colony autonomy and expansion. Rather, he wrote, it was because the colonists had insisted on moving BCC headquarters from Edison to Equality. An obviously better option, in Lermond's view, was the scenic seaport of Anacortes, several miles west of Edison, across Padilla Bay, where city leaders had offered to host BCC headquarters. The colonists, however, saw it differently. They "raised a rumpus," he wrote, "and acted more like anarchists than Bellamy Socialists, threatening to move our headquarters to the colony by force!"

"I saw the futility of the whole project, became homesick, and beat it back to Maine and the farm!"

The founding father was gone, but McDevitt, Pelton, Halladay and others pressed on, and new arrivals kept a glimmer of hope alive.

Chapter 11

From Republican to Radical

As Lermond headed back East, he practically crossed paths with a westbound Arkansan who would become one of Equality's most memorable characters. His name was David Burgess.

At first glance, Burgess would seem an unlikely admirer of socialism or of the Equality colony. Unlike Lermond, he had not spent years theorizing about radicalism and a new social order. Unlike George Boomer, he had not filled newspaper columns with calls to action on behalf of the downtrodden. Unlike Harry Ault, his parents were not socialists.

For more than half his life, Burgess followed the beaten path. He abided by the capitalist conventions of 19th century America: work hard, take calculated risks, invest wisely. In the Arkansas towns in which he raised a family for the better part of two decades, he was an adaptive entrepreneur. At various times he was a dairyman, a lumber mill owner, an accountant, a book agent, a grocer, a school teacher, and, briefly, a newspaper editor. Also devoted to civic duties, he did a stint as justice of the peace, presiding over minor legal odds and ends. Before that, in Burlington, Iowa, he served on the city council and was principal at a business college. He had the instincts of a community booster, the patience of an educator, and the charm of a silver-tongued salesman. He was endowed with what a friend described as a "rich and musical oratorical voice." Despite having no formal training in the law, he once persuaded an Arkansas trial jury to acquit a man who had admitted pulling a loaded gun on a business partner.[1]

Burgess had guile and gumption in the style of men of his generation who believed free enterprise was golden. He was an enthusiastic Republican in the years before the Grand Old Party transitioned from champion of civil rights to promoter of business interests. In middle age he served on his county's Republican central committee and helped start a Republican Club.

All seemed grand. Then, suddenly, it was not. Everything changed. Just months before turning fifty, he packed up his family and moved to Equality.

On the surface, this switch to radicalism seems abrupt and out of character. The impulse, however, was deeply rooted. His parents were Quakers, the Protestant Christians who were shunned and persecuted in England in the 17th century as a perceived threat to the existing social order. Quakers have a rebellious streak, in a distinctly peaceful way. In worship they tolerate no ritual, no preacher, no hierarchy. They are not socialists in the political sense, but community and the idea of a social body and bond are central to their way of life, as implied by the Quakers' formal name, the Religious Society of Friends. Their interest in utopian communities in the late 19th century was what historian T.D. Seymour Bassett called "a natural if extreme development of essential Quaker ideas and testimonies."[2]

Growing up in the 1850s on a farm in southeastern Ohio,

along the Muskingum River in the Appalachian foothills, Burgess absorbed core Quaker teachings: quiet piety, pacifism, the importance of education, spiritual equality for men and women, and the immorality of slavery. The Burgesses were abolitionists. Morgan County, where David spent his boyhood, was a common destination on the Underground Railroad for escaped slaves heading north to freedom. At age nineteen he left home to attend school in Mt. Pleasant, a Quaker settlement and former fugitive slave sanctuary in eastern Ohio near the West Virginia border. There he likely attended a Quaker academy known at the time as the Friends Boarding School.

True to tradition, Burgess married a Quaker. Her name was Anna Bonsall, an Ohio native with strong family connections to the 1850s anti-slavery movement. Her ancestors were Quakers who immigrated to Pennsylvania Colony in the late 1600s from the village of Bonsall in Derbyshire, England.[3] Anna's parents were active in the Ohio-based Western Anti-Slavery Society, whose vision of a reconstructed social order based on human equality could be seen as anticipating the dream of utopian socialists like those who started the Equality colony.

Anna became a devoted socialist in her own right, and not the first in her extended family. A cousin, Charles Bonsall,[4] was among Quaker activists who helped accommodate the Coxey protest "army" when it reached the Quaker stronghold of Salem, Ohio, on its march to Washington, D.C., in 1894. The Bonsall family was partners for decades in Salem's highly successful Buckeye Engine Co., maker of steam engines used to power grain, saw and shingle mills. Nonetheless, Charles was "a live and energetic socialist," according to a 1944 account of the Coxey march written by William McDevitt and Carl Browne.[5]

As a child, Anna moved with her family to Keokuk County, Iowa, from Mahoning County, Ohio, where her paternal grandfather had been an early settler of Green township near Salem.[6] The Bonsalls' move west was part of a broader, post-Civil War migration of Quakers to Iowa's coal country. In 1871, David moved there—near a town by the improbable name of What Cheer— and he and Anna were married in Des Moines County four days before Christmas the following year. David spent a couple of years as a principal at the Burlington Business College, which was owned by a J. Bonsall, probably Anna's older brother Joseph.[7] David and Anna started a family in Burlington before moving back to Ohio.

In 1879, a year after the birth of their third child, David and Anna left Ohio for a second time. They resettled in a remote part of south-central Arkansas, in Caddo township north of the Ouachita River town of Arkadelphia, which had been a manufacturing center for the Confederacy. Here lay painful and vivid memories of what some in Arkadelphia called the South's "war of separation,"[8] and bitterness over its failure. The Burgess family arrived shortly after Reconstruction in a state that was so devastated by war and civil strife that it struggled for many decades with unsettled and corrupt politics, a chronically weak economy, and a crippled education system.

Burgess left no known explanation for his and Anna's move to Arkansas, but it may have reflected an adventurous impulse as well as a Quaker missionary drive to help the poor and to contribute in direct ways to the recovery of a stricken region. He had a particularly strong interest in public education; he helped establish the first school in the new Arkansas town of St. Paul, where he was a teacher and later served on the school board. He argued strenuously for greater taxpayer support for public schools, an unpopular stance in Arkansas at a time when education was widely seen as a private matter, a privilege of the rich, and therefore not to be supported with tax dollars.

The Burgesses were among a number of Quaker families,

mostly from Ohio and Iowa, who migrated to Arkansas in the late 1870s. In 1879 they received formal Quaker approval to establish a new meeting house and worship group in Arkadelphia. The town welcomed them as solid, God-fearing folk and donated land for a meeting house. Two years later, however, the plan was dropped, possibly because an expected expansion of the Quaker contingent failed to materialize.

Quaker affairs were not Burgess's only focus. In January 1880, less than a year after arriving in the Arkadelphia area, he became a tenant dairyman. A one-year contract with the owners of a farm just outside of town entitled Burgess to sell all the milk and butter he could produce from a herd of dairy cows he managed for the farm's owners. The owners received one-third of Burgess's monthly sales revenue, and they provided not only the livestock and a furnished residence for the Burgess family but also the cans, kettles and other vessels necessary to store the milk and make the butter. The deal went sour after eight months, however, and Burgess became entangled in a lawsuit that likely left a bad taste.[9]

Soon Burgess was ready to start over again—and not for the last time. In a move that may have foretold his attraction to Equality, he and Anna pulled up stakes and resettled in the remote White River valley of northwestern Arkansas, where he helped create a new town from scratch. This was a relatively primitive, isolated area in the Boston Mountains, at the highest elevations of the fabled Ozark mountain range, about thirty miles south of Fayetteville. Times were hard, but life here could be as simple as a bird's song. In their two-room log cabin, Anna cooked meals in the fireplace, which was the only source of light other than candles. The Burgess children roamed freely, barefoot except in winter; years later, one recalled that they didn't need store-bought toys because "nature provided us with more interesting things."[10]

Burgess arrived in the White River valley amid a timber boom triggered by an extension of the St. Louis & San Francisco Railroad into that thinly populated part of Madison County in 1887. The new settlement at the rail terminus was named St. Paul, and Burgess joined the effort to grow the town and attract businesses. That made him a "boomer," in the lingo of the day. He was co-leader of a committee that wrote plans for establishing a schoolhouse and a public school system.

He partnered with Augustus Lowe, a grandson of former Arkansas governor Isaac Murphy,[11] to start the town's first newspaper, the *St. Paul Republican.* Burgess was the editor-in-chief, Lowe the publisher. Typical of the times and as the name implied, the paper was openly partisan; it advocated for Republican political causes and opposed Democrats. A hallmark of Burgess's editorial policy was support for public schools as the civic heart of democracy—where equality of educational opportunity meets the equality of informed judgment.

Under Burgess's editorship, the paper was bold and unbending—a lot like his politics of later years. "It speaks its convictions forcibly," he wrote shortly after the *Republican* got started, "and is ever ready to take a stand for whatever it believes to be for the interests of the masses."

In true Quaker fashion, Burgess had little tolerance for dishonesty, and during his short stint as editor of the weekly he crusaded relentlessly against what he saw as inexcusable corruption in county government. He named names. Whether it was these attacks on officialdom that led to his sudden departure from the newspaper is difficult to know, but it seems possible, given the timing of his most sharply worded blast. "It is very evident," his editorial page roared, "that the citizens of Madison County are being robbed by a corrupt ring of politicians who care not for the good of the people."[12] If common sense were any guide, he wrote, voters would toss out "the gang in power."

One week later he resigned from the paper. In a brief note announcing his departure, Burgess wrote with apparently purposeful haziness that "circumstances seem to require" that he go. "For many reasons I regret this step, but recognizing the logic of recent events, I yield as cheerfully as my nature will allow." He wished the paper well.

For the next ten years he did what came naturally—he adapted, and that meant moving the family. In 1890 he loaded a railroad boxcar with everything he and Anna owned, including horses, cows, and a two-seat wagon, and resettled near two of his sisters in Cherokee County, Kansas, in the extreme southeastern corner of the state. This was an area of Quaker settlements, including one called Lowell, where the Burgess family battled extreme weather, malaria, and the loss of four-year-old Bertha, who was buried in a Quaker cemetery. "The most miserable time of my life," recalled older sister Myrta, who wrote years later that malaria had attacked and nearly killed her and a sibling.[13]

Two years later, Burgess was ready to return to Arkansas. He bought an acre of land and a house in Fayetteville, moved the family, and began operating a sawmill and a grocery store, apparently in the vicinity of St. Paul. This was the kind of backwoods life where boys shot squirrels to trade for groceries at the Burgess store. The 1890s, however, were not kind to small-time entrepreneurs in rural northwest Arkansas. The lumber market followed the national economy into depression.

"The financial panic of 1894 was very disastrous to the lumber business of St. Paul," the local newspaper said in reporting the following spring that only 434 rail carloads of lumber—oak, walnut and cherry—were shipped in the first quarter of 1895. It was the smallest total for any three-month period on record. Shipments had been ten times higher in the first years of the boom. By the mid-90s, business was so slow that Burgess tried to trade several of his lumber wagons for food or cash.

The collapse of his mill business seems to have been the last straw for Burgess, possibly the tipping point in his shift to radicalism. Although the available record on this is thin, he may have believed that his business was sunk by big-money influence. By one account, the crowning blow was a decision by the region's main railroad company, the St. Louis & San Francisco —under pressure from Burgess's larger competitors—to not build an additional spur near his mill. "This ruined him financially, laying the basis for his interest in radicalism," a fellow socialist, Marvin Sanford, wrote decades later.[14] Sanford was not in Arkansas at the time but got to know Burgess much later. In his only known public comment on the demise of his mill business, Burgess said years later that it "was sold out."[15] With this vague formulation, he distanced himself from an unpleasant episode. As for what had steered him to socialism, a candidate biography for his Socialist campaign for a United States House seat in 1902 was slightly more revealing. It said his experiences in Arkansas had convinced him that the two dominant political parties were tools of industrial capitalism and that neither offered hope for social justice.

In a memoir written in 1973 at age ninety-three, Myrta Burgess Cooper, the Burgess daughter who survived the Kansas malaria scare, recalled in detail the family's many moves and her father's work ethic. Her only comment about his politics was that by the late 1890s, "my father had become much interested in socialism." She had fond memories of Equality and seemed to share her father's political beliefs. "If socialism ever comes, all people will have much more to live for," she wrote, "and this world would be a better place to live. Someday it may come, but I doubt if I live to see it."[16]

By 1897, the year Equality was established, David Burgess was pushing the socialist cause in Fayetteville, and he and Anna began donating small sums to Lermond's Brotherhood. In September, just as Pelton was trekking westward to find suitable land for the colony, *The Appeal to Reason* published a brief note from Burgess asking for enough copies of the socialist newspaper to drop one on every doorstep in Fayetteville.

The following year, when word reached St. Paul that Burgess had moved to Equality, the town's *Mountain Air* newspaper mocked the colony as a "socialist society that proposes to revolutionize the world" and concluded with regret that Burgess was "chasing a shadow." Burgess, however, had the last word. As editor of *Industrial Freedom*, he republished the *Mountain Air* comment and countered by writing that if socialists were chasing shadows, then Democrats and Republicans were "rainbow chasing" —pursuing unattainable hopes for capitalism.

"For too long, people have fallen for the broken promises of capitalism," he wrote, adding, "That is why they are now enlisted under the sunny banners of socialism."[17]

With their three youngest children in hand, David and Anna Burgess left Fayetteville on August 10, 1898, a Sunday that was sweltering even by Arkansas standards. The mercury touched 110 degrees, turning seasonal humidity into a steamy blanket and setting the Burgesses up for a pleasant surprise when they reached the cool, dry air of western Washington. The bigger surprise on arrival was their discovery that

Lermond had vanished a few days earlier. In his absence they found colonists groping for a way forward in a summer of turmoil and dashed hopes.

By chance, the month of August brought a second newcomer with an entrepreneurial background, William Hummel. What distinguished him at Equality was a business experience which, unlike Burgess's, was largely positive—and profitable. Hummel defied the stereotype of a political radical. Yes, he was a lifelong advocate for social reform. But at sixty-five, he was twice the age of most Equality recruits. And as a prosperous merchant and local civic leader, he did not fit the mold of a left-wing dreamer.[18]

When Hummel handed his wife the keys to his dry goods store in New Ulm, Minnesota, in late summer 1898 and headed for Puget Sound, his hometown paper thought it possible he would never return.

"His New Ulm friends will regret this in all sincerity, for Mr. Hummel has been identified with the town for so long that he has become almost a landmark," the *New Ulm Review* declared solemnly. "He was one of its founders and to its best interests he has always been loyal."

Like any good businessman, Hummel looked before he leaped. In early 1898 he spent several weeks at Equality as an observer. Unlike Lewis Ayer, the Minneapolis populist who took one look at Equality and declared it a loser, Hummel was mightily encouraged by what he saw. He returned home in April to tidy up his personal affairs and to pump up other prospective recruits. "We will establish a new industrial condition based on justice to all to overcome our present unjust and barbarous social and industrial conditions," he assured them.

He was eager to get started.

"I can't help thinking of the colony every day," he wrote from New Ulm.

Once he settled in, Hummel took over as the BCC's distributor, meaning he sold colony-made products and commodities that were surplus to the colony's own needs and exchanged some of the surplus for items on the "outside" that the colonists wanted but couldn't make themselves.

Hummel knew a lot about new beginnings—hard ones. He was twelve and hungry when he arrived in America from Germany with his parents and four younger siblings. In Hummel's telling, all emigrant passengers on the Atlantic crossing were required to bring their own food, which did not last because the sailing crew pilfered any meats that were not locked up or nailed down. Twenty-eight passengers died during the ocean crossing; food ran so low that they made an unplanned stop at an island for provisions to complete the voyage.

The Hummel family settled in New Orleans, and one year later the father died of yellow fever. As the eldest son and now the family provider, William moved to Cincinnati to earn what he could as an apprentice to a harness maker and later a trunk maker. His wages were so meager that he could not afford underwear or socks, but his fortunes improved when he began working aboard steamers on the Ohio and Mississippi rivers. In 1852 he moved to Chicago, where he joined the city's Turner Society, a German-American organization that promoted physical fitness, German culture and liberal politics.

The Turner Society gave him his first exposure to frontier colonizing—and to the bloodshed it sometimes faced. The group bought land in southern Minnesota Territory, and in 1856 a Turner settler party, including 23-year-old Hummel, established from scratch a German-American colony that is now the city of New Ulm, about 100 miles southwest of Minneapolis. Hummel bought a 160-acre property on a lake and farmed it for more than a decade. This area of Minnesota, near the confluence of the Minnesota and Cottonwood rivers, was a traditional homeland of Santee Dakota tribes (sometimes called Santee Sioux) who in 1851 had ceded millions of acres to the U.S. government in treaties that promised cash and other support. The support was not fully forthcoming, and in 1862 the Dakotas' frustration, hunger, and desperation boiled over. They burned much of New Ulm and killed hundreds of white civilians across a broad swath of south-central Minnesota.[19] Hundreds more were made refugees. Thousands were terrorized.[20] A judge in New Ulm formed a militia to strike back, and Hummel signed up. In an unpublished autobiography, Hummel recalled that the Dakota attacks had "caused me great damage," apparently including the loss of his farm crop. He offered few details beyond this: "We escaped with our lives."

With a contingent of government troops stationed on his farm to deter further violence, Hummel's family hunkered down while he served two years with the Union army during the Civil War. After the war he returned to his farm, worked himself out of debt, and in 1868 sold the farm, moved into town, and opened a New Ulm saloon. Later he built and ran a profitable creamery and then established a dry goods store, which he called The People's Store.

In his autobiography, Hummel made no mention of his time at Equality, but there is little doubt about his initial enthusiasm for the idea of creating a new, more just society. Perhaps he saw Equality as his chance to recreate the new-settlement success he had witnessed in Minnesota. He and New Ulm's other early settlers were unabashed socialists. In an article on the 50th anniversary of the town's founding, the local newspaper said Hummel and other Turner Society members had sought fertile ground to plant their liberal ideas.

"Believing that socialism in proper doses regulates the movements of humanity, adjusts the differences between right and wrong, steps in and arbitrates between labor and capital; defends the poor and holds checkrein upon the rich, the founders of the city were in that sense socialists," the paper said in recalling New Ulm's unusual origins.[21]

Hummel had been active in the People's Party in Brown County, and although his devotion to socialism was welcomed at Equality, he did not bring Burgess's level of fervor.[22] *Industrial Freedom* trumpeted Burgess's arrival as if it might mark the coming of a savior: "Socialism is his theme, and he wants to help us work it out if it suits him. We are on our best behavior."

A few weeks later the paper said Burgess, who arrived on about August 11, had "rolled up his sleeves, spit on his hands, and pitched into the work as though he meant it."

Mean it, indeed. Burgess was as committed to socialism as anyone at Equality and more than most. He took inspiration from such obscure socialists as Stephen Maybell, a poet whose 1889 book, *Civilization Civilized*, advocated a gradual and peaceful evolution to "nationalism." By this he meant public ownership of land and industry. "Nationalism marches with thought, not daggers," Maybell wrote.[23]

In time, Burgess's notions about socialism would turn so radical that, like Boomer, he came to see the Equality model as too tame. Also like Boomer, he relished verbal combat. "I am a believer in the joy of fighting—not military fighting, but intellectual and spiritual fighting," he told a friend years after leaving Equality.[24] Neither he nor Boomer, however, went so far as to endorse anarchism; both, in fact, rejected it. In 1901 Burgess called anarchism "the product of despotism." In later years, however, he became something of a contradiction. He embraced one of anarchism's central themes, arguing that an absence of government would be tenable, even preferable, if capitalism and its economic class divisions were eliminated. In 1905 he traveled to Chicago to attend the inaugural convention of the Industrial Workers of the World, the "Wobblies" whose stated mission was "emancipation of the working class from the slave bondage of capitalism"—class warfare. And yet, he also ran for public office numerous times to become part of a government he despised.

In his tamer days at Equality, Burgess was among the most energetic leaders. He served as school principal, took a turn as president of the colony, and was editor of *Industrial Freedom*. True to his activist instincts, he was the leadoff speaker at the first meeting of Equality's lyceum, a forum for weekly public lectures, debates and entertainment. At one such event he recounted his visit to a failed socialist utopian colony called Topolobampo on the Pacific coast of Mexico. The content of his remarks is unrecorded, and the timing, purpose, and length of his visit at Topolobampo is unclear.[25]

Burgess managed to keep hope alive at Equality, but he could not stop a dispiriting series of crises. On the last day of August, shortly after his arrival and just as the dust was settling on the autonomy debate, the BCC national board decided to hold a referendum on an unresolved debate about whether to move BCC headquarters out of Edison. This was the issue that Lermond said years later was the main reason he quit without waiting for the referendum's results.

This debate was about more than logistics. At bottom it was about Equality's path and purpose. Pelton and some other colonists argued for moving BCC offices from Edison to Equality. In Pelton's mind, the presence of BCC staff in Edison was perversely providing support for the very capitalist system that Lermond's movement sought to destroy. He asked: "Did we break up homes, sacrifice property, sever associations both near and dear, and travel hundreds and thousands of miles" to spend the movement's funds on rent and food in a capitalist town? "In brief, what is this movement for and why are we here?"[26]

The counterargument was that moving headquarters to Equality was tantamount to killing the BCC and blowing up the whole project. The national organization could not fulfill its mission of creating a statewide, let alone a nationwide, network of colonies if it was under the thumb of a single colony. "In order to unite all socialists, you must provide for various industries at points where they can be made remunerative, and it has been thoroughly demonstrated that this cannot be done in one colony," one non-resident BCC member asserted.

When the votes were counted in early October, the Pelton argument prevailed.

Before the matter had been settled, the leading alternative to Equality as a new location for BCC headquarters was the place Lermond had favored: Anacortes, a rough-and-tumble port town of salmon canneries, saw mills, and broken dreams. Situated on the north end of Fidalgo Island, Anacortes was sprinkled with saloons and other haunts of farmers, woodsmen, smugglers and adventurers. George Boomer, too, strongly favored relocating to Anacortes. Years later he said it was part of a grand proposal by Anacortes businessmen to make their town a host of several Equality offices and factories.[27]

In Boomer's recollection, most at Equality refused to consider the proposition, and this marked the beginning of the end.

Burgess saw the Anacortes idea much differently. To him, the argument for moving BCC headquarters anywhere but Equality implied that the colonists were rubes and that non-resident socialists (like Lermond) knew better than the colonists what was good for them and for their cause. He could not resist also taking a swipe at the town of Anacortes.

"It is in its decadence, a veritable graveyard," he sniffed in an article in *Industrial Freedom*.

That comment was too much for William Kaufman, the

paper's editor at the time, whose own utterances years later would test the wartime limits of free speech. He added a note at the end of Burgess's article: "The question as to whether or not Anacortes is a dead or live town cuts no figure in this argument. It is a deep-water harbor we argue for, whether at Seattle, Anacortes or any other place."

Two weeks later, Burgess replaced Kaufman as editor, and soon the Kaufmans would leave Equality and take up farming farther north, in Whatcom County. At this point, public expressions of unity—not to be confused with *actual* unity—came back into fashion at the colony, perhaps because, as the colony newspaper's editorial column put it, outside supporters were writing to "express fears that we are not harmonious in Equality." Not to worry. "There has never, at any time, been greater harmony, nor have our people ever been so hopeful as at the present time," the unsigned editorial claimed. If true, they also had never been so delusional.

Burgess's challenge as the new editor was to avoid undercutting the colonists' morale while also offering them, and socialists elsewhere, something close to an honest picture of how the colony's experiment in socialism was going, now that Lermond had fled and left the Brotherhood for dead.

In November, when Equality marked its first anniversary, the tone of Burgess's editorial page remained one of cautious optimism. Tensions were openly acknowledged but shrugged off as mere growing pains. One editorial said experience had shown that a clash of ideas and opinions produced "some of our most valuable lessons." If so, the colonists must have been learning a lot because conflict within this diverse pool of humanity was frequent, if not continuous.

"We are learning the lesson of tolerance," Oliver P. Darr, the transplanted Missouri dreamer, insisted as he announced in late October one bit of indisputably good news: enough donations had been collected from BCC members, after months of pleading, to buy a portable 35-horsepower steam-driven winch, known in the logging trade as a donkey engine. The device, resembling a flatcar on skids with a mounted steam engine and cables, was used to lift and drag logs to the sawmill from the hillside where they had been felled. It cost nearly $900 and marked a vast improvement from the previous practice of using horses and men to drag logs.

"Do you wonder at us being jubilant here at Equality?" Darr wrote. Soon the donkey engine would be puffing and snorting in the woods, and work could begin on individual homes for colony families, he said, a step toward ending the overcrowded, communal living arrangements that many found tiresome and that would soon ignite a new crisis. The donkey engine arrived at nearby Blanchard in January aboard the steamer *May Queen*; it took fifteen men to unload the beast, put it on a pair of rail trucks borrowed from a nearby commercial logging camp, and push the load to the colony sawmill.

"A scream of welcome bellowed forth from our sawmill whistle as the donkey was slid to the ground," the paper reported.

This was one lonely bit of good news during a period crowded with setbacks.

STILL, newcomers kept arriving, none more colorful than William Hogan. A wiry, mustachioed man of average height and a receding line of dark brown hair, he was the sort of fellow who saw little point in steering a careful course through life. Rambunctious is not too strong a word to describe a man who took chances, sometimes recklessly, to chase adventure and to champion the cause of the underdog, the ordinary laborer.

A devotee of English and Irish literature and the bowler hat, Hogan tried his hand at a remarkable array of work and play—cowboy, union organizer, self-taught Shakespeare expert, boatsman, local government official, silver miner, populist rabble rouser, and, most memorably, instigator of one of the most dazzling capers of late-19th century America.

Born in central Massachusetts to Irish immigrant parents, Hogan was two when his father died of tuberculosis. His mother, whom he would recall as an angelic presence, taught him to live by the Golden Rule, treating others as he wished to be treated. At age twenty he ventured west to taste new freedoms. He rode the cattle ranges of Dakota Territory in the mid-1880s, then drifted farther west, hoping to strike it rich in Montana's gold and silver mines. Instead, he struck a vein of fame—some would call it infamy.

In April 1894 he "borrowed" a Northern Pacific locomotive from a roundhouse in Butte in the dead of night, attached a box car and six empty coal cars, and loaded several hundred members of the Montana branch of Coxey's "army" for a daring dash eastward across the Continental Divide, hoping to reach Washington, D.C., to join the protest against joblessness.[28] This was not an impulse grab. For weeks, Hogan had pleaded with railroad officials to give his men free passage to Washington. They refused but also hinted that at the right moment they might look the other way.[29] Finally, Hogan's patience expired, and in the wee hours of April 25 the renegade locomotive roared out of Butte in the northern Rockies, "nostrils distended and steam chests heaving," as one witness put it.[30] Hogan had opened what an accompanying newspaper reporter called "a chapter in American history that will be read with wonder and amazement by future generations."[31]

At the time, the Northern Pacific was bankrupt and in federal receivership, which meant it could not turn a blind eye to Hogan's audacious grab. It also meant the administration of President Cleveland had skin in Hogan's game and was determined not to lose.

The Hoganites, as the newspapers called his "army," gave Cleveland a good scare. They outran a posse of 80-plus armed federal deputies for more than 200 miles until they reached Billings. There the deputies—a cobbled-together band of mercenaries who had been scraped off the floor of several Butte saloons—caught up with Hogan and demanded he surrender or be shot.

"Shoot and be damned," he retorted.

They shot, oblivious of the risk to a crowd of innocent onlookers, including children. Neither Hogan nor any of his men was seriously wounded, but an unlucky bystander who happened to be a disabled Civil War veteran[32] took a bullet through a lung. (And improbably lived to tell about it.) The shooting triggered such outrage from fellow townsmen that they overpowered the deputies, smashed their Winchester rifles against the iron rails, and ran them out of town.

Hogan and his hijacked train got up a new head of steam and made it another hundred miles to the Yellowstone River town of Forsyth, where they were met by the long arm of the United States military. A blocking force of about 500 soldiers of the Army's 22nd Infantry Regiment had been ordered into action from nearby Fort Keogh, with other forces on call in Bismarck, North Dakota. The Hoganites were captured without a fight.

Such stories tend toward embellishment in the retelling, but in Hogan's description of the Forsyth scene for a newspaper two decades later, he was whittling with a penknife when he acknowledged to the arresting Army officer[33] that he was leader of the unarmed Butte pack. "Do you surrender?" the officer puffed. Hogan casually reversed his penknife to offer the handle to the officer, and with a sigh and low bow replied, "Please accept my sword."[34]

Hogan's hijinks were over. He was convicted of contempt of court for violating a federal order protecting the bankrupt railroad's property and served three months in a Helena jail. At his sentencing, a melodramatic prosecutor cast the episode in dark tones. The commandeering of the train, he said, was reminiscent of the rebelliousness— "mutterings of thunder" he called it—seen and heard in the weeks leading up to the fight at Fort Sumter that opened the Civil War. He was exaggerating for effect, but he was not wrong to suggest there had been a fraying of the social order in western Montana, where capitalism ruled supreme, copper was king and mining tycoons like William A. Clark dominated the state's economy and corrupted its politics.

Even the *St. Louis Post-Dispatch*, which savaged the Coxey movement and Hogan's role in it as misguided folly, saw this as evidence of deep-seated trouble in American society. "The hopelessness and helplessness which induced great masses of men to embark in so mad and dangerous a mission indicate the existence of radical wrongs, the righting of which is vital to the preservation of peace and just government,"[35] it wrote after a group of more than 200 men—minus Hogan, who was still behind bars—made a subsequent (and entirely legal) attempt to reach the nation's capital by building and piloting a fleet of barge-like flatboats down the Missouri River from Fort Benton, Montana, to St. Louis, where they finally gave up.

Hogan, too, had sensed a basic failing of government—indifference to the suffering of the unemployed and underfed, or as he might have quoted Shakespeare on the subject, "poor naked wretches, wheresoever you are"[36]—and tried to do something about it. In a jailhouse interview, he told a newspaper reporter that common people, particularly the jobless, were fed up with being trampled by the rich and powerful. His solution may have been foolish, but even critics admired his motive and style. The *Helena Daily Independent* called the Butte caper wrongheaded and deserving of criminal penalty, but it took a mildly sympathetic view of Hogan— "the unflinching leader of a mistaken cause, wrong in his ideas but right in his heart." That sentiment might as easily fit Lermond, Pelton, Halladay, Burgess and others at the Equality colony, where Hogan would settle a few years later.

For much of his life, Hogan was not keen on polite society. But after regaining his freedom in Montana[37] he served as deputy auditor for Silver Bow County, got married, and became active in the state's trade union movement. Referred to in some newspapers as General Hogan in a nod to his role in the Coxey "army" episode of 1894, he became a regional folk hero. He also turned to socialism and had his eye on Equality from its earliest days.

In February 1899, Hogan and his wife Virginia moved to Equality where by one account he was received as a modern-day Robin Hood. *Industrial Freedom* welcomed him as "a big beam in the timbers that are to build up Equality."[38] A few months later he told a Butte newspaper that Lermond's original scheme was still alive— "to take the reins and drive the government wagon along the road to the cooperative commonwealth ... as fast as the Socialist vote will permit." He had his doubts, however. The Lermond model, he wrote, will be adopted from coast to coast once the capture of Washington is accomplished — "if it ever is."

Hogan spent a quiet two years at the colony, including a period as editor of *Industrial Freedom,* succeeding Burgess, who submitted a brief resignation letter one day before Hogan arrived. In 1900, Hogan ran unsuccessfully for Congress as a socialist, and the following year he and Virginia moved to nearby Orcas Island, where they operated an apple and pear orchard. He took up pleasure boating and made occasional excursions to Seattle to visit a friend who was a yachtsman and taught English literature at the University of Washington.[39] The Hogans lived their final years in Anacortes; he died there in 1940, she in 1960.[40]

Chapter 12

Rough Seas, Choppy Progress

One of the Equality colony's selling points was its proximity to Puget Sound, an inland estuary linked to the Pacific Ocean through Admiralty Inlet and the Strait of Juan de Fuca. Framed by the Olympic and Cascade mountain ranges and fed by thousands of rivers and streams, the Sound features 1,300 miles of shoreline and more than 100 islands.

To their lasting regret, the colonists failed to capitalize on this natural asset.

In addition to offering a bounty of seafood, including salmon, halibut, perch, crab, herring, clams, oysters and mussels, the Sound in the 1890s was a marine superhighway. Steamboats carried passengers and cargo along its shores and between its cities and islands, but for Equality the problem was access. The closest wharf, Fravel's Landing, was a mile away near Blanchard in water so shallow that large boats could reach it only at high tide. This gave rise to an enterprising idea: If the colony could improve the landing and acquire a steamboat, it could handle its own transportation needs, saving freight costs.

They might even capture a share of the commercial shipping trade in a Puget Sound region of about 200,000 people.

Enterprise, however, was never these socialists' strong suit. The BCC solicited donations for a steamboat fund, but the hoped-for golden stream never grew to more than a trickle. The plan was abandoned before the colony came close to raising the required $500.

A related effort to exploit the area's fishing potential gained more traction. The colony created a fishing department and bought a seine net to catch herring. The plan seemed on course when an Oregon woman signed over ownership of a small sailboat, *Progress*, valued at $150, in return for an Equality membership. A Swedish immigrant member was assigned as captain, and for a few years the sloop and a small fleet of row boats supplied the colony with chinook and sockeye salmon, voyaging as far north as Point Roberts on the Canadian border. In subsequent years this venture stalled as they struggled to find willing crew members. Then, construction of a Great Northern rail line through Blanchard destroyed Fravel's Landing, effectively ending the colony's hopes for a fishing bonanza.

Luck was lacking, too.

In November 1898, *Progress* made a trip to Seattle to retrieve several tons of freight. In what might be seen as a metaphor for the fate of Equality itself, the sloop hit rough seas early in its voyage and capsized in the Swinomish slough. The crew, which included Halladay and Pelton, were thrown overboard. The ship's captain managed to release the sheet line that controls the direction of the sails "in time to save the crew from a watery grave," according to an account by an unidentified member of the group. *Progress* was righted and the crew recovered sufficiently to complete the voyage.

Progress in the broader sense was equally unsteady. Lermond's ambition to make Equality the first in a wide network of colonies was largely discarded by now. With it went any realistic hope of validating his economic theory and acquiring the political clout to capture Washington for socialism. In that sense, the Lermond experiment in socialism fizzled before it could be fully tested in the laboratory of real life.

And yet, at the one-year mark, the colonists at Equality could claim they had laid the foundation for improved housing, sustainable food production, and other practical advancements.

By now the men had built two apartment houses, which were supposed to serve as temporary quarters until Lermond's envisioned permanent city was constructed nearby. The first apartment house was twenty-four feet by fifty feet with rooms for twelve families and an attic dormitory for bachelors. The second was twice that size with room for thirty families. They also erected four log cabins and three habitable tents. Even that was insufficient amid the influx of families; houses and rooms in and near Edison were rented for new arrivals and for the growing number of visitors who had come to observe for a few days.

Visitors were welcomed as a means of spreading the colony message, although the message they communicated was not always the desired one. Most regrettable was the harsh criticism that Lewis Ayer of Minneapolis dished out in Seattle and Minneapolis newspapers. Other visitors proved to be of better propaganda value; Ed Pelton's younger brother Charles, for example, spent several weeks at Equality in December 1898 while on leave from the Army to recuperate from an illness acquired during his Spanish-American War service in Puerto Rico. *Industrial Freedom* called him "a staunch believer" in socialism and made a similar assertion about John Abbey, a brother of colony member Grace Lewis, who visited in June 1899 after returning from Army counterinsurgency duty in the Philippines. "He is a socialist," the newspaper said, "and says that he never lacked for congenial company in the army and never suffered for any lack of socialistic literature."

Whatever the value of these visits, they did nothing to solve two big problems that hung threateningly over the little colony like storm clouds over Puget Sound: overcrowding and the failure to build individual residences as promised at the permanent townsite on the hill. These were the kind of failures that Morrison Swift, the Lermond recruit who quickly soured on colonization, had foreseen in December 1897 at the outset of Equality's first winter of discontent.

Optimism, however, had not yet died. "We are quite crowded, but there is little complaint, as we feel it is only temporary," Oliver Darr wrote in a special November edition of *Industrial Freedom* marking Equality's first anniversary. Darr was now BCC secretary, succeeding the recently departed McDevitt. Darr listed the other structures that had begun to give Equality the look of a real town—a schoolhouse, a bakery, a saw and shingle mill, and shops for shoe making, tailoring, dress making, coopering (barrel and bucket making), blacksmithing and furniture making. A newly built barn was a point of pride —and later a source of conflict and crisis.

But it was a different, more important dimension—the human one—that was proving unmanageable. Pelton by now was more willing than most to acknowledge this. He had not lost hope that Equality would succeed eventually, but to those prospective recruits on the "outside" who imagined they would arrive to find ideal people he offered a blunt message: "Drop that weak idea."[1]

Conflict persisted even when the home building finally began. One colonist recalled years later that others resented her family for adding special touches to their home at their own expense. "Then, of course, jealousy could sit on the shoulders of a good many—and did," she said. "And all kinds of trouble commenced."[2]

Aside from internal friction, Pelton and the remaining leaders at Equality also had to contend with verbal fire from former colleagues like Boomer, who moved to Tacoma in November 1898 to start his own radical newspaper. He named it *The Spirit of '76* in reference to the original American rebels, and he promoted it as a faithful reflection of the Founding Fathers' commitment to equal justice and to avoiding entanglement in foreign wars. Boomer's cocksure nature was evident in the blurb he published beside his paper's masthead: "It doesn't make any difference whether you want Socialism or not. It's coming."

An admirer called *The Spirit of '76* the state's first "simon-pure," or authentic, socialist paper.[3] Another applauded it as "a lulu and a hummer."[4] In any case, it was not enough to keep Boomer in business long. The paper, which he operated in partnership with an adventurous gold miner and BCC member named Alfred B. Hicks, lasted only half a year.

In print, Burgess and Boomer exchanged gentle, long-distance jabs, neither mentioning the other by name. Burgess, still editor of *Industrial Freedom*, referred to the "leading light" of the Tacoma paper; he took issue with Boomer writing that Equality practiced a weak brand of socialism.

"We do not claim that our colonies represent pure socialism," Burgess wrote. "We know they do not, and we as well know that there is no pure socialism anywhere else, nor can there be any such so long as competition [capitalism] is in the ascendancy."[5]

Boomer had come to see the Equality experiment as escapism, doomed to fail because the colony members had retreated from the arena of political competition in the mistaken belief that they could build socialism organically, from the ground up. Burgess took note of this implied criticism. It comes, Burgess wrote, "with ill grace from one who advises the poor victim of thousands of political schemes to 'Go straight for the citadel of your enemy, capitalism, by the better of the only two roads to reach it—the ballot.'"[6] In Burgess's view, the electoral system was rotten to the core, although in coming years he would take multiple bites at the campaign apple.

Pioneering for socialism was serious business, but colony life had its lighter side.

Kids found their fun on nature's playground. They explored the woods, meadows, trails, and mountain streams, and the adults organized evening songfests, amateur plays, and Saturday night dances. A partial basement was dug out of the downhill side of the schoolhouse to serve as a dance hall, complete with wooden bleacher seats and coal lamps fastened to the walls. Neighbors flocked to the festivities and reciprocated with invitations to dances in Blanchard and Edison.

Choral singing was a crowd pleaser, led by an Equality quartette starring A.L. Young, a multi-talented musician from Maine, and W.C. Davis, a diminutive Welsh baker. The lineup varied, but the other two members of the foursome sometimes were soprano singer Grace Lewis, wife of the eccentric Carey Lewis, and James Potts, a cabinetmaker who sang baritone and had a knack for accompaniment on a concertina, the little accordion-like instrument.

Another favorite was mass singing, which had become a staple of socialist and populist rallies around the country. "These 'sings' were an especial delight to the kids," one colonist recalled. "They could shout their heads off, and the louder they yelled the better everyone seemed to feel."[7]

As the colony's fortunes faded, so, too, did the singing, the shouting, and the good feeling.

For its many financial failings, Equality did achieve one commercial success: a homemade coffee substitute cooked up by blacksmith Robert Barton.

Barton, whose main job was shoeing the colony's horses and sharpening its plows, made what he called cereal coffee by roasting locally grown grains in a copper-bottom pan in a brick furnace. The formula was secret, but molasses was a known ingredient—perhaps the additive that made the bland beverage palatable. The caffeine-free drink was touted by colonists as "health coffee" and reportedly was the colony's leading commercial export. "Made from selected material, guaranteed to be pure, wholesome and healthful," a colony advertisement boasted, it was a bargain at ten cents a pound or six dollars for a hundred pounds. They enlisted an agent in San Francisco to expand sales, but available records are silent on how he fared. The colony newspaper, however, was loud and clear about Barton's performance. He was a "champion cereal coffee roaster."

Less clear is how Barton acquired his formula and roasting technique. Some believed he had once worked for the Kellogg family in Battle Creek, his home town. The Kellogg brothers, John and Will, were best known for inventing and popularizing breakfast cereals like Corn Flakes, but they also made a grain-based coffee substitute in the 1890s. They called it Caramel-Cereal and produced it at their Battle Creek Sanitarium Health Food Company, but there is no available evidence that Barton ever worked for them.

Barton was an easy fit at Equality, or so he said in postcards and letters to his wife and to the Battle Creek newspaper, the *Moon.* "I am perfectly contented and happy here," he wrote in May, two months after arrival. "It is a new life, so much different from the old that I can hardly find words to express myself and the satisfaction I have of being here among a united and harmonious people." He was working with a fellow Battle Creeker, John T. Oldham, to simplify the collective laundry chore by building a water wheel on the mountain stream that ran through the colony. Barton already was speaking the language of the Lermond socialists: "We propose by our persistent efforts to show the world that cooperation is the only way by which labor will ever gain the just share of the products of its own efforts."

Barton was an irrepressible optimist. In January 1900, one year after a fire[8] destroyed the little building in which he concocted his coffee, he wrote to the *Moon:*

> This is the first time that I could write you with any feelings of certainty that we would be a success as a colony. Now the doubt is removed from my mind. In fact, I was personally sure when I left my family and friends in my dear old home in Battle Creek that the colony would be a success, with God's help.[9]

He added:

> I have received some encouraging letters from my old friends in Battle Creek, which has had a tendency to nerve me on. I enjoy the courage of my convictions and the freedom I have here, and with God's help I will fight the battle to the finish.

Not long after he wrote those words he moved to Tacoma, where he joined the local socialist movement and drew notice for a "missionary wagon" he began building for a tour across the state to promote the socialist cause.

Barton's "battle" ended eight years later. In March 1909 a judge in Tacoma ordered him committed to an insane asylum, and he died there three days later. The circumstances of his apparently sudden demise at age fifty-nine are curious and may never be fully explained. He was arrested on the streets of Tacoma for, in the words of a local newspaper report, "trying to persuade the proprietor of a restaurant into giving the girls higher wages." His punishment was admittance to Western Washington Hospital for the Insane (now Western State Hospital) at Fort Steilacoom, about a half-dozen miles south of Tacoma.[10] His death certificate says he died there of "acute peritonitis following perforation from gastric ulcer." In simpler terms, an ulcer tore a hole in the lining of his stomach or small intestine. His only recorded possessions were a pocket watch and $27 in cash.

Chapter 13

Equality For Women, Too

Lermond and his followers were more forward-thinking on women's issues than most Americans of that era, and yet Equality was indisputably a man's colony. Women had voting rights in the General Assembly and earned equal pay for a day's work, which is remarkable in itself. However, only one woman held a management position of consequence; several contributed behind the scenes, but few spoke out publicly.[1]

The voices that mattered most were male. The women largely kept their own counsel. Two exceptions were Annie Billingsley and Anna Burgess, and even their influence was relatively modest and short-lived.

Billingsley, who had been as active as her husband in the Farmers' Alliance and populist movements back home in Buffalo County, Nebraska, served briefly as editor of "Equality Notes," a breezy fixture in *Industrial Freedom.* In June 1898 she wrote a tribute to the recently deceased Edward Bellamy, whose first utopian novel was Lermond's original inspiration and whose second, *Equality*, was the colony's namesake. She seemed inclined to embrace his view that women deserved liberation. In *Equality*, Bellamy wrote of women: "They were all their lives in a state of subjection both to the personal dictation of some individual man, and to a set of irksome and mind-benumbing conventions representing traditional standards of opinion as to their proper conduct fixed in accordance with the masculine sentiment."

On the very day her tribute appeared in print, the Billingsleys' seven-year-old daughter Hazel died. The following week's paper said Annie was sick in bed, and a week later she resigned her newspaper role. Later that summer she wrote a 32-line poem expressing her family's heartbreak. It began:

Yes, our darling is waiting for us
In God's own heavenly land;
But our hearts are still left longing
For the touch of her little hand.[2]

Verse was her medium. At about the time of her family's move from Nebraska to Equality, *The Appeal to Reason* published her lament of the lust for money.

Oh, Lord! How long must suffering
come,
How long their hearts be cold.
How long their eyes be closed to woe,
In this mad thirst for gold? [3]

Anna Burgess, who arrived at Equality several months after Annie Billingsley, was a more enduring presence on the *Industrial Freedom* staff. Her husband, David, was one of the busiest colony leaders, and they had several children at home, yet Anna knew how to make her voice heard. In fact, it was she who had talked David into leaving Arkansas to join Equality; she initially was drawn to the colonization movement by the power of Eugene Debs' call for socialists to join hands.

As editor of the "Equality Colony Woman's Column," Anna wanted to share the writing responsibilities but found few takers. In her typically mild tone, she complained: "The women of Equality seem to have had their say, at least they do not seem disposed to write for our column." Like her husband, she was a gentle optimist, a devout Christian, a prohibitionist, and a staunch socialist—and her pen was at least as sharp as his.

"The real is not the ideal," she wrote in explaining why newcomers to Equality had to temper their expectations; they should not think they were joining a socialist movement on easy street.

Anna started her column shortly after Equality's first anniversary. She described her goal as telling "the truth, the whole truth, and nothing but the truth, about Equality." That pledge unnerved some male members, Anna wrote, "for fear we would tell something we ought not to."

In her debut column she said she aimed to inform women elsewhere of what home life was like at Equality. That sounds innocuous but in fact was among the touchier subjects because some wives, including Ed Pelton's, found colony life intolerably difficult. This undercurrent of unhappiness was hardly the sort of thing Equality's leaders wanted to advertise.

Anna Burgess occasionally made brief mention of socialism and of women's rights, but mostly she limited herself to light commentary on progress toward normalizing colony life, the challenges of living in a marine climate (she was not a fan of the incessant late-autumn rainstorms that blew in off the Pacific and turned dirt paths into mud streams), and the generally sunny disposition of the colony's dozens of children.

On women's issues, she was relentlessly positive.

"What has impressed me much is the independence of our women," she wrote. "We have equal rights here, we vote as we please, not as our husbands tell us, and this is because we are economically free; what we earn is our very own, consequently we have peace in the family."[4]

In Anna's view, Equality was no place for women who lacked conviction.

"A woman who comes here just because her husband wants her to is almost sure to be discontented," she wrote.[5] Or, as another young woman put it, "A woman coming here must make up her mind to grin and bear much. We must live for the future."[6] At times Anna spoke the language of the revolutionary. "We need women to come to the front who are both able and willing to deprive themselves of the comforts and conveniences of life."

Deprivation of course was not for everyone. In eastern Kansas, a comfortable socialist named Bina A. Otis supported Equality in spirit. She offered words of encouragement and donated small sums but left the heavy lifting to others. "We almost envy you who are permitted to lay the foundation of this great, ever-growing movement in the very desirable state of Washington," she wrote in a July 1898 letter to Equality. When her husband, former Congressman John G. Otis, moved to the colony two years later, she chose to stay in Kansas with their three youngest children and pursue her own socialist agenda. This was not her husband's first fling with a socialist colony. He had moved to Montrose County, Colorado, a few years earlier to join the Colorado Cooperative Colony but was expelled with seven others in April 1896 for being "fault finders and mischief makers."[7]

Bina was plenty busy on her own. She was a leader in the woman suffrage[8] movement in Kansas, and she helped organize a Topeka women's group, the Commonwealth Club, whose members included the wife of the chief justice of the Kansas Supreme Court. The women discussed domestic and foreign policy issues of the day and embraced socialism as a natural evolution of democracy. At their first meeting, the club members discussed a paper on socialism's role in resolving what they believed was the nation's main problem in the final years of the 19th century—joblessness. "An idle citizenship is a menace to the republic," the discussion paper said; work was essential, and reliable employment "can only be secured through a nationalized system of commerce and industry."[9]

Bina hoped for Equality's success but, like many progressives, was unwilling to uproot herself and become one of the deprived. She figured her husband was better suited for that.

"Mr. Otis is a born reformer," she told a newspaper reporter at their dairy farm outside Topeka several weeks after her husband left for Skagit County. "We are both socialists, and while not believing entirely alike on all phases of the question, we are in the main in sympathy with each other."[10] She remained on the farm and advocated for temperance and other social issues she had supported for years, including during her mid-1890s presidency of the Women's Progressive Political League and as a writer for *The Farmer's Wife*, a monthly journal of the Kansas Farmers' Alliance.

"He has more of the pioneer in his makeup than I have," she said of her husband, who at age sixty-two was among the oldest at Equality. "But frankly, I hope that he may conclude not to join the colony at Equality just now but may decide to come back instead." He did join, but after eight months he gave it up, possibly because Bina had fallen ill. Home again, he spoke admiringly of the colony on Samish Bay. "Were I younger," he said, "I would certainly move there. It is an ideal life."[11]

Anna Burgess knew that outsiders like Bina Otis who enjoyed a degree of local prominence and influence might find it hard to believe that life at Equality could be more liberating and meaningful. After all, no woman held a position on the BCC national board after Helen Mason quit in late 1898. Anna herself was unsure how to explain this.

"I know of no answer except that an office here is considered a burden instead of an honor, and our brothers no doubt wish to shield us from all burdens," she wrote.[12] Those do not seem like the words of someone who believed women should share leadership responsibilities. Indeed, few women of her time did. She nonetheless saw something wrong in a society that held women to be intellectually inferior and denied them the most basic of rights in a democracy—the right to choose who will govern. It was among the most glaring examples of inequality in a country that professed to offer equal rights for all.

Women's rights was a subject much discussed at Equality. One member, Sadie Smith Long, wrote sarcastically that in the outside world her status as a woman "condemns me to stand in rank with criminals and idiots—like them, denied the ballot." For her, social equality was the colony's calling card. "We enjoy here the right of free thinking, of free speech, and of a free ballot for both men and women," she wrote.[13]

Even as the suffrage movement grew and accelerated in the post-Civil War period, it remained conventional wisdom—and not just among men—that women were unsuited to enter the political life of the nation. As irrational as it might sound in the 21st century, many believed that giving women the right to vote would do nothing to strengthen American democracy. Some, in fact, asserted that it would hasten the demise of the republic.

Sarah B. Cooper, a religious educator of national repute, argued in 1872 that "wifehood and motherhood" were better remedies than suffrage for what ailed society. The right to vote, she wrote, "will never accomplish what the patient, severe, well-disciplined strength of the guiding maternal arm may do, directed and energized by a God-given faith and love."[14] Still, as with many women of her era, Cooper's views evolved, and in the 1890s she became a leader of the suffrage movement in San Francisco.

And yet, as the new century approached, traditional arguments against women's voting rights remained in the nation's embrace. Chief among them was the idea once espoused by Cooper—that allowing women to vote would distract them from maternal duties and weaken their contribution to society. In a word, voting was "unwomanly." Worse, warned one Democratic member of Congress, it would "mar the beauty and dim the luster of the glorious womanhood with which we have been familiar."[15] Alas, in 1920, with ratification of the 19th Amendment, women won the right to vote and lost neither looks nor luster.

In addition to their personal prejudices, men had their pocketbook reasons for wanting to keep half the adult population out of the voting booth. They knew, for instance, that women were the driving force behind the temperance movement against alcohol use. If allowed to vote, women doubtless would endanger men's booze business.

Women of that era likewise were deemed ill-fitted for leadership positions in business and public life, although they made modest headway in certain professions. Between 1870 and 1890, the number of women lawyers in the United States grew from five—yes, just five—to 288; physicians and surgeons from 544 to 4,557, and architects from one to twenty-two. By far the largest number of working women were in fields considered "woman's work"—teaching school (so long as they were unmarried and thus "free" of homemaker duties), bookkeeping, stenography, and other clerical jobs.[16]

Anna Burgess supported the suffrage movement as well as temperance, but in her *Industrial Freedom* columns she addressed neither issue in detail. She believed those two reforms would prove inadequate to women's needs if pursued separately from the most important change of all—substituting socialism for capitalism.

"Through socialism we will get all other needed reforms," she wrote in her typically tidy way.

An anonymous donor sent Anna a copy of a recently published novel whose theme surely shocked many in this late-Victorian era when women were expected to keep house, bear and nurture children, and leave nearly all other consequential affairs to men. The novel was *The Strike of a Sex*. The premise was that all women in a fictional city had gone on strike, leaving their husbands to fend for themselves. "They have struck for their rights as a sex," one of the deprived husbands told an astonished visitor. "They say that the chains which have bound them for unnumbered ages, although artfully garlanded with flowers and called by sentimental and endearing names, are older and more galling than those of any bondspeople on the globe. They have decided that the time has come to throw off those chains."[17]

Anna mentioned the book and its author, George N. Miller, in one of her columns but left unclear how she felt about it.

Her only comment was, "This book contains much food for thought."

Anna's independent streak reflected her upbringing. Like her husband David, she was raised among Quakers, whose core values, including equality for women in spiritual leadership, sometimes put them at odds with social convention. The most famous suffragist, Susan B. Anthony, founder of the National Woman Suffrage Association, was a Quaker.

Anna's interest in public affairs did not begin at Equality. In Arkansas, she and David led a local group, affiliated with the Woman's Christian Temperance Union, that instructed St. Paul's children in the virtues of abstinence from alcohol. David won public applause for helping block issuance of a saloon license, which was no small matter in St. Paul. The hill country of northwest Arkansas was known as a "land of blind tigers," meaning it welcomed (or at least tolerated) speakeasies, moonshine hideouts, and other illicit booze establishments.

The Burgesses spent a total of eleven months at Equality. They left in July 1899 and moved up the road to New Whatcom, where David recited "the cheery optimism of socialism"[18] and claimed to hear a "thunderous roar of the rising tide" of believers in capitalism's coming demise. He and Anna later moved to Seattle and, finally, Tacoma, but they never fully escaped the world of "wage slavery." In Tacoma, Anna worked as a tailoress, altering clothing for customers at a fabric store called Stone, Fisher & Lane. David did manual labor at the Wheeler, Osgood & Company millworks, penned articles for socialist newspapers, wrote ads for a socialist dentist,[19] worked in a Tacoma bookstore owned by a Minneapolis-based socialist,[20] and traveled across Washington to push the socialist case on the public lecture circuit.

Anna Burgess's call for more of Equality's women to write for *Industrial Freedom* didn't get much result—with one remarkable exception. Sarah Ward Temple, who had arrived at the colony in the fall of 1898, wrote things for the "Woman's

Column" that may have made even Burgess cringe. In fact, it likely was Temple's outspokenness more than Burgess's that left the men of Equality "trembling," as Burgess put it,[21] with fear that the women would say too much.

Temple had a lot to say. She made her writing debut in January 1899 by offering a twist on Anna Burgess's comment about women coming to Equality for the right reasons. Temple saw two kinds of women there—those of a "gentle, wifely character" who had been dragged by their husbands, and those, like her, who had come to change the world. In both cases, women thinking of joining Equality needed to awaken to some hard facts, she wrote, or they would pay in homesickness and regret. They must understand that after a day's work—be it waiting tables in the community dining hall or caring for the children or the sick—there was no escaping the burdens of communal life.

The worst hardship for women, she wrote, was "finding one's home life of quiet and seclusion gone—crushed into one twelve-by-fourteen-foot room of a large, barn-like apartment house whose stovepipes poking intrusively out of every window frequently go on a strike and smoke you out of house and home." Not to mention the annoyance of having one's rest or sleep interrupted by "meanderings of melody from a violin in one room, an organ in another, a debate in mixed American upstairs, and a resentful baby heaven knows where!"

Temple worried that, like most American women, those at Equality had resigned themselves to male dominance and accepted what she called "the chains of domestic slavery." In her view, they had given up hope of liberation, like the character in Lord Byron's narrative poem, *Prisoner of Chillon*, who murmured:

My very chains and I grew friends,
So much a long communion tends

To make us what we are – even I
Regained my freedom with a sigh.

After just three months at Equality, Temple was unhappy, and her mood grew steadily darker. She was not wrong about the overcrowded conditions; more than a year after the colony's founding, housing was still in such short supply that families with four or five children were sleeping in a single room. Even an Equality promoter acknowledged earlier in the year that the housing problem had "taxed the pioneers to the utmost."[22] Other necessities were lacking, too. Nourishment was barely adequate. Sanitation was worse.

In the spring of 1899 Temple abruptly left, reportedly citing "failing health." Soon afterward, she publicly lambasted the colony. She claimed it had devolved into anarchy—years before that actually happened. Without evidence, she accused Equality's leaders of misspending or stealing funds from the community treasury, a charge they firmly denied.

"I say without fear of successful contradiction that Equality colony as managed now is a fraud, a failure, and a disgrace to the name of socialism," she wrote in a tirade published by the colony newspaper on June 3. She was immediately contradicted in a rebuttal that regretted her "sad wail" and accused her of pursuing a vendetta. It said that at a meeting of the General Assembly just before quitting the colony, Temple vowed that if her $160 membership fee was not returned (which it was not) she would "never cease to use tongue and pen to destroy Equality."

Her main complaint was that $160 had not put her in her own home, as was promised to each new member. Instead, she and her young son Andrew lived in the dreaded apartment house, leaving her to choose between "going insane or getting away," as she put it.

The first of those two choices—insanity—was probably not meant literally, but in fact a short time later Temple was hauled off to the county jail in New Whatcom on a charge her jailers recorded with a single word: "insane."[23] On the authority of Whatcom County Superior Court Judge Hiram E. Hadley, she spent one night behind bars and then was transferred to nearby St. Luke's Hospital,[24] which was not a mental health institute. Exactly why she was jailed and then hospitalized, and what happened next, are mysteries. Her case file was removed from the county courthouse at some point and has not been found.[25]

One year after her "insane" episode, Temple was living in a fruit-growing area of northern California with a younger brother, Edwin, who was leasing an orchard with another brother, William. Sarah was forty-one. Also in the household was her 11-year-old son Andrew and her mother, Emmaline. The 1900 census listed Sarah as a widow. Remarkably, by 1902 all three of Sarah's housemates were dead.[26] Influenza killed Edwin, Andrew drowned, and Emmaline died of "senility" at age sixty-seven. At that point, clues to Sarah's life path disappear.

Sarah Ward Temple was born and raised on a relatively prosperous farm about a mile east of the village of Virden on the tallgrass prairie of west-central Illinois. Her father, John P. Ward, was a Civil War veteran and prominent member of the community. Sarah remembered him as "the most gentle and generous man I have ever known."[27]

Shortly after the war, Virden became a coal-mining center, and this would be its ticket to a tragic place in history books. Situated about twenty miles south of Springfield, the state capital, Virden was the scene of a violent labor struggle in October

1898 that left thirteen men dead, including eight coal miners. The miners had gone on strike to protest the Chicago-Virden Coal Company's refusal to honor a nationwide wage agreement between coal operators and the United Mine Workers. When Chicago-Virden Coal imported a trainload of black non-union miners from Alabama to break the strike, emotions boiled over. The striking miners and company guards exchanged gunfire, with tragic results. The episode is largely forgotten elsewhere, but Virden remembers. A downtown park features a bronze-and-granite memorial to the massacre. At the time, the battle reinforced a core belief among many Americans, including the socialists at Equality, that industrial capitalism was rigged against ordinary workers and that excessive corporate power was a deadly threat.

Temple had just arrived at Equality when the Virden battle erupted. She responded with venom. The shooting of miners by Thiel Detective Service agents hired to enforce the coal company's strike-breaking operation was nothing less, in her view, than cold-blooded murder.

"These slimy red marks upon the bosom of outraged Mother Earth are the glancing footprints of monstrous War!" she wrote.[28]

As her choice of words suggests, Temple was not a newcomer to radicalism. In her late twenties, as the nation was emerging from the severe recession of the mid-1880s, she and her older sister Julia gave up a relatively comfortable life in Virden to get an up-close look at the seamier side of capitalism. They moved to Chicago and got jobs in a large factory "at the starvation wages usually paid to that class of labor."[29] It's unclear how long they lasted, but this episode foretold their eventual embrace of socialism.

After giving up the Chicago jobs, both sisters got married, Sarah to Charles R. Temple and Julia to Willard Pennington.

Both couples moved to Carroll County in the Ozarks of northern Arkansas. Together, Sarah and Julia started a commune with a strange theme. "We call our organization one of 'common homes for understanding friends'—that is, people whose tastes, beliefs, habits and manner of life are in harmony," Sarah said. How the plan would achieve that harmony was unclear from her description.

"It is our pet hobby," Sarah told a local newspaper, suggesting her commitment was more casual than financial. "We shall be woefully disappointed if it proves a failure."

Fail it did. Sarah and Julia may have been disappointed, but Sarah was not about to give up on her belief that some form of collectivism would make the world a happier place. It was a cause she shared with Julia, a regionally acclaimed singer of populist ballads. Julia attended the 1896 People's Party presidential nominating convention in St. Louis, where she may have caught wind of Norman Lermond's Brotherhood idea. That may have been the connection that led Sarah to Equality two years later.

In the early 1890s, Sarah Temple taught in public schools, lectured at community gatherings, and organized a communal fruit orchard near Maple, Arkansas. Maple was "an ideal situation for a colony 'far from the madding crowd,'" she wrote in an 1897 article for a Kansas newspaper, *Progressive Thought and Dawn of Equity,* the official voice of the labor exchange movement, a sort of twist on socialism. The basic idea of a labor exchange, or workers' cooperative, was that members deposited their work products, such as farm produce or small manufactured items, in a central warehouse and in return received "labor checks," or scrip, based on the wholesale value of the item. The scrip could be exchanged at the same warehouse for commodities produced by others and sold at a retail price; the difference between the wholesale and retail charges went to the original depositor.

This alternative to classic capitalism was in some respects a forerunner of today's co-op food stores—rooted in ideas of self-reliance and community-based solutions to price competition. The labor exchange was the brainchild of an Italian immigrant, Giovanni B. DeBernardi, who took up farming in Missouri and organized the first exchange in about 1890. The idea spread across the Middle West but the exchanges had largely disappeared by the turn of the century.[30]

By the spring of 1897, Temple had her Labor Exchange Branch No. 82 up and running in Maple. A few months later she was calling herself vice president of the colony and describing it as a "proposed industrial city and reform health resort." Then the "resort" concept veered in a new direction. In September, just as Pelton was arriving in Skagit County, Temple, still in Maple, was publicly urging labor unions across the nation to buy up cheap land near all coal mining centers to create farms that would serve as sanctuaries—she called them "summer resorts"—for striking miners and for the sick and elderly.

These big ideas apparently failed. She left for Equality about a year later.

Sarah Ward Temple was one of several at Equality who had previously dabbled in socialist-style colonies. George Boomer was reported in 1896 to be planning a colony in Maryland's Allegany County across the Potomac River from the West Virginia town of Paw Paw. He foresaw an economy centered on an industry that harkened to his childhood—a woolen mill. It seems not to have gotten beyond the planning stage. Another aspirant was William Kaufman, the Minnesota newspaper editor whose wife feasted on visions of Puget Sound seafood during their train ride west. Nearly a year before they joined Equality, he announced plans for a "cooperative colony" south of Minneapolis on 300 acres donated by a farmer.

"We will have freedom from rent, profits, worry, etc.," Kaufman wrote. "This is practical Christianity."[31]

Although he was an ordained minister and considered himself a disciple of Christian Socialism, his colony venture won no divine favor and by late 1897 had passed to the Great Beyond.

Kaufman was a devoted follower of Henry George, the writer and reformer who started the "single tax" movement in the 1880s with his wildly popular book, *Progress and Poverty*. The single tax was George's proposed solution to the puzzle implied by his book title: Why must there be so much poverty amid riches? That question gnawed at the Equality colonists and is one still asked in the 21st century.

Among the questions George posed in aiming for a fairer society was this: "Why should a man benefit merely from the act of ownership, when he may render no services to the community in exchange?"[32] George, who was not a socialist, was referring in part to real estate speculators. He argued that a tax on unimproved land—that is, a property in its natural state, with no buildings or other improvements—would transform the economic system as land values grew. This single tax would produce so much public revenue, he argued, that no others would be necessary.

Kaufman preached this point: Profits from rising land values are unearned and thus should be taxed as a form of economic rent because land naturally belongs to society as a whole, not to any individual. He took this further, however. Citing what he called the laws that God had imparted to Israelites through Moses, he argued in a sermon in 1886 that all real estate should be redistributed every fifty years. "Impractical? Was Moses a fool?" he asked.

Kaufman was a contrarian in the Boomer mold, and in his post-Equality years he did Boomer one better. He attracted even more public outrage for his anti-war rhetoric than Boomer had gained two decades earlier in Kansas for his "painted rag" comment about the flag.

In a speech in Olympia on Labor Day in 1917, a few months after the United States declared war on Germany and American troops landed in France to enter the First World War, Kaufman asserted that the American government had been "buncoed into this war" by profiteering arms manufacturers. Liberty Bonds used to finance the allied cause were "a disgrace to America," he said, because the government should have taxed arms merchants rather than using "Lady Liberty" to shame ordinary people into believing it was their civic duty to buy at least $150 in bonds yielding a lower rate of return than their bank savings. Justified or not, the government did resort to scare tactics in its marketing; one of its widely published advertisements was titled "Bonds or Bondage—Which?" It warned that if Germany won the war, "the fate of your home would be the fate of those of Belgium. You would have no choice as to what would be done with your money. It would be taken from you by force." Refusing to buy bonds, it said, was "selfishness" tantamount to betraying one's own child. In some towns, "anti-slacker" vigilantes splashed yellow paint on homes or barns of people who hesitated to buy bonds.[33]

For offering his unpopular opinion, Kaufman was arrested, indicted, tried and convicted of violating a section of the newly enacted Espionage Act that outlawed speech intended to interfere with military operations or to obstruct military recruiting—anti-war speech, in other words. He was sentenced to five years in prison but on appeal his case was dismissed a year later at the request of the government, which—after having publicly denounced Kaufman as a traitor and a "dangerous propagandist"—admitted it had misapplied the law. This was a mumbo-jumbo admission that it had violated his rights.[34]

The decision to dismiss the charges was made by U.S. Attorney General A. Mitchell Palmer, who two years later would launch what became known as the Palmer Raids, a legally questionable campaign to stamp out radicals by ordering the arrest and deportation of thousands of suspected communist sympathizers and anarchists, including Emma Goldman, who lived her remaining years mostly in Europe and Canada.

Kaufman faced trials of a different kind during his several months at Equality. Early on, Pelton and other leading members tried to get him fired by removing him from the BCC board of trustees. They invoked a provision of the BCC constitution allowing for a special election to remove any board member. In a handwritten letter to Lermond, three dozen colonists declared themselves "aggrieved and injured because of the delays and hindrances thrown in the way of our progress by the failures" of Kaufman to fulfill promises he had made when elected to the board. The letter specified neither his promises nor his failures, and the available record is silent on whether a recall election was actually held. Some unhappiness with Kaufman may have originated with his promise to ship a printing press from Minnesota, where he had been editor of a small-town newspaper. The contraption turned out to be useless and carried a $400 freight charge, to boot. The colony spent another $1,200 to buy a press in Tacoma.

Away from Equality, Kaufman did have admirers. He was elected Whatcom County's assessor in 1910; he ran on the Republican ticket, then promptly disowned the Republican party.

Many were unsure what to make of him.

"An unusual man is this man Kaufman," the *Tacoma Times* wrote in a mostly flattering article about his candidacy for governor in 1911. "People around here swear by him—those who don't swear *at* him."

If Sarah Ward Temple was one of the loudest and most eccentric people at Equality, Helen M. Mason was her opposite. She made no waves. Quietly competent, she worked behind the scenes as BCC treasurer, one of the group's more thankless jobs. She was a sober, God-fearing, untiring advocate for social justice, driven by a special passion for improving the lives of the poor, the orphaned, the working mother, and the unemployed.

In a word, she was a saint. Or so one could conclude from a life that included a rigorous religious education, many years as a public-school teacher, a lifelong abstinence from alcohol, and nine months of work at Equality that would have tested the patience of Job. She never married, which might explain her enduring calm.

The daughter of a clockmaker, she grew up in the Hudson River town of Glens Falls, New York. Her parents raised her in the Methodist Episcopal faith, which emphasized social obligations and moral responsibility, including working to abolish slavery and fight poverty. She attended a private secondary school and then a teacher-training school in the nearby town of North Granville.

Like William McDevitt, Helen was an academic at heart. She taught English at Castleton Seminary (now a campus of Vermont State University), just across the New York state line, before moving to St. Louis in about 1871.

She spent more than twenty years teaching in St. Louis public schools, but, like David Burgess in his final years in Arkansas, her focus shifted in a radical direction as the nation's economic ills mounted. This transformation in the late 1880s and early 1890s may have been a product of her experiences in St. Louis classrooms and as an observer of alcohol's social costs. She had seen enough of urban poverty and despair. She decided to try to do something about it.

For starters, she did a lot of writing. In the late 1880s she helped lead the Missouri Prohibition Society and edited its quarterly journal, the *Temperance Advocate*. Broader questions of social justice were never far from her mind, perhaps due to her Methodist Episcopal upbringing. In the early '90s she began bombarding the *St. Louis Post-Dispatch* with letters shining a light on the consequences of inner-city neglect. While working as a *Post-Dispatch* proofreader she pleaded for federal and local action on an issue that fit neatly with Lermond's agenda—getting government more involved in leveling the economic playing field and assisting the poor, the weak, and the jobless.

"Let Congress at once inaugurate some needed public work on a gigantic scale, which will employ the unemployed, and tax incomes at a graduated rate for the expense," she wrote[35] in the *Post-Dispatch,* whose editorial policy strongly opposed public assistance of any kind. Mason argued that this large-scale program should be enacted as an emergency measure and then made permanent nationwide "at the expense of the wealthy." She didn't buy the popular argument that taxing the wealthy amounted to stealing from the successful. "Through blunder or design," she wrote, rich Americans had been entrusted with a metaphorical scepter, or symbol of power, to assist others in need. "If they are to give or withhold relief according to their pleasure, it is a tyrant's scepter."

She was passionate, also, about what she saw as an equally pressing problem—alcohol and the social problems it created and perpetuated. Alcohol abuse among men was hurting and in some cases destroying families in an age when few wives had the economic independence or the legal means to protect themselves from their husband's excesses. In this era, the two movements—socialism and prohibition—were broadly related in the sense that they placed a higher priority on the welfare of society than on the liberty of the individual.

Prohibition was not an official priority at Equality or in the broader socialist movement, although it became the law of the land with ratification of the 18th Amendment to the Constitution in 1919. To Mason, countering the ills of alcohol abuse was a moral issue inseparable from others like support for the poor and the jobless and protection of children. These were issues that had attracted her to Lermond's Brotherhood in the first place. Evidence of her devotion to achieving an alcohol-free society is the fact that despite her relatively obscure role in the movement, she established a personal tie to its leading voice —Frances E. Willard, national president of the Woman's Christian Temperance Union. Early in Mason's tenure with the BCC she asked Willard to accept an honorary membership.

"Of course I will be an honorary member. I believe in the things that Christian socialism stands for, and were I not teetotally occupied, would go into the movement heart and soul," Willard replied.[36]

For several years in St. Louis, while a member of the Carondelet branch of the Woman's Christian Temperance Union, Helen served as Missouri correspondent for the organization's national newspaper, *The Union Signal*. Her writing could be as gnarly as a Bristlecone pine tree, but from time to time the contours of an important insight emerged from the dense tangle of words. In an 1892 article, she used a medical metaphor to argue that inner city neighborhoods were "sick with inflammation and ulcer" because of poisonous business practices like hiring children for factory jobs.[37]

Legislating the protection of children in the work force was high on the reform agenda of socialists and populists. Not all children of that era were performing dangerous work or putting in long hours, but their role was a source of growing national debate. The numbers explain why. In 1870, 19 percent of boys aged 10 to 15 were working for pay, and the figure climbed steadily until peaking in 1900 at 26 percent. It then declined rapidly, dipping just below 17 percent in 1920 and 6 percent a decade later. In an analysis of this data, the Census Bureau in 1940 noted that most working children were employed on family farms, in many cases under the supervision of their own parents. But for those in non-farm jobs away from home, the work "is so arduous and continuous as to be injurious," it said.[38]

The practice of employing children in factories and mines, sometimes even in their pre-teen years, seems extreme and even cruel by today's moral standards. But in the late 19th century it was seen by many as an economic necessity; an extra dollar here and there put food on the family table. More broadly, it was viewed as a matter of individual choice, not to be limited by government.

"Parents do not have their children work in factories for the love of it, but 'dire want dictates,'" was how one person put it in response to a survey of working-class Pennsylvanians in 1889.[39] Another argued that by age twelve a child is ready to learn the value of work. "Early training in the duties of labor would be a realization of the old adage—'just as the twig is bent the tree is inclined.'"[40]

For employers it was a matter of expedience and economic self-interest. Child labor was cheap.

Some adults, however, viewed the practice as immoral, harmful to children's health and a constraint on their education. It was stealing from the nation's future.

The children at Equality were not excused from lessons in

the value of work, but school attendance was an equal priority. Boys and girls aged 10 to 17 were required to work one hour before school and one hour after, plus five hours on Saturdays. Summer hours were longer. Girls assisted the adult housekeepers, helped in the meal service and did some cooking. Boys had a wider range of options—feeding the hogs, tending to the chickens, delivering official messages, helping in the dining hall, and working at the sawmill.

Like several other pieces of the 1890s socialist agenda, limits on child labor eventually became a mainstream political priority. It was pushed in that direction in the 1910's by aggressive reformers like George E. Creel, a writer who rejected socialism but echoed its attack on corporate greed.[41] Creel viewed child labor as a fundamental evil and a stain on capitalism. "Child labor, no less than the tariff, the trusts and monopoly, is a foundation stone in the towering structure of Big Business; and in every state it will be seen that the interests that fight political, industrial and economic advancement are also bitter in their antagonism to child labor reform," he and his co-authors wrote in 1914 in *Children in Bondage*, a book which included the revelation that kids as young as six were working in cotton mills.[42]

In 1916, Congress passed the first federal law to regulate child labor. It limited the working hours of children and forbade the interstate sale of goods produced by child labor, but two years later the law was ruled unconstitutional. Federal laws protecting children in the workplace did not become permanent until passage of the Fair Labor Standards Act of 1938. Helen Mason would have been unhappy to learn that by the 2020s, Republican-led legislatures in some states, including Iowa and Arkansas, were citing worker shortages during the Covid-19 pandemic as justification to scale back child labor standards, including limits on the number of hours children could work during the school year.

MASON WAS the only woman to serve on the BCC's national board of trustees. When she took over as treasurer a few months after Equality was established, the coffers contained $136.57, and the BCC's ledgers were in such disarray that the outgoing bookkeeper informed her it would take the bank at least a week to sort out the accounts.

The historical record offers few details of Mason's short tenure at Equality. She kept her head down. On November 1, the first anniversary of Equality's founding, she quit the board, but this was not reported by the colony paper. Unhappy with the BCC's new direction, Mason wrote in an unpublished resignation letter that "the theory under which the work of the BCC is now to go on is not the theory under which I have worked and have hoped to work."[43] She seemed to refer to recent decisions to grant self-governing status to Equality and to move BCC headquarters to colony grounds, actions which broke Lermond's spirit and all but crushed his original goal of creating a broad network of colonies that could capture the state for socialism.

True to character, she agreed to stay on to do clerical work "to carry out the wishes of the Brotherhood."

Mason had outlasted and perhaps outworked most of the original BCC officers, yet her material reward was meager. Shortly before Christmas, at about the time she left to resettle in a nearby village, the resident BCC trustees published a tribute in *Industrial Freedom*.

"When all the other national officers had grown weary, she remained at her post, true to the cause," they wrote. As a token of appreciation, they proposed to give her 20 percent of funds collected for new newspaper subscriptions on a single day, December 20. That likely amounted to no more than several dollars—about what it would have cost her for a new pocket watch. It also was roughly equal to the sums she donated to the Brotherhood from outside sales of a 16-page astronomy pamphlet that she wrote and illustrated for classroom use.[44]

Mason returned to her first love: education. She taught at a two-room schoolhouse at Pleasant Ridge, a hamlet a couple of miles east of La Conner and about a dozen miles south of Edison. The school, built in 1891 and abandoned in 1930, was still standing in the 2020s with its stone foundation intact, its bell cupola perched atop a moss-covered shake roof, and echoes of its past still lingering. A year later she moved to the village of Cherry Valley (now Duvall), east of Seattle on the banks of the Snoqualmie River. She also served as an officer in the Washington Woman Suffrage Association but did not live to see its success in 1910, when the state granted women the right to vote.

In January 1901, the state board of education awarded Mason a "life diploma" for her career of public service. Two weeks later she died of colorectal cancer in a Seattle hospital.

A Seattle chapel hosted Mason's funeral service, and she was buried in the shadow of a cedar tree at Mount Pleasant Cemetery on the city's Queen Anne hill.[45] The cemetery was a fitting choice. It originally was a fraternal burial ground of the International Order of Odd Fellows, whose building in Edison served as the BCC's first headquarters. Notably, the cemetery holds the remains of three union agitators killed in one of labor's most famous 20th century confrontations with capitalism—the Everett Massacre, a 1916 gun battle between radical unionists and a sheriff's posse of deputized Everett businessmen. Helen Mason, an advocate of worker rights and peaceful revolution, would have deplored the violence but acknowledged the deadly risks in challenging capitalism.

One of Equality's most publicly active women was not even a member. Helen J. Wescott wrote a "Children's Column" for *Industrial Freedom*, mostly by mail from Manhattan, Kansas, where she was a librarian at the Kansas State Agricultural College (now Kansas State University). In 1898, she spent her summer break working at BCC headquarters in Edison. William McDevitt, the bookworm and former government clerk who served as Lermond's legal aid, recalled Wescott as his secretary and "my most intimate chum."[46]

Adventurous and ambitious, Wescott was more a social reformer than a political radical. She advocated for women's rights with a boldness that would have served her well in the women's liberation movement of the 1960s. You might have called her a protofeminist.

In the summer of 1893, at age twenty-three, she and three other women traveled from Boston to the World's Fair in Chicago to showcase a Wescott-designed bicyclist outfit. Writing afterward for a Boston magazine, she described the outfit—known as a "costume" in the lingo of the day—as Syrian style. Made "as tastefully as possible," its distinguishing feature was a loose skirt hemmed above the ankle and accented with a sash that hung from the hips.[47] Her creation was featured as part of the "rational dress movement" of the 1890s, an attempt to free women of the irrationally constricting clothing demanded by society in the Victorian period—the tightly laced corset and wire-frame bustle worn over voluminous layers of petticoat designed to enhance modesty by hiding the shape of the leg. In some circles it was deemed scandalous to even suggest a liberation, for this was an era in which the female body in public was assumed to stop at the chin, only revealing itself again at the instep, and a woman's virtue was measured in bolts of cloth.

To her surprise, Wescott and her bicycling companions attracted compliments but few criticisms. "Where can I get the pattern?" was asked of them over and over.

"Day after day this was what we heard, and in our whole trip of two weeks, during which we wore our suits on the trains, in the city, and at the [fair] grounds, not one unpleasant experience have we to record, of all that our conservative friends so confidently prophesied," she wrote. "We returned feeling that the time is ripe for such a movement."

Her optimism about liberalizing women's style was well placed, but in matters of women's rights more generally, late-1890s culture was not even close to abandoning traditional views of what was still called "the fairer sex." The same page of a newspaper that commented approvingly on Wescott's Boston magazine article also featured an advertisement for a concoction to cure women of the "sallow faces, dull eyes, hollow cheeks and low spirits" caused by the "disorders, derangements and weaknesses peculiar to their sex."

After her Chicago adventure, Wescott spent two years studying law under the private tutelage of Frank Parsons, whom she likely met during his time as a Boston University law school professor, before he became a BCC board member. She was admitted to the Suffolk Bar Association in Boston in March 1897—an achievement so rare for a woman that it made national headlines. Several months after Parsons began teaching at the Kansas State Agricultural College in the summer of 1897, Wescott took the librarian position there, likely on Parson's recommendation.

Nicknamed "Hattie" as a child, Helen Josephine Wescott

was born in Merrimack County, New Hampshire, in a small town just east of Concord, and grew up in rural northeastern Maine. She was remarkably accomplished by her late 20s—attorney, stenographer, lecturer and writer.

After her summer at Equality, Helen returned to Kansas and wrote a lengthy account of her impressions. She saw the colony as "a large city in miniature," with families from towns and villages across the country.[48] The sublime setting in the Cascade range made a lasting impression. She marveled at how the forest canopy blocked most rays of sunlight, bathing the ground in a "perpetual soft green twilight, inexpressibly restful and fascinating."

She recalled a newsboy on her Great Northern train saying as they pulled into Belfast station, "Oh, yes, this is God's own country where you've come to now." She figured he was being sarcastic but changed her mind on the walk to Edison.

"We started out after an admiring look across the track at the tall, straight ranks of trees, forming long, pillared avenues like cathedral aisles," she wrote. From there, the scene left her at a loss for words. "I can only try to give a faint idea and leave the rest to the reader's imagination. The road winds among primeval giants such as would dwarf the mightiest in the woods of Maine or the Adirondacks."

She made no forecast of Equality's future but said the time she had spent talking to and working with BCC officers convinced her of the genuineness of their devotion to socialism.

She admired the colonists' grit and patience.

"At one time their fare consisted for several weeks of beans, potatoes, bread without butter, and sauce made from some prunes that were donated for their use," she wrote in her essay. (Those prunes again!)

Spending a summer with a colorful ring of radicals was an education, but colony life was not for Helen. She sympathized with the socialists, but it's not clear she wanted to be one. The law was her calling.

When a Boston Globe reporter in 1897 asked what had motivated her to become a lawyer, she replied, "I wanted to be something more than a stenographer, and now I want to be something more than a lawyer." Her friends had assured her that in time she would, like others in the profession, succumb to the temptation to cut ethical corners. "But I intend to be that rare thing, a perfectly honest lawyer," she said.

Her noble ambition was left unfulfilled. Tuberculosis took her life in the Boston suburb of Medford the summer after her Equality visit. At just twenty-nine, she was stopped short of what seemed her destiny—to confront and perhaps shatter what a century later would be called the glass ceiling.

Years later, McDevitt wrote that Wescott fought a prolonged battle with tuberculosis, the infectious disease that in the 19th century was incurable and commonly called consumption, capturing in a word its ravaging effects on the body. It was a feared killer for centuries until the development of effective drug treatments, a vaccine, and preventive therapies.

McDevitt claimed to have learned from prior experience that sufferers of tuberculosis were capable of extraordinary displays of courage. "Young persons convinced of their liability to chronic invalidism or worse from consumption are immune to the usual fear of danger or peril," he wrote.[49]

McDevitt remembered a weekend sailboat ride with Wescott to the tiny island of Eliza at the entrance to Bellingham Bay, just off the southern tip of Lummi Island. (McDevitt said some BCC members wanted to buy Eliza, once home to a large chicken farm and reputed to be haunted by ghosts, and he claimed it could have been had for $1,700. But that's another story.) The single-mast boat, the *Dora*, was simple to sail, but on this excursion Mother Nature added an unwelcome complication—a storm so frightful that on the return voyage one man in their party of four insisted he be put ashore a dozen miles before they reached home. McDevitt recalled Wescott as "so thoroughly unperturbed that she compelled me to screw up my courage to the sticking point." They made it back safely, and it was not the last time he would witness her steady nerve. "Once, I recall, she and I rode horseback into close contact with a raging forest fire in the woods near Equality, and once again she displayed more courage than I had."

As Equality's fortunes faded in the spring of 1899, so, too, did women's voices. Anna Burgess gave up her "Equality Colony Woman's Column" in May, and two months later she and David moved to New Whatcom. Anna's successor, Rhoda C. Eddy, lasted only a couple of weeks before her father's sudden death prompted her and her husband, Bige Eddy, to quit and return to their home south of Olympia, where he owned a small weekly newspaper.

More women would arrive in the years ahead, including one whose knack for disruption would rival that of Sarah Ward Temple. But their public visibility was greatly diminished, not just because of the shrinking ambitions of the BCC and its lonesome colony but also because *Industrial Freedom* became a shell of its former self. For reasons that have gone unrecorded, the Postmaster General revoked the newspaper's second-class mailing privilege in 1899, causing it to temporarily cease publication. The final weekly edition appeared on June 24, although it reappeared the following year as a monthly, with teenager Harry Ault in charge, until shutting down permanently in November 1901.[50]

Chapter 14

Pelton's Last Stand

The rush to the exits that began with Lermond had nearly emptied the colony of its original leadership by the end of 1898, just fourteen months into the Equality experiment.

This reflected two major features of the utopian socialist movement of that era. First, some devotees like Charles Swigart came to recognize its limitations and returned to mainstream America. Second, others like David Burgess were inclined to double down—to leave in pursuit of a more radical agenda.[1] This was a magnified version of the split between Lewis Ayer and George Boomer in Equality's earliest days; too radical for one, too timid for the other.

Swigart left a few months after Lermond to build a conventional career in civil engineering. He was followed by McDevitt, who served briefly as Lermond's successor and then left for new adventures and more radical pursuits. Helen Mason left soon after McDevitt; she quit on the Brotherhood because she felt it had quit on her.

Non-resident BCC trustees who contributed their name

(but little else) to Lermond's movement also faded away; Myron Reed, the Denver preacher who served as the Brotherhood's first president, died in January 1899. George Candee, who ran the recruiting operation from his home in Toledo, Ohio, gave it up just weeks after Lermond's exit, although he did not go quietly. He used the pages of *Industrial Freedom* to criticize the colony he had never visited in person; he argued, as had Ayer before him, that its distance from a deep-water port was an insurmountable problem. A fellow member of the BCC board, not mentioned by name, had written to alert him to an Equality exodus. "'This was no news to me," Candee wrote. "Equality is not adapted to growth ... It can never furnish employment for the great numbers of cooperators who are anxious to go to Washington."[2]

Of the early leaders who remained at the colony beyond the first year, Ed Pelton, the wizened woodsman, stood out for his principled devotion, his troubled family circumstance, and, ultimately, his shocking demise in the woods just beyond the colony property line. His confidence in Equality's course had started strong but eventually waned. He faulted the Brotherhood's more radical elements for insisting on an uncompromising approach to combatting capitalism. In a poke almost certainly aimed at Boomer, without mentioning him by name, Pelton wrote in June 1899 that an "ex-editor of national reputation" who was "keen, fearless and aggressive" had abandoned the Equality cause to start a "spicy socialist weekly" of his own. The publication, most likely Boomer's *Spirit of '76* newspaper, met an early end, Pelton noted; in his view this was the kind of scattershot effort that only strengthened critics' argument that socialists were unreliable.

Pelton took over as BCC president when Myron Reed died, leaving it largely to him to referee what he called a fight between his colleagues' socialist and individualist instincts—a conflict that lay at the heart of that era's broader debate about radical alternatives to capitalism. In the moment, Pelton recognized this tension as the central threat to Equality's existence; it was the main reason people were quitting.

In a remarkably candid article published in the colony newspaper in May 1899, he lamented that so many felt free to give up, though he acknowledged their right to do so. The problem, he wrote, was that these quitters had ignored a moral obligation.

> There was a contract implied when we banded together, that we would support one another in carrying the load, and every useful member that dropped out left the burden that much heavier on the remainder. Had most of us realized that so many of our comrades would have failed us, we would have stayed where we came from and not have made the sacrifices we did in breaking up our homes and coming here. The worst part of this dropping-out business is the gratification it gives the enemies of Socialism who are continually encouraged in believing that they scent another 'socialistic fizzle.[3]

He called socialism a "sacred cause," but if that was his true feeling it didn't stop him from dividing his loyalties once Equality started to fade. In August 1900, while still at the colony, he took a leadership position with the People's Party of Skagit County—a step down from socialism that men like Burgess and Boomer would have found hard to fathom or accept.

A man of little formal education, Pelton had an instinctive understanding of people and of what it took to build a community. He knew that Equality needed men and women who could resist the temptation to see governance as someone else's responsibility and who would avoid the trap of regarding the colony's elected leaders as "them," as if they were not part of "us." This insight resonates in 21st century America, where people often regard "the government" as an irritant, if not an enemy, somehow run in the shadows by "them," not us.

Pelton stood tall at Equality, above average in physical size and in community respect. "He is considerable of a 'skyscraper' is Ed, but his feet are on solid ground," a fellow colonist[4] wrote of the man who took on even the most disagreeable jobs. Another remembered "a big, warm, pulsating soul" who rose with the sun, "bareheaded, with sleeves rolled up, face tanned almost as dark as an Indian," the first to grab an ax or crosscut saw to do whatever needed doing. "[We] had an eight-hour workday there, but Pelton never knew it."[5]

Pelton's reputation for self-sacrifice was well earned. During the second winter at Equality, the colony newspaper ribbed him for being the one who "slops around in any old pair of leaky shoes." Comrades finally "caught Pelton in a snare and shod him as a blacksmith shoes an unwilling bronco. That's the only way you can handle Pelton."

One ex-colonist asked of another, years later, "Were you there when Ed Pelton used to get up at 4:00 a.m. on Sundays and make New England hot bread and baked beans for Sunday dinner? What a relief from sauerkraut boiled, fried and raw!"[6]

Pelton worried that too many at Equality failed to see that success or failure was in their hands, and to remember they were working *for* a common cause, not *against* some absent adversary.

"The predominating thought until very recently seemed to be that the colony was a separate and distinct entity of which we individually were not a component part, and with which we had no connection," he wrote. His "until very recently" phrase suggests that attitudes had shifted, but the broad context of Pelton's article indicates otherwise.[7]

The feeling of detachment from Equality's central purpose was so strong that some colonists saw it almost as their duty to try to outsmart the colony, as if it were an antagonist. Pelton likely knew that other "cooperative" colonies in the West had faced similar resistance. As one leader of a Colorado colony put it in 1896, "In the very nature of the case, men and women who take hold of an enterprise of this kind have strong individuality. They are earnest, and earnestness is close kin to intolerance."[8]

Even the colony's megaphone for socialism, *Industrial Freedom*, sometimes sounded a jarringly discordant note. In one of his "humor" columns, Bige Eddy wrote, "I thank the Lord that the older I get the more bigoted, intolerant and hide-bound I become." A reader in Pennsylvania was so offended that he cancelled his subscription. "I thought brotherly love was one of the essentials of a socialist, but I was mistaken," he wrote.

Frederick Smith, the author who studied Equality years after its collapse and interviewed a number who had lived there as children, put it this way: "The spirit of individualism refused to give up; its impulse was to fight the group rather than submit to it." It was that impulse, as much as anything, that doomed the Lermond dream of a socialist triumph over capitalism. One famously reviled radical unaffiliated with Equality described the nature of this tension between individual and social instincts this way: "The one a most potent factor for individual endeavor, for growth, aspiration, self-realization; the other an equally potent factor for mutual helpfulness and social well-being."[9] Those were the words of Emma Goldman, the unapologetic anarchist and under-appreciated student of the human psyche.

True to form, Pelton held out hope for a change of attitude, even as he feared the cause was lost.

"The mainspring of all our troubles has been, as usual, the

childish weakness of human nature, intensified by our poverty," he wrote in 1899, adding that the problems, while sometimes only an annoyance, were "exceedingly irritating in their nature and almost continual in their recurrence."[10]

Without naming names, he added: "A few drones got mixed into the human hive from time to time and caused almost no end of trouble."

Some of the trouble was in Pelton's own home, although that was not the "hive" to which he referred. His wife, Annie, was unhappy with colony life and didn't mind saying so. She was no stranger to disappointment or to hard times. As an eight-year-old she and her family trekked some 800 miles by covered wagon from tiny Fearing township in southeastern Ohio to central Minnesota, where she would meet and marry her first husband, Ernest Pelton, then lose him in a Grey Eagle street fight. She was a hardy woman; she outlived five husbands. On her 100th birthday she consented to a newspaper interview and may even have approved of the paper's reference to her as "peppery-tongued," for she seemed to enjoy giving the business to all within earshot.[11] She was photographed in an easy chair, her feet propped up, one hand clutching a bouquet of golden orchids. She told the interviewer she wouldn't talk about Equality, claiming she remembered almost nothing of it. The full picture of what had troubled her at Equality cannot be reconstructed from the fragmentary record that remained a century-plus later. She seemed to suffer the effects of at least two psychological wounds, one from colonists' constant carping at her husband and the other from their spreading of agonizing gossip about her.

Harry Ault, a teenager during his years at Equality, remembered Annie as "jolly and friendly" and her teenage daughter Eva as fun-loving and free-spirited in ways that made her and her mother easy targets for gossip and innuendo in this insular community. Annie did not show the deference to men that was considered proper in that era, even at liberal-minded Equality. This created jealousies that eventually exhausted her patience with pettiness. In the late spring or early summer of 1900, more than two years after arriving at Equality, she left with daughters Eva and Florence to work as a cook on a nearby farm, whose owner, George T. Stevens, had joined the rush to gold in Alaska.

This forced Ed to choose between his fractured colony and his fractured family. He chose his family. Understandably, he was prioritizing his individual needs over those of the socialist movement. He chose pragmatism over radicalism, not unlike those colonists whom he criticized for making that same choice in quitting the cause.

The Pelton family moved to Seattle, and Ed found a job in construction. After a few months his employer's firm folded, and what little money Ed had saved quickly dried up. In a letter to colleagues at Equality, he seemed torn between hopelessness for capitalism— "This monopolistic botch of a system" —and grave doubt about the great experiment he had helped Lermond launch three years earlier. The cooperative commonwealth they had hoped to build, he wrote, "seems but an iridescent dream."[12]

A Seattle boarding house operator and friend of Equality, William H. Benson, offered to pay to move the Peltons back to Skagit County. They accepted and Ed resumed working at Equality, but at Annie's insistence they did not move into colony housing. They settled instead on a rental property nearby at an abandoned logging camp just east of Blanchard in the Chuckanut hills.

Several weeks later, on a Sunday morning in late February 1901, Pelton was felling a fir tree about a hundred yards up the hill from his house. Accounts of what happened next vary; one version is that when the tree landed it struck the end of a smaller cedar log on which Pelton was standing. The force of the collision catapulted him into the air, breaking his neck in the fall.[13]

At age forty-five, he died as he had lived—working in the woods. Gone, too, was any hope for Equality.

Chapter 15

Chaos and the Joslyns

Even as the colony population dwindled from an early peak of more than 300 to half that by the end of 1899, new hopefuls kept trickling in. It was not always clear why.

In the summer of 1900, the Brotherhood was showing little sign of organizational life, although it still existed on paper and the colony continued to function. In July, an Equality officer wrote in response to a federal Department of Labor survey of socialist and socialist-like communities that the BCC had been missing in action lately: "There seems but little to say except that the movement was conspicuous for its lack of activity." The unidentified officer was described in the Labor Department's published report[1] as Equality's secretary. That would have been Arthur Knud Hanson, a 27-year-old Nebraska native and son of Danish immigrants. The colony population had shrunk to 120, Hanson wrote, and most were "more reflective and argumentative than practical." Even so, he insisted the colony had made measurable progress despite suffering from what he called an excess of democracy and a shortage of expertise. The author of the Labor report was less charitable. The colony, he wrote, was locked in a "hard struggle to resist the discouraging influences of an unfriendly environment and the disintegrating tendencies of a selfish individualistic spirit."[2]

On Hanson's watch, the colony quietly abandoned the original Lermond mission and revolutionary vision by revising the membership application. Instead of pledging to "do all in my power" to help build a socialist society, an aspiring member now was required to promise only to abide by colony rules and to "work faithfully at whatever work may be assigned me." Gone were the words "socialism" and "cooperative commonwealth." The revolutionary spirit had departed and, with it, any hope for making the colony more than a pale imitation of the social order it meant to replace.

With its receding ambition, Equality now stood at a financial low tide, forcing the colonists to grub for dollars. When a woman writing from Oregon offered to buy heaps of Puget Sound clam shells, *Industrial Freedom* advised the colony's best clammers to strap on their boots and start digging, most likely on one of the beaches of nearby Samish Island, a favored destination for bite-size butter clams and burrowing geoduck clams weighing up to ten pounds. "We believe in turning everything into money that we can," the newspaper said.

Equality was searching, too, for new dues-paying members, and they had some success that summer. At this point, motivations for throwing in with a group of strangers in a strange land ranged from the mundane to the fantastic. Rumor had it that a headstrong young woman from Illinois had been directed by a tribal spirit to travel west to save a colony in trouble.[3]

That woman was Inza Joslyn, who rather than rescue the colony helped deepen its divisions.

In her own telling, Joslyn became a spiritualist at an early age, convinced that she could communicate with the dead beyond the grave. She said she realized at five or six that God had endowed her with the ability to serve as a medium for the spiritual realm. "I get it from above," she told an interviewer.[4] She led seances at Equality and likely was the originator of the oft-repeated tale that a tribal spirit had steered her west.

Spiritualism may sound goofy now, but in the late 19th century it was so popular that it was practically a craze in the United States, energized by such well-known converts as the British writer Sir Arthur Conan Doyle, creator of the Sherlock Holmes stories. Influential American journalist Horace Greeley also was a believer. Mark Twain was said to have attended a séance but dismissed spiritualism as a "wildcat religion." The fad sometimes made news. In 1881, a small-town Arkansas newspaper reported that "excitement in spiritualism has broken out in our city," enchanting "some of our best citizens."[5]

The middle child of three, Inza Joslyn was born to John and Margaret Joslyn in 1872 on a farm near the small town of Sycamore in DeKalb County, Illinois, about fifty miles west of Chicago. She grew up there and in an even smaller town in rural southeastern Minnesota. At twenty-eight she came to Equality with her parents from the southside Chicago suburb of West Pullman, where she worked as an office clerk. In an interview in 1966 shortly before she died, Inza said little about what drew her parents to Equality. They had seemed anchored in Illinois; she recalled her father saying of their West Pullman place, "This is the last home that I'll ever build."[6] It was not.

The Joslyns arrived at Equality on about July 1, 1900, with little to suggest a history of radicalism. Margaret was born in upstate New York (coincidentally, barely ten miles from Helen

Mason's hometown of Glens Falls), to Douglass and Emily Thompson—he a laborer and farmer and she a mother of thirteen. Margaret was number eight, arriving in 1842. In the 1850s the Thompsons moved to DeKalb County in northern Illinois, where Margaret met her future husband, John Joslyn, whose family lived in a neighboring township.

Margaret and John were everyday people. Born in 1840, he was raised in a farm family of modest means, solid reputation, and traditional values. There did not seem to be a socialist bone in the Joslyn body. Among John's close relatives were a judge, a corporate executive, a county sheriff, a real estate agent, a tax collector, and a supervisor of the county poor house. His family roots reached deep into colonial times and spread from Connecticut to western New York as the young nation grew.

John's paternal grandfather, Reuben Joslyn, served with a Connecticut regiment in the Revolutionary War. His story is straight from the history books; he fought under the command of Gen. George Washington in the Battle of Trenton in December 1776, a pivotal momentum-builder for the rebels that is commemorated in the famous painting depicting a heroic Washington crossing the icy Delaware River. Reuben's story also touches on the generations-long debate over the proper role of government and the meaning of social welfare. When he applied for a military-service pension in 1818, he wrote that his "reduced circumstances" at age 62 meant he was no longer capable of manual labor and was "in need of the assistance of his country."[7] He got his pension, and in the passage of time, thanks in part to more than a century of agitation by people like Reuben's grandson, it became Americans' consensus view that the federal government should assist with basic needs of the disadvantaged and the elderly—and not just broken-down former soldiers.

John's father, Phineas Vison Joslyn, served with the New

York militia in the War of 1812 against the British. In about 1838, after the Black Hawk War had opened northern Illinois for white settlement, Phineas brought the family to DeKalb County. He acquired a forty-acre parcel near Sycamore and began coaxing crops from the rich prairie soil.[8]

DeKalb County in those days was a typical slice of frontier America, hardly a magnet for radicalism. Most folks were God-fearing, law-abiding patriots, but the diabolical had their day, too. Grave robbers became a local curse in the late 1840s. When a nearby medical school ran low on cadavers for dissection, a band of "resurrectionists" put their picks and shovels to work stealthily emptying freshly dug graves. One day in 1849, word got around that the fresh grave of a 17-year-old Sycamore girl had been violated, and John Joslyn's older brother Harry pitched in with a few outraged neighbors to catch the body snatchers. They succeeded but let the suspects go for lack of evidence. Frontier justice was delivered a short time later, however, in gunfire that killed one of the grave robbers as well as the medical school president who had hired them and then falsely denied possessing the girl's remains. What was left of her body was found in a blanket buried in a shallow hole on a riverbank.[9]

From an early age, John E. Joslyn seemed in search of something beyond the Illinois prairie, beyond Sycamore and the circle-shaped pattern of trees known as the Ohio Grove that stood near his family's farm, barely a mile from the little cemetery whose graves had been robbed. He was not, however, looking for military adventure. When the Union army scoured northern Illinois for eligible recruits in the summer of 1863, John was listed as an unmarried farmer "on the way to California," and thus not immediately available. Six months later he turned up on a similar list of military-age men in northern California; recorded as a "ranchman," he somehow avoided serving in uniform.

After marrying in 1865, he and Margaret wandered a good bit, from northern Illinois to the isolation of southeastern Minnesota in the mid-1870s, then back to Illinois. Before yet another move back to Minnesota, the Joslyns ventured in 1880 to a gold-mining region of California's Sierra Nevada that had been the epicenter of the gold rush of 1849. The five of them, including Inza and her brothers Clayton and Harry, lived for a time with Margaret's brother, Jesse S. Thompson, who made his living in one of the area's most productive businesses—the sale of ice harvested from surrounding lakes. The Sierra Nevada had drawn John's attention for many years. During a visit in 1869 to the Carson Valley area in Nevada Territory, he wrote home to say that despite not hearing from family members since leaving Sycamore, he was not homesick and had just experienced something that people back home could only dream about: soaking in a hot springs. "This place is a very nice one," he wrote.[10]

Farming was in John Joslyn's blood, but he also had an instinct for entrepreneurship. In the 1870s he linked up in Mower County, Minnesota, with a local inventor to manufacture and market a clothes-washing machine that Joslyn's newspaper ads claimed was so simple that it could be operated by a ten-year-old and so gentle that a dollar bill could be washed without tearing. The inventor, Irvin A. Shaw, had the device patented in 1875 and assigned the rights jointly to himself and Joslyn.[11] Joslyn was so sure this machine was a winner that he offered $25 cash—almost a princely sum in those days—to any woman who could credibly claim that his washer did not equal or exceed the performance of her "old-fashioned, back-breaking washboard."

"None can afford to do without it!" his newspaper ad shouted. But many did. The business gained little traction and apparently folded, perhaps shaking John's confidence in capitalism. He showed no sign, however, of embracing radicalism; during his Minnesota farming years he held an auctioneer's license, served on a county grand jury, bought and sold property, and flirted with mainstream politics. He served on the board of supervisors for the town in which he and Margaret lived, and he was a delegate to the Republican county convention.

Margaret, too, showed entrepreneurial spirit. She came up with an invention of her own. It was a funnel-shaped device that attached to a gasoline-burning residential stove to capture soot and smoke emitted by the burner. She applied for a patent in 1886 and received it a little over a year later,[12] but like many inventions it seemed to die an early death.

In 1892 the Joslyns finally gave up their Minnesota farm, touted by a local newspaper as "one of the finest" in Mower County. They sold it for $5,000 and moved to West Pullman, just in time for the 1893 financial crisis.

West Pullman was a newly established neighborhood on Chicago's south side, just west of Lake Calumet. Next door was Pullman, a so-called "model city" established a decade earlier by its namesake, George M. Pullman, manufacturer of the hugely successful Pullman sleeper, a luxury railroad car. Pullman envisioned his designed city as a working man's utopia. It housed the industrial plants that made his rail cars, as well as several thousand Pullman workers and their families. The historical record provides no evidence that either John or Margaret Joslyn worked for Pullman, but the unusual nature of the company town and the suddenness of its demise may have influenced their thinking about starting a new chapter of their lives.

John and Margaret could see that Pullman was, in effect, a social experiment gone wrong. It was not a socialist but a capitalist idea in which one man, George Pullman, lorded over the land; every resident paid him rent because owning was not an option. He owned everything—even the town's church. The Joslyns may have viewed it in the same light as an economist who visited in the early years and judged the town to be a new form of capitalist excess, a "benevolent, well-wishing feudalism" that put workers at the mercy of an all-powerful master. The economist, Richard Ely, saw much to admire in George Pullman's orderly, efficient and physically attractive town but concluded nonetheless that it was a "gilded cage." It was un-American, he wrote, in the sense that a resident had no say in governance. "Everything is done for him, nothing by him."[13]

On the surface, Pullman had appeal. The houses were modest but neat and modern; they offered amenities unusual for a working-class town, including indoor plumbing and well-trimmed lawns that abutted clean streets lined with young saplings. But the conveniences came at a cost that ultimately destroyed the Pullman experiment, perhaps giving the Joslyns new ideas. Pullman workers chafed at the corporate paternalism and the red tape, and most annoyingly, the rising rents that George Pullman deducted from stagnant paychecks.

Worker discontent grew, and in May 1894, Pullman reduced wages by one-quarter without any corresponding relief in rent payments. The workers walked out, and in June they won backing from Eugene Debs's newly created American Railway Union, which itself was destined for destruction. The strike and the associated boycott of trains pulling Pullman cars halted much of the nation's rail traffic west of Chicago, prompting Attorney General Richard Olney to claim the country had been pushed to "the ragged edge of anarchy."[14] Olney won a court injunction by arguing that the strike was disrupting interstate commerce, opening the way for President Cleveland to send federal troops to put down the strikers and their supporters, at times with deadly force. Using military muscle against civilian strikers was a short-term expedient; it saved George Pullman and turned public opinion against the labor movement, but in the long run it solidified the image of government as a tool of big business. Debs' union was crushed. He was convicted of contempt of court for violating Olney's court injunction and served six months in jail. He emerged a socialist and a working man's hero.

Without a known record of their own thoughts on the Pullman debacle at their doorstep or on Debs' conversion to socialism, it's hard to say with certainty what drew the Joslyns to the idea of starting over at Equality among the tall timber where, yes, John would build another house.

In June 1900, Margaret and Inza made a brief return to Mower County, Minnesota, to visit old friends and then joined John in Minneapolis for the train trip to Washington state. One of the Joslyns' two sons came with them. The other had volunteered for Army duty in the Spanish-American war.[15] On June 26, *Industrial Freedom* announced the arrival at Equality of four "two-horse loads" of household goods, including an organ, that John had sent ahead from Chicago.

"The family is somewhere on the road here, intending to arrive the last of this month," it said.

On the day of their arrival, as they walked along the wood-plank trail through the woods between Belfast station and Equality, John and Margaret stopped to pose for a photograph, he with hat in hand, she clutching what appears to be a bouquet of flowers. The black-and-white image captured the stark reality that awaited every man and woman who came to

Equality sight unseen. Dressed in what looks like their Sunday best, determined to make a good impression but unsure what awaited them, the Joslyns stood among sprawling ferns, against the backdrop of giant evergreens. They were rebels in the wild.

By the time the Joslyns got to Equality, it was lurching toward a level of chaos that within months would make a mockery of the motto of the colony's social club: "Always be cheerful."

An episode the following spring ended in spilled blood. Not surprisingly, Inza Joslyn was mixed up in it, though not as a combatant. She had her eye on the Equality postmaster job—"postmistress," as they said in those days—following the death in May 1901 of the occupant of that post, Harry Ault's father, James. The assistant postmaster was in line to succeed Ault, but Joslyn had an ace in the hole. The brother of her friend and fellow spiritualist Grace Lewis was the postmaster at a nearby village and, more importantly, was chairman of the county Republican party.[16] This was significant because postmaster positions in that era were doled out as political patronage by the party in power in Washington, D.C., which happened to be the Republicans. So, with Grace pulling strings, it looked like Joslyn's appointment was a cinch. Neither woman figured, however, on an angry backlash from their backroom maneuvering.

Some colonists took offense at Grace's interference, and for the first time, violence erupted in the General Assembly. Charlie F. Hart, a man of big muscles, wide belly, and short temper, wasn't going to abide these political shenanigans. He aimed a barrage of verbal abuse at Grace— "this political pimp" he called her, in Harry Ault's recollection—and at her indignant husband Carey. The 39-year-old Carey leaped across the room and got his hands on Hart's throat. At that point events took a turn whose details vary in the retelling. By one account, Hart drew a pistol, intending to smack Carey with its butt end. Instead, something sharp—possibly the gunsight—collided with Carey's skull and tore a long gash. To restrain Hart, two men locked his arms, and in an instant the bloodied Carey was "merrily pounding Hart to a pulp."[17]

Inza Joslyn's appointment was voided, but the fight it provoked was hardly the last.

Chapter 16

'Boy Bandit'

Despite its remoteness, or perhaps because of it, Equality had accidental connections with two remarkable characters of that era. One was famous, the other infamous.

The famous one was Russell A. Alger, the epitome of a successful late-19th century capitalist. A Civil War veteran and retired Army general, Alger served one term as Michigan governor in the mid-1880s, twice ran unsuccessfully for the Republican nomination for president, and served as President McKinley's secretary of war during the Spanish-American war.[1] He made millions in timber and real estate, and his interests in Whatcom and Skagit counties included hundreds of acres of old-growth forest.[2] This millionaire's reach, nearly to Equality's doorstep, was a reminder to the struggling colony members of the wealth divide in America—the very divide that animated their socialist dream.

Alger visited some of these properties in the 1880s, long before Lermond had arrived.[3] And while Alger may never have known of the colonists' existence, they certainly knew of his.

They complained bitterly that his logging company denied them permission to build a road that, by crossing a narrow strip of his land, would have shortened by three miles the wagon ride between the colony and the Belfast rail station.

Still standing as a reminder of his influence is a namesake hamlet—Alger, just east of Interstate 5 and about four miles north of Belfast.

(Easily the most famous American from the Equality neighborhood was Edward R. Murrow, the legendary CBS News radio and television broadcaster, although the colony had been disbanded for several years by the time he and his family arrived in the area in 1913 from North Carolina. Born Egbert R. Murrow, he grew up in Blanchard, a stone's throw from the colony site, and graduated from Edison High School. His parents, Roscoe and Ethel Murrow, are buried just east of Edison at Bow Cemetery.)

The infamous one among Equality's neighbors was an outlaw named Bill Miner, born Ezra Allen Miner, whose list of aliases was nearly as long as his jail record. The "Grey Fox," as he was known late in his career of horse thievery, stagecoach holdups and train robberies, came to the Puget Sound area after serving almost twenty years in the California State Penitentiary at San Quentin. Ostensibly his purpose in Washington was to visit a sister near Bellingham, but in fact he was plotting a rendezvous with a former San Quentin cell mate. While lying low, Miner worked at an oyster farm on Samish Bay, within walking distance of Equality. Soon he managed to befriend one of the colony's unluckier teenagers, Charlie Hoehn, whose already hard-knocks existence was about to get a lot harder.[4]

Charles Lewis Hoehn was an orphan. His mother, Anna, died of tuberculosis in their hometown of Cleveland when he was nine. Four years later, his father, Leonard, moved the family to Equality, only to be killed a few months later, in April

1900, when he lost control of his horse-drawn mail wagon and was thrown against a stump. The death stunned the colonists, who held Leonard in high regard. Writing several weeks after the accident, a former colonist recalled him as "a fine man, a true cooperator," which was high praise from a fellow socialist.

"Were there more such, the name of socialism would not be synonymous with insanity and hypocrisy, as it is fast coming to be," the former colonist wrote in a private letter,[5] revealing a depth of disillusionment among Equality's socialists that was rarely voiced publicly.

Having lost both parents, Charlie and his three siblings were surrounded, and undoubtedly supported in part, by other colony families. Though well intentioned, that help was not enough to keep Charlie from falling under the spell of 54-year-old Miner, who recruited the 17-year-old in the summer of 1903 for an adventure of a lifetime.

Miner was planning to rob an Oregon Railroad & Navigation passenger train as it headed east from Portland along the Columbia River.[6] After boarding at the Troutdale station, two of his compatriots donned black cloth masks, jumped the engineer, and ordered him to stop near Corbett, about twenty miles east of Portland, at the western edge of the Columbia River Gorge.[7] The plan was to blow the door off the baggage car to gain access to the safe. The dynamite, however, proved insufficient, and in the ensuing excitement, a third member of the masked gang, a convicted counterfeiter named Zebulon G. "Gay" Harshman, known in some parts as the Kansas Kid, was shot in the face by the train's express messenger, Fred A. Korner, whose job it was to guard the safe.[8] Realizing their peril, Miner and Hoehn fled to the riverbank, dodging a final blast from Korner's sawed-off shotgun. They made it back across the Columbia on a rowboat they had stashed in advance, leaving their wounded comrade for dead. As it turned out,

Harshman lived to tell the story. Police retrieved him from a ditch beside the train track and deposited him at Portland's Good Samaritan Hospital. There he spilled the beans on his co-conspirators, including their names and likely whereabouts in Washington.[9] Within days, the Pinkerton detective agency had a man operating under cover at the Equality sawmill where Hoehn had returned to work. The boy was arrested and taken to Portland, where he pleaded guilty in Multnomah County Circuit Court to a charge of assault with a deadly weapon.

"Boy Bandit," an Oregon newspaper called him.[10] He was front-page news. "Bad Man Nabbed," was the harsh headline in the *Argus* at Mount Vernon.

Hoehn's lawyer told the court that Hoehn had been "overcome by the superior will of Miner," who fooled the boy into believing they were merely taking a joy ride to Mexico.[11] In the lawyer's account, Hoehn didn't realize the true purpose of the trip until Miner put a rifle in his hands at the scene of the robbery and told him to stop passengers from exiting the cars while Miner attempted to blast the door off the baggage car. In the prosecuting attorney's version of events, however, Hoehn not only fired his weapon during the botched heist but also made off with fellow bandit Harshman's weapons and money after Harshman went down with a load of lead pellets in his skull.

(After investigators extracted a confession from Harshman and he'd been sent to prison, doctors drilled a hole in his skull and removed bone fragments and a chunk of lead from his brain. He eventually recovered and returned to counterfeiting —and then to prison.)[12]

Having escaped back to Washington with Hoehn, ringleader Miner made his way further north across the border into British Columbia. There he resumed his lifelong cycle of crime and incarceration.

Hoehn, whose only previous brush with the law was a botched attempt to forge scrip at Equality, was sentenced to ten years in the Oregon State Penitentiary at Salem. In an official penitentiary photo, inmate No. 4792, weighing 143 pounds and measuring five feet, five inches tall, looked blankly at the camera, showing little of the emotion that must have coursed through the veins of a teenager facing ten years behind bars. His penitentiary file contains hints that he had been in tough scrapes; he bore many scars, including what were recorded as "cut scars" on both sides of his head and "a long cut scar" on his back.[13]

Hoehn served four years before Governor George E. Chamberlain commuted his sentence. He was released in November 1907.

After regaining his freedom, Hoehn returned to Skagit County and took up farm work. He married a recent immigrant from New Brunswick, Canada;[14] they had two children and lived a quiet life. He died in 1944 and was buried in Bow Cemetery, a mile and a half from Equality.

Chapter 17

'Reign of Terror'

By the time Charlie Hoehn won a new lease on life, Equality was dead.

The fatal spiral began, fittingly, with a blow from boom-and-bust capitalism, followed by a blast from Mother Nature. A depression squeezed the region's saw and shingle mill industry in 1903, and the economic pain hit especially hard in Skagit County, home to more mills than all but three other counties in the state.[1] That summer, Equality's remaining members, numbering fewer than thirty adults, were compelled to hire out their mill, a prized asset that had lost most of its market for shingles and a steady workforce to produce them.

A year later, at about noon on the final day of summer, the mill compound burst into flames. The mill roof, as described by author Smith, was "crackling and snapping like gunfire,"[2] barely visible in a "roaring ball of flame larger than the mill structure." Feeding the inferno was paper-dry, downy-fine sawdust that lay on every surface. The blaze destroyed not just the sawmill but also the shingle mill and shed, the planer and grist mills, and the woodworking and machine shops. It incinerated, too, what remained of the dream that had come west with Lermond's pioneering radicals seven years earlier.

Equality's fate was sealed, but it did not go quietly. Its death throes, as one newspaper put it, were "terrible to look upon."[3]

The loss of the mill forced more soul searching. It resurfaced the question Pelton had posed in the colony's first year: "What is this movement for and why are we here?" Instead of yielding answers, this latest rethinking produced new divisions that degenerated into hostility. Two factions emerged. One wanted to continue what Smith called the "quiet farm life spiced with a little socialist agitation but without grand ambitions." The other faction, led by John Joslyn, his daughter Inza and her husband, David Barry, believed it was time to admit failure and find a new course to recapture the original vision of a socialist revolution.

The Joslyn-Barry faction prevailed or at least made sure that the quiet life was over.

Quiet had suited David Barry. But then the Joslyns arrived and he seemed to change. What drew him to socialism, and how he wound up at Equality, are enduring mysteries. He was born in New York City in 1860 to Irish immigrants who had fled the potato famine of the late 1840s. They raised him and his younger siblings mostly in Irish immigrant areas of Manhattan, including in what was then a rural neighborhood known as Tubby Hook on the island's wooded upper tip. He left no known clues to his adult life's path until he turned up in New Whatcom at about the age of thirty-one. For at least three years starting in 1891 he lived in a working-class New Whatcom neighborhood known as York, just east of today's downtown Bellingham and south of Whatcom Creek.[4] He became a dues-paying member of Lermond's BCC in 1896 and moved to Equality on

December 15, 1897, just as Pelton was sealing his deal for colony land.

In time, Barry would become one of Equality's most controversial figures—a truth teller to some, a troublemaker to others, and a treasured life partner to Inza Joslyn, whom he married in December 1901.

THE MAN most responsible for turning Equality's discord into defeat had no connection whatever to the colony's early years. His name was Alexander Horr, and his game was, well, no one seemed sure *what* it was. He arrived, perhaps coincidentally, four days after the mill fire and was quick to fan the flames of trouble in a colony that could ill afford it.

Horr was a New York bookbinder, used-book dealer, rabble rouser, philosophizer, and convicted felon whose anarchist credentials and criminal record the colonists either overlooked or didn't know about when they welcomed him. If they were ignorant of his history, it would mean they missed sensational news headlines across the country— "*Shot by an Anarchist*" was a common one—in December 1901 reporting Horr's arrest for shooting a New York *Daily News* editorial writer.[5] Despite taking four bullets, including one in the chest, Francis McGinnis-Iveagh lived to tell about it. The 28-year-old Horr was convicted of first-degree assault and sent to a "reformatory" at Elmira, New York—a prison reimagined as the nation's first institutional test of the idea that incarceration should rehabilitate rather than punish criminals, especially young ones.

One year before the shooting, Horr gave a speech to a gathering of anarchists in New York. It made national news and he was quoted in papers as near and familiar to the Equality colonists as the *Anacortes American*. His words were widely interpreted as an implied threat to kill President McKinley—ten months before he was assassinated in Buffalo by a declared anarchist, Leon Czolgosz. "If anyone in control of government here persists in prohibiting the right of free speech, if the mayor of the city does it, or the governor of the state, or the president of the United States, he does it at his peril," Horr was reported to have said.[6]

Whether or not Elmira cured Horr of his violent tendencies, he remained a committed anarchist with an urge for sensationalism, a nose for trouble, and a knack for dividing people. He might not have been delusional, but he seemed imperfectly acquainted with reality. Shortly before he shot the *Daily News* writer, Horr made headlines with an announced plan to raise half a million dollars through memberships in a group that would purchase a township in Rhode Island and turn it into an "economic utopia."

Standing barely five feet tall, with curly red hair framing a wide forehead, he peered out from behind wire-rimmed glasses with eyes that "dance and sparkle like bits of radium."[7] He could be charming, even disarming. Acquaintances described him as a fast talker, a quarrelsome but not unpleasant man. Lucy Robins Lang, a fellow anarchist, remembered him from his pre-World War One years in San Francisco as a frequent visitor to her vegetarian restaurant— "but for argument, not for food. Why should anyone be concerned about the body, he asked, when only the spirit mattered?"[8]

Paradoxically, the Equality member who invited Horr to join the colony would turn out to be his worst enemy—Charlie Hart, who a few years earlier had clubbed Carey Lewis with a pistol. By the summer of 1904, with the colony in dire straits, Hart was among the most vocal advocates of seeking a radical new approach. On his own initiative, he wrote to Horr in New York praising his ideas on politics and economics. He provided a copy of colony bylaws and urged Horr to give Equality a try. Horr arrived in late September, and soon he and Hart were at each other's throats. In Horr's view, Hart was easy to despise because he was a low-life authoritarian with "the most ungovernable temper and unlimited brutality."[9] Horr once alluded to Hart having been challenged to a pistol duel, "where Charlie appeared only by proxy, for while Charlie is a bully, he is an arrant [complete] coward."

The enmity between Horr and Hart, now leaders of opposing factions, was so intense that it's hard to judge the credence of stories told later. David Barry, a Horr ally, claimed Hart was so instinctively violent that he once drew a sword during an argument.[10] That sharp-edged confrontation ended poorly for Hart. The unidentified target of his threat responded by clubbing him with a chair, sending him sprawling onto a stove.

By the end of 1904, Horr had attained such influence at Equality that he was able to win agreement to change the colony's name to Freeland and to fundamentally revise the BCC's constitution. He was feeling cocky, even Caesar-like. "I came, I saw, I conquered," Horr wrote before events turned so decisively against him that he was forced to give up his conquest.[11]

The historical record is unclear on how much Horr's rivals at Equality knew of his criminally violent past or his politics. He gave no outward indication of being an extremist when he applied for Equality membership. "I am fairly well read on the literature of socialism," he wrote on his application form. Asked what he considered the best incentive to work, he replied with a characteristic lack of clarity, "Permanent guarantee in maintaining the law of equal freedom."

His core objection to both democracy and Equality-style socialism, as best can be deduced from his writings, was the primacy of majority rule. He equated it with tyranny. Nor did he accept the legitimacy of manmade law as a constraint on individual behavior; he and his anarchist friends later captured this idea in a slogan posted to a wall in their Seattle meetinghouse: "Supremacy of the Individual."[12] In his view, individuals should be naturally free to act as they wish, separately or as a minority group. This may have been what he meant by "the law of equal freedom."

Soon after arriving at Equality, Horr cleverly positioned himself and the colony as a ready source of news for the main local newspaper, the Mount Vernon *Argus*. The paper's management in 1903 had switched its editorial viewpoint from liberal to conservative, and, until Horr appeared on the scene in 1904, the word "Equality" almost never appeared on its printed pages. Then, quite suddenly, short articles began appearing. One in early December reported that the colony would change its name to "The Land of the Free," adding (without citing Horr by name) that "a wealthy Jew of New York is at the bottom of the scheme." A few weeks later, the paper reported that the new name would be "Liberty," and it quoted an anonymous person "informed on sociological matters"—no doubt Horr—as saying the colony henceforth would adhere to a libertarian form of socialism, a veiled reference to anarchism. ("Liberty" never caught on, and the new name became Freeland, not to be confused with a utopian community of the same name that had been established a few years earlier on nearby Whidbey Island.)

In January, Horr made a return visit to New York, staying just long enough to demonstrate his skill at attracting publicity. He enthralled a reporter for *The Sun* newspaper with his ideas for achieving nothing less than the salvation of society. He would turn the entire state of Washington into what he called an "individualistic" community. This sounded like anarchism, but he insisted it was not. Nor did he use the term socialism. "We are Anticrats," he declared,[13] using an invented term suggesting opposition to bureaucracy, or organized government. "I do not wish to create the impression that we are Anarchists," he said, but they were exactly that.

He took potshots at Equality's founders, claiming they had performed so poorly before his arrival that the colonists had been reduced to a diet of nothing but cabbage for an entire year, surely an exaggeration. (It is true, however, that they ate more than their share of sauerkraut— "boiled, fried, and raw," as one recalled.)

Horr went on to describe how he would stretch his envisioned empire from Puget Sound to the east side of the Cascades. He would build a "water tunnel" through the mountains to connect a proposed canal from the upper Skagit River on the west side to the Columbia River on the east by way of Lake Chelan. Ships, he said, could sail through the tunnel by lowering their masts.

While in New York he also gave an address at the renown Cooper Union for the Advancement of Science and Art in which he foresaw the little colony in Skagit County growing within five years to a population of 5,000, a territory of 50,000 acres, and most improbably of all, a capital budget of $5 million. "By then we will have taught the people what the right to work really means, and in the state of Washington we will see to it that the wrong people are not elected to office," he said.

Soon he was back in the Pacific Northwest winning upbeat headlines.

"*Equality Colony Is Rejuvenated*," the *Argus* reported in February, noting Horr had taken charge. The colony was now "completely reorganized" and anticipating an injection of capital and talent with the impending arrival of twenty-five people from New York, each bearing a $200 entry fee.

The wave of New Yorkers never arrived, nor did an infusion of cash.

Attentive but not particularly inquisitive, the *Argus* reported Horr had visited Mount Vernon to share the good news that Freeland's affairs were "in a prosperous condition," a claim the newspaper took at face value. It said the colony was going to build and operate a high-capacity fruit and vegetable cannery in the coming year. Horr was said to consider Skagit County an ideal place for such a business, a consideration he may have borrowed from recent *Argus* headlines making that very argument.

Alas, Horr's cannery idea died a quick death. Nor would there be any rejuvenation of the colony. Horr, however, was still scheming. In February he made a recruiting pitch to members of an openly anarchist community known as Home, on Kitsap Peninsula west of Tacoma, where Emma Goldman had lectured in 1898. He painted a rosy picture of his newly renamed Freeland colony— "the finest location and natural resources of any colony in existence," he boasted—and called for thirty anarchists to make the move immediately.[14] Few, if any, did.

LERMOND and his fellow founders of Equality likely were horrified to learn from afar what unfolded after Horr arrived. He didn't just suffocate the Brotherhood of the Cooperative Commonwealth and kill off Equality, he undermined their democratic foundations. Divisions among the remaining colonists made them easy pickings. Horr sold them on his "Anticrat" scheme to convert the colony from Bellamy-inspired socialism to what he called libertarianism, based on a rejection of majority rule. The Horr plan was, in other words, anarchy by another name. It was based on an 1890 utopian novel, *Freeland: A Social Anticipation*, by Theodor Hertzka, an Austrian economist, about a fictional, poverty-free society established in the east African nation of Kenya.

"The news of the Freeland system converting the world—even though only in a story book—was a tonic and a trap for tired and baffled utopians of Equality," Smith wrote. "They were thirsty to be persuaded, and Alex Horr was a persuader."[15]

Horr was a restless sort with a gift for gab and self-promotion. After immigrating from Hungary in 1888 at age fifteen, he spent several years in central Texas, where he showed an early talent for sniffing out centers of political restiveness and for tooting his own horn.[16] In 1894 a Fort Worth newspaper ran an admiring account, casting him as "a unique character" and the ablest advocate of Henry George's single tax theory. The "single taxers," as George's followers were known, would abolish all taxes except one based on market-driven increases in land values, arguing that since land is a natural resource, its economic benefits should be shared by all.

"He is such an ardent supporter of his belief that he will go without his dinner or his sleep at any time to argue with an opponent or a prospective convert," the story gushed.

In Waco, then a hotbed of populist agitation, he published a monthly journal, *Social Problems,* welcomed by the Waco *Evening News* as the product of "our gifted young friend, Mr. Alexander Horr," who was publishing the journal not to make money but "to give play and scope to his restless mental faculties" and to convert more Texans to the single tax theory. Another Waco paper called Horr's knowledge of the issue "as all-prevailing as his personality."

He had a foot in two unconventional camps. The more radical one was the Dallas Freethinkers, a group of religious dissenters—agnostics, atheists and other non-conformists; Horr was elected a Freethinkers vice president in 1894. He also maneuvered inside the People's Party, which was progressive but not socialist and was a far cry from anarchism.

When he moved to New York he changed—or revealed—his political stripes. He joined the ranks of the anarchists, but the transformation didn't get far before he shot the *Daily News* writer. After completing his prison term, he returned to Manhattan and gave anarchism another shot. He became a disciple of Benjamin R. Tucker, an American writer who called himself an "individualist anarchist," meaning he believed in unlimited individual freedom and argued for abolishing statutory law.

Horr and his partner, a Russian immigrant named Jenny, lived in Manhattan on East 13th Street in an apartment shared with their friend Emma Goldman. Goldman had little use for socialists. She saw them as too soft, so it's doubtful she ever visited Equality. About a year after the colony collapsed, however, she made a memorable stop in nearby Bellingham. Detectives met her arriving train, followed her and her companion to their hotel, and arrested them on the flimsy charge (later dropped) of conspiring to hold an unlawful assembly. "We were given the choice between leaving Bellingham at once or going to the city jail. It being the first hospitality offered us in the state of Washington, we decided in favor of jail," she recalled.[17] In a long story about her short visit, the local newspaper denounced her views, mocked her looks and mannerisms, and suggested she was insane—yet seemed almost grateful that so colorful a character had given the city something new to talk about.

At Equality, Horr won the support of John Joslyn, Henry Halladay, and Inza and David Barry—none of them anarchists but each believing, perhaps naively, that Horr's rescue plan was worth a desperate try. They were in the minority. Most correctly suspected Horr of subterfuge. In the summer of 1905, he convened an unannounced meeting of BCC trustees, which included himself and his allies as well as representatives of a larger opposing bloc led by Hart and a man named Kingsmill Commander, a dedicated socialist and national secretary of the BCC. By one account, the Horr group improperly engineered a rules revision that enabled it to win disputed approval of a 99-year lease on 165 acres of colony land at $160 a year. Trouble ensued. BCC properties were mortgaged—by competing mortgagors in at least one case, setting the stage for court battles to come.

Tensions mounted, and on a Monday evening in early September, one year after Horr's arrival, his opponents used a meeting of the General Assembly to try to expel the New Yorker. The proceedings ended early and inconclusively when someone (apparently Horr or an associate) blew out the lamplight. Fisticuffs erupted. Horr slipped away in the confusion, escaping expulsion.

"By cunning and violence, Horr had thwarted the legal vote that would have ended his days at the colony," Smith wrote.

For the first time in the colony's history, the Mount Vernon newspaper became more than just a little interested. A lengthy front-page article[18] described a colony "all torn with strife" by a fistfight that produced "a perfect pandemonium of noise and confusion." In tone and substance, the story had Horr's fingerprints all over it. A savvy influencer, he managed to get the story told in a way that portrayed him as not just the central character but also the chief victim.

Horr, the story said, had lately become a target of unjust sniping.

"It made little difference that Mr. Horr was one of the best-informed speakers on political economy ever in the state and that he knew all about cooperative colonies everywhere and the precise rocks upon which each cooperative failure had split, [yet] the majority of the people of the colony refused to listen to Mr. Horr's counsels," the story said.

The *Argus* almost certainly had no reporter present at the Monday night fight. Its account was based mainly—perhaps solely—on Horr's version of events, which may have been largely accurate, if incomplete.

The fracas, it said, began with a breakdown in decorum on the floor of the Assembly.

"Suddenly several powerful enemies of Alexander Horr moved in his direction in a manner that indicated more plainly than words bodily harm," it said. "Suddenly the light was blown out and the warring factions went at each other, striking out from the shoulder."

In the darkness the combatants could not distinguish friend from foe—a circumstance that favored Horr, since his group was outnumbered four-to-one. Left untold after the free-for-all, at least in public, was the injury count. The next day each faction hired lawyers in Mount Vernon. The Horr group's proposed solution was to split the colony by dividing its property into separate holdings—one for it and the other for the group headed by Hart and Commander, which opposed a split. In the meantime, the *Argus* worried about worsening violence.

"Unless a speedy settlement of the difficulties is reached it will be strange if Freeland colony is not the scene of some dire tragedy," it warned, as if foreseeing events of coming months.

After an October meeting that was meant (but failed) to find a compromise settlement to avoid court action, Horr on

November 2 took his lumps in another fight featuring Hart, now serving as colony president. The *Argus* again published a front-page story, this time skipping the pretense of doing its own reporting. It simply handed over its columns to Horr.

"The brute Hart assaulted me and beat me unmercifully," Horr wrote, adding that two Hart allies stood by and watched the pummeling. "If the majority [referring to the Hart-Commander faction] think that tactics of this character will have any other effect than to strengthen the minority's determination to resist their encroachments and brutalities, they are mistaken."[19]

With a Boomer-like flourish, Horr concluded defiantly: "We will die in the last ditch."

This was followed by weeks of arguing over whether and how to wind up colony affairs. The anti-Horr group sued in Skagit County Superior Court to void Horr's 99-year lease. Tossing in every colorful adverb that came to mind, the plaintiffs charged that Horr and his allies had "wickedly, corruptly, purposely, maliciously, traitorously, unlawfully and surreptitiously" conspired to write, authorize, and execute an illegal lease.[20] In January 1906 the court voided the lease but allowed Horr to remain at the colony.

At a special meeting of the General Assembly on February 1, Hart, Horr and others kicked around ideas (instead of each other) for paying off the colony's debts, including renting out portions of the land or requesting a court-appointed receiver to sell it all. Selling was a tricky matter, since the BCC's bylaws stated that all colony land was held in trust by the board of trustees and "cannot be sold as long as any colonists remain to cooperate." That last phrase, "remain to cooperate," might have provided legal cover to sell the land, since it could be argued that the cooperative spirit had long since departed.

As tensions grew, disaster struck yet again. On the evening

of February 6, the building that arguably was the most valuable of all colony structures—the barn—suddenly and suspiciously burst into flames. Forty-two feet wide, a hundred feet long, and fifty-two feet high, the barn housed about two dozen head of cattle and an unspecified number of horses as well as nearly all the colony's stores of hay and grain—totaling about a hundred tons. Of the animals, all but three horses burned to death. The odor of burnt hair and hide was said to be detectable a mile away in Blanchard. No colony member was injured, but the fire destroyed vital farm machinery and spread to an adjacent root house filled with nearly the entirety of the colony's homegrown root vegetables. All was lost, save for a few sacks of potatoes.[21]

The enormity of the setback could hardly be overstated, even by newspapers for which the drama offered an opportunity to poke another stick in the eye of the hapless radicals at Equality.

"It looks as if complete ruination stares it in the face," a Tacoma newspaper reported two days later.[22]

Adding to the tragedy was the painful likelihood that the fire was deliberately set, perhaps to so decisively extinguish the colonists' hope for the future that court action to dissolve it would be their only viable option. Arson was never officially established; each faction blamed the other. Horr was quoted in newspaper reports as saying that it was obviously arson, yet "it would be folly" to accuse anyone in the absence of proof. "I look for more trouble from the same source, as the members of the majority have shown that they are capable of more desperate deeds," he said.[23]

Two weeks later, the anti-Horr majority presented a petition to the colony's General Assembly citing irreconcilable differences between "warring factions" and a fear of "further incendiarism, violence, assault and perhaps murder." Given the intensity of the conflict and the fact that some had already been assaulted "by certain members of the colony with deadly weapons," the time had come to ask a court to end the nightmare before someone got killed.[24]

And so began a new sequence of litigation in Skagit County Superior Court, starting with a request for appointment of a receiver to wind down the affairs of the Brotherhood and its colony, untangle a thicket of conflicting claims of ownership, and sell off the remaining property.

The anti-Horr group painted a picture of fear and loathing where peace and quiet once stood.

"There is now a reign of terror existing in said association to such an extent that some of its members are fleeing therefrom, not only through fear of having their homes burned over them, but through fear of their lives," the petitioners declared.[25] Indeed, Roland L. Lewis, whose father was the victim of Charlie Hart's pistol-whipping, recalled that guns, or "shooting irons," as he called them, had become a regular feature of General Assembly meetings. "You'd better bring them along 'cause you might need them, see," he told an interviewer years later.[26]

Some colonists regularly armed themselves with boxes of rocks for self-defense.[27]

Hart and his allies in the majority told the court that the colony's schoolteacher was so afraid for her safety that she spent nights in a boarding room off colony grounds. "In truth and in fact such conditions prevail in said colony as should not be tolerated in any civilized or law-abiding community," they wrote in their request for a court receiver.

Horr and his allies opposed a receivership. They wanted the land for themselves. The case went to trial in March, and Superior Court Judge George A. Joiner ruled in Hart's favor. Joiner gave the receiver appointment to Edward W. Ferris, who just weeks earlier had resigned as court stenographer to go into the real estate business. The judge withheld his final decree until Ferris's work was finished a year later, at which point Joiner formally ordered the BCC and the colony dissolved and the land sold to pay debts, which included $1,400 in mortgages.

For all its seriousness, the business of dissolving Equality and selling its property had a lighter moment.

"At the time your receiver took charge of said property there was on hand one bull," Ferris reported to Joiner. "Said bull was causing great annoyance and was destroying the fences on said property and other property." His solution: sell the bull without waiting for court approval. The beast fetched $25.

In June 1907, the 440 acres of colony land subject to Joiner's order was auctioned on the doorstep of the Skagit County courthouse. The winning bidder was John J. Peth, a well-off local farmer who coincidentally in the 1880s had been a business partner of Mathias Decker, the man who sold the original 280 acres to Pelton for $2,800. Peth paid $12,400 for the 440 acres, plus $768 in delinquent taxes. A thirty-acre portion of the property originally intended as the site of Equality's "new city" up the hill and a bit southeast of the "temporary" village, was set aside and several of its lots sold to final hangers-on, including Henry and Josie Halladay, John Joslyn, William R. Giles, and David and Inza Barry. (The court explicitly excluded the colony's little graveyard from the land sale, with no indication of whether this was meant to preserve it in some quasi-public status. The graveyard today is on private property.)

In his final decree, Judge Joiner minced no words.[28] The colonists, he wrote, were "guilty of violent and irreconcilable discord and have been guilty of practices inimical to the peace and quiethood [quietude] of the community in which they reside." Having abandoned their own purposes, the colony and the Brotherhood were therefore ordered dissolved. Earlier in the legal wrangling, Joiner, a self-described progressive Republican, showed his disdain for socialism by mockingly quoting a phrase from the BCC's own founding document. In explaining Equality's descent to ruin, he applied the same reasoning the BCC constitution used to justify killing capitalism— "that the present civilization of warring interests has reached its climax of development."

This was an inglorious and humiliating end for Lermond's promised "new civilization."

"*'Equality' Is Wiped Off Earth*," the *Bellingham Herald* declared.[29]

The story made headlines across the country. Some editors could not resist the temptation to cast Equality's collapse as a triumph of good over evil. "*Court Dissolves Free Love Colony*," an Illinois newspaper declared on its front page, perpetuating the tiresome but catchy myth that these socialists were not only radical but immoral.

Horr moved to Seattle, then to San Francisco, where he had numerous run-ins with the law, was threatened with deportation, became a naturalized citizen, and ran for governor as a Socialist. Eventually he shed his most radical baggage and married Louise M. Harding, daughter of a Michigan newspaper editor who, it must be noted, listed his occupation as "capitalist."[30]

Horr died in October 1947 in San Mateo County, California.

MORE THAN A CENTURY after Equality's demise, it is not so much a ghost town as a lost town. The physical footprint has vanished—the homes, the schoolhouse, the mill, the last of the rudimentary building blocks of Lermond's dream. Gone, too, is any hint of the striving, the struggle, the hope, the doubt, the moments of celebration, the days of grief, the little successes and the big failures. It all dissolved into nothingness, like so much stardust scattered by an indifferent wind. Even the memories are mostly gone. The only visible reminders are a few road and place names—Colony Road, Colony Mountain Road, and Colony Creek, which still tumbles silently down the wooded hill.

Aside from the stray ceramic shard, bit of rusted metal, and other small pieces of the past that surface from time to time,[31] no recognizable remnant survives on the hillside where Robert Barton the blacksmith shaped hot steel into horseshoes, where David Burgess the smooth-talking Quaker forged a sturdier argument for socialism, where Harry Ault the boy editor crafted his *Young Socialist* newspaper, and where dozens of dreamers simply lived their daily lives.

What does remain, though hidden from public view, is the tiny graveyard, an enduring symbol of the colony's humanity and its eternal loss. An estimated thirty men, women and children are interred there, although no burial list is known to exist and by the 21st century no grave marker could be seen. They include Ed Pelton, the Maine woodsman and Lermond partner who ventured west to acquire the colony's land and whose sudden death in 1901 extinguished its leading light. He was preceded by his sister's 19-year-old son, Levi Amby Irish, killed in a winch accident at the colony sawmill.[32]

Disease, including pneumonia, took numerous lives at Equality, and accidents were sometimes fatal. Forty-eight-year-old Ernest J. Richter fell to his death in 1900 from the upper-story porch of a colony apartment building.

Equality's first burial was a baby boy, Archie William

Stoney. Born May 1, 1898, he died four days later— "too tiny and frail to battle with life," as the colony put it in announcing the Stoney family's loss. He keeps silent company with the graveyard's second entry, 7-year-old Hazel Billingsley, whose parents would always long for the touch of her little hand.

The anguish of child deaths hit Equality all too often. On the evening of May 1, 1899, the parents of 3-year-old Jimmie Mooney were outdoors and thought he was asleep in bed when he accidentally set his clothes on fire while playing with matches in the communal apartment building. "The cotton material went off like a flash, and before the fire could be quenched the flames had done their deadly work," the colony newspaper said. He was buried the next day at a Catholic cemetery in a nearby village. The newspaper captured the mood: "His little velvet cap still covers his chestnut locks, but the musical voice is silent, and gone is the jaunt air." The Mooneys had arrived the previous summer from the coal mines of Indian Territory. "My papa's a red-hot socialist," Jimmie's older sister wrote shortly before the move. After the tragic death, the enthusiasm cooled; the Mooneys moved to nearby New Whatcom.

Shortly before Christmas 1898, Orchil Gifford, age seven, was taking his turn in a daredevil game of tempting the flames of an enclosed brush fire. He fell in, and although an adult pulled him out, he could not be saved. The Gifford family had arrived at Equality in 1897 from Colorado, where Orchil's father, Levi L. Gifford, had been expelled from a socialist colony for being a troublemaker. (Levi went on to become a prominent labor leader in Bellingham.) *Industrial Freedom*'s report of the boy's death drew sympathetic notes from beyond the colony; a woman in a little town east of Tacoma wrote a poem for the boy's grieving mother, Susie.

Do not think of the seared and
wasted form
Of your precious darling boy;
But think of the Innocence, Purity, Love,
Which fire can never destroy.

The last to be interred, in April 1928, was William R. Giles, a British immigrant and transplanted Kansas farmer who arrived at Equality in its second year—leaving his unwilling wife behind—and remained on the hillside long after the colony collapsed.

The cemetery also holds the remains of Margaret Joslyn, who died at Equality in February 1903 at age sixty, and James B. Ault, the atheist with a knack for nicknames. Ault was forty-four when he succumbed to kidney disease in May 1901; his widow married Julius Monnich, the family friend and bicycle enthusiast who had accompanied the Aults from Kentucky. Thirty years later, Harry Ault returned to visit his father's grave and to see what remained of the little village of his teenage years. The apartment building in which the Ault family had lived was now a makeshift barn; cows inhabited the room in which Harry's sister Miskel was born in 1900, and torn patches of wallpaper told of a homier time.

With difficulty, Harry found the cemetery.

"Dad's grave was overgrown, but the cedar marker was still standing," he recalled.[33]

Time has buried most memories of the cemetery. Nor would a passerby detect its presence. The graves repose, like ancient crypts, beneath a natural cover—a century's deposit of leaves, twigs and branches disturbed only by the relentless spread of salmonberry shoots, salal, ferns, and English ivy.[34] On a sunny day, rays pierce the tops of cedar, cottonwood and maple trees standing watch over the tiny burial ground atop a narrow ridge on the lowest slope of Colony Mountain, just north and east of the creek that once was the lifeblood of Lermond's vision of Utopia.

A half-century after Equality was gone, a retired Seattle newspaper columnist reflected unsympathetically on the colony's life and death. A "futile and ill-advised experiment," he called it.[35] He concluded his account with a comment on the graveyard that fairly summed up the whole affair.

There lay men and women, he wrote, who searched for equality in life but found it only in death.

Chapter 18

A Dream Destroyed

Norman Lermond's vision of launching a revolution by capturing Washington for socialism collapsed so quickly that most memories of the little colony on Samish Bay evaporated like a coastal fog in a warming sun.

What should not be forgotten is that American capitalism might not have evolved from its untamed 1890s state to a more sustainable form—with constraints meant to limit the misuse of private power—were it not for decades of agitating by idealists like Lermond, venturesome radicals like Harry Ault, reformed ruffians like Ed Pelton, and rabble-rousers like George Boomer. Their efforts helped set the stage for more successful reformers of succeeding generations—women like consumer-rights activist Frances Perkins, who helped design President Franklin D. Roosevelt's Social Security Act, and Helen Keller, the blind-deaf activist who as a socialist in the 1910s and 1920s fought for workers' rights and woman suffrage, and men like Woodrow Wilson, whose economic reform ideas helped define the Progressive Era.

It would be an exaggeration to say the Equality episode

accelerated the arrival of a more just economic system and the rise of a welfare state. But it played a role to be remembered, as the colony's leaders seemed to foresee when they wrote one year into the project: "Every strike of a labor union, every former labor and reform organization, no matter how short lived or how narrow in its aims and methods, was a healthy—even if blind—protest against what all felt to be an injustice somewhere."[1]

In other words, Equality touched a nerve.

> Many a rebellious working man, fed up with factory slavery in the East, headed West as a result, not always, perhaps, to join a colony, but to be in a section of the land where the voice of dissent could be heard.[2]

Those are the words of the late Harvey O'Connor, a socialist chronicler of Seattle's radical heyday of the 1910s, whose rebel-in-arms wife, Jessie Lloyd O'Connor, was a granddaughter of Henry Demarest Lloyd, the acclaimed journalist and social activist. In Harvey O'Connor's view, Equality sowed seeds from which grew "some of the most daring and radical experiments ever seen on this continent,"[3] including the general strike that shut down Seattle in February 1919 and cemented the city's reputation for social militancy.

Americans have always viewed capitalism much more positively than socialism, but Gallup polls since 2010 indicate the gap has narrowed. This may reflect the fact that today's economic system is a blend of the two and that there remains an unquenched thirst for greater equality.[4]

Lermond and his followers may never have believed they would make a success of socialism, much less achieve a revolution. Yet it would be wrong to call them losers. They were dreamers—motivated by idealism, guided by hope, blind to their faults, and doomed by a naivety born of a belief that on the cusp of the 20th century, anything—even social justice and a fair shake for all—was possible. Like the snake that Lermond once gripped in his baby teeth, these dreamers' brand of radicalism proved a slippery solution to America's growing pains. Still, in their strivings are echoes of Henrik Irbsen: The pursuit of ideals, more than their attainment, is what gives life meaning.

Lermond was wrong to think that the fractured socialist movement of the late 1890s, even with better leadership, could have escaped the political wilderness and risen to power by carving colonies out of Washington's woods. Perhaps he sensed this mistake sooner than others and so fled the scene even before his creation's first anniversary. His idealism, however, was more enduring. Upon returning to Maine, where he would live out his remaining years, he began a new organization to shake up society. He called it the Industrial Brotherhood, another attempt to unite all socialist movements—minus the failed focus on colonizing.[5] He wrote to McDevitt in Olympia, urging him (unsuccessfully) to join this rejiggered and short-lived socialist cause.

Lermond remained a letter-writing dynamo. He contacted Albert Einstein in 1931, two years before the famed physicist and pacifist renounced his German citizenship and immigrated to the United States. Addressing him as "Dear Fellow Scientist," Lermond urged Einstein to aim his antiwar efforts at what Lermond considered the central cause of war—the profit motive. "If wars are to cease," Lermond wrote, "capitalism must be abolished." Einstein responded: "The theory that wars are made exclusively or chiefly by capitalists is in my opinion not tenable." Better to focus on stopping war by persuading young men to refuse military service, Einstein wrote, and force nations to settle their differences by arbitration.[6]

Back home at *The Willows*, Lermond kept searching for a winning way to combine his first loves—nature and politics. He created an outdoor arena, a sort of public playground, to serve as both a nature reserve and a venue for socialist lectures. He called it Utopia Park, and there, in perfect symmetry, he was interred in an unmarked grave in 1944.

David Burgess also gave up on Equality, but he stayed loyal to the idea that American democracy was capable of producing a fairer economic system. During a court trial over the colony's breakup, Burgess was asked why he had walked away in Equality's second year. "I concluded I would engineer myself better outside," he replied, and when asked if that meant he had abandoned the colony, he said, "No sir, not entirely. I would never abandon the idea. I never could do that."[7]

In the early 1900s, Burgess engaged in what he called "educational warfare"—recruiting for the socialist cause. He didn't just instruct from a distance; he taught in the trenches. On a spring evening in 1908, for example, at a rail crossing in Missoula County, Montana, Burgess shared an outdoor meal with a couple dozen hobos, the wandering homeless of that era. "The dinner was cooked in tin cans; we ate standing," Burgess recalled.[8] Having no home meant these men had no vote, and thus they had no faith in politics. They deserved respect, however, as men of intelligence— "men of skill, men of training in the schools, men of travel," as Burgess put it. To him, the emptiness of their lives was evidence of the dark side of capitalism, but it also was a reminder of socialism's unkept promise.

"They are looking for something visible, tangible—something that will enable them to occupy a home and have some of the comforts and luxuries of life," Burgess wrote of his hobo acquaintances.[9] They had no quarrel with socialism. "But they did tell me that they could not live upon mere theory."

What made Burgess different, aside from his hopefulness, was his fearlessness. Unlike 21st century blowhards who dish out drivel from the comfort and safety of a television studio, radio booth, or internet site, Burgess and other activists of his era stood on street corners to state their case and face whatever might come from anyone who cared to confront them.

After leaving Equality, Burgess pursued radical politics in a more direct way, taking leadership positions in a newly created Washington State Socialist Party, and, after the party collapsed in 1919, in the more radical Socialist Labor Party. By then he had concluded that garden-variety socialism was too timid; rather than push for an economic revolution, it sought only to make capitalism tolerable. He ran multiple races for state office, losing each. After a bid for governor in 1904 he tried again in 1908, a year of national hysteria over anarchists that ensnared socialists in a web of suspicion about loyalties.

The anarchist scare reflected an enduring fear of radicalism, which surged after a string of unsettling events: labor strikes in the 1890s; the attempted assassination of Carnegie Steel chairman Henry C. Frick in 1892 by Emma Goldman's anarchist friend, Alexander Berkman; the assassination of President McKinley in Buffalo in 1901, and the killing in February 1908 of Father Leo Heinrichs in Denver by an Italian immigrant who claimed to be an anarchist.

As political scientist Robert J. Goldstein put it years later: "The Heinrichs murder threw a shiver of fear into a society which was already in a mood to accept reports of radical conspiracies and to demand measures of repression."[10] Within a decade, socialism as an organized movement in American political life would be not just weakened but mortally wounded.

The year after he lost his second campaign for the Washington governorship, Burgess revealed a hint of regret that his socialist dreams, at Equality and afterward, had gone unfulfilled. From Seattle, he wrote to his former hometown newspaper in Arkansas: "I have a big notion to run away and go back to St. Paul, for I cannot ever find something that they have there."[11] He didn't say what it was that had eluded him, but perhaps it was the "shadow" that an Arkansas critic once said Burgess was chasing when he took up his socialist quest.

Burgess pressed on, even after Anna died in 1912, but his heart was not in it. The hope that grew from his Quaker upbringing and that sustained him at Equality had finally expired. His future was behind him. In 1927 he wrote with uncharacteristic melancholy: "Nearly fifteen years ago my life's companion left my side, and since then I have been wandering along life's dreary path alone, feeling that there is little left for me that is worth striving for."[12]

He died in Tacoma in 1929.

If Burgess brought hope to Equality and Lermond brought idealism, Inza Barry added a kind of blinding naivety that prevented her and others from seeing that they were reaching for the unattainable.

Barry lived to be ninety-four and apparently never did overcome her divorce from reality. She and her husband David and her father, John Joslyn, stayed put on the colony hillside until 1914, when they packed their household goods into a Great Northern rail car and made their way to the central coast of California. There they bought a parcel of land and built a little six-room bungalow—this home really would be her father's last[13]—in a new fruit-growing colony called Atascadero that did not label itself socialist but in some respects took cooperative living and collective enterprise to a higher level than Equality ever did.

From her new home, Inza helped promote an investment scam that demonstrated the wisdom of P.T. Barnum's line about suckers.[14] In 1927 the California State Corporation Commission concluded that she and an Atascadero business partner, Lewis M. Thornburgh, had swindled hundreds of Californians. The two were accused of soliciting "investment" in a fraudulent legal fund to settle the estate of Sir Francis Drake, the English explorer whose defeat of the Spanish armada in the late 16th century helped England become a global power and made him fabulously rich. Investors were promised that once a centuries-old battle for the Drake inheritance was settled in a London court and his $350 million estate was distributed, they would collect a fabulous return: between $100 and $1,800 for every dollar they had invested. The lure was so strong that some in Atascadero were said to have borrowed money or sold their homes to buy stakes in the Drake scheme.

The payoff never appeared because there was no unsettled Drake estate. This was one of a series of multi-million-dollar Drake inheritance con games—some predating the one involving Barry—that eventually were exposed as frauds. California's investigation concluded that she and Thornburgh had sold fraudulent "shares" in league with Sudie B. Whittaker, a Chicago genealogist and scam artist whom Barry had never met. The Corporation Commission recommended Barry and Thornburgh be prosecuted for violating corporate securities laws, but the case was never pursued.

In 1931, California renewed its effort to stop Barry by issuing a cease-and-desist order. She acknowledged collecting Drake legal fund "investments" but argued in a public rebuttal that she had broken no state law because she was not paid for her work on behalf of Whittaker.[15] The controversy faded and seemed to do no lasting damage to her reputation in Atascadero. In 1963 the city declared her queen of its 50-year municipal commemoration.[16]

She died in Atascadero in 1967, outliving her husband by twenty-four years.

ABANDONED AS an infant and sickly in childhood, William McDevitt defied the odds by living to ninety. By the time he died in San Francisco in 1959 he had lived nearly half his country's history, from Reconstruction to the Cold War, from the Gilded Age to the Great Depression, from horse-and-buggy days to the dawn of the Space Age.

Twice McDevitt ran for mayor of San Francisco. After his second defeat, in 1911, the Socialist Party expelled him for accepting an offer from the elected mayor, a Democrat, to serve on the city's Election Commission.

He dabbled in radical newspapering in Oakland and San Francisco, and in the 1930s often contributed to a *San Francisco News* feature, "Pulse of the Public." The left-leaning paper's editor remembered him as a man of "great tranquility," and "representative of the very best in human kind," adding, "We shall not see his like again in our day."[17]

McDevitt never fully restored his relationship with John B. Tabb, his adoptive father. In 1905, after moving to California after a brief period in Portland, Oregon, one more Tabb letter arrived at McDevitt's door.[18] Sadness was the theme. Apparently having seen a recent photo of his former pupil, Tabb began by writing, "If socialism makes you, son, as sad as you look, it is strange that men follow you." He ended with a reminder that McDevitt was always in his thoughts, "though nothing would be sadder to me than to meet you."[19]

McDevitt entered the antiquarian book business in 1907 as San Francisco was recovering from the devastating quake and fire of the prior year—not to make money but to create a winter refuge from street-corner oratory. Alexander Horr, the anarchist from Equality, was his first partner. Their Liberty Book Store on Golden Gate Avenue at Fillmore Street became a popular gathering place for radicals; McDevitt later ran his own store, The People's Library, where, his advertisements proclaimed, "anything that's radical may be found."

His enthusiasm for debate was long-lived. On a spring day in 1911 he took on Emma Goldman at San Francisco's Recreation Park; they argued the relative merits of socialism and anarchism, with McDevitt declaring that she and her followers were "thoroughly right at heart but thoroughly wrong in head."

Publicly an idealist and privately a realist, McDevitt eventually accumulated hundreds of shares of stock in corporations such as Bank of America, the Radio Corporation of America and Twentieth Century Fox.[20] In the late 1940s he arranged to bequeath these securities to a special friend, Veronica J. Sexton.[21] She was a librarian, born and raised in Berkeley, whom he had befriended and, by mutual and notarized agreement, adopted as his daughter—an echo of Father Tabb's embrace in McDevitt's youth. Single and nearly thirty years younger than McDevitt, she had patronized his bookstores; in the recollection of a friend, in the mid-1950s she found McDevitt had become "old, cold and forlorn," and so gave him an upstairs room in her house near Golden Gate Park[22] and allowed him to store there what remained of his vast collection of old books and magazines.

Books were as close to McDevitt's heart as mollusks were to Lermond's, as central to his identity as newspapers were to

Boomer's. He loved to mine the literary depths for hidden gems, and among his discoveries was Jack London's first for-pay published story—so obscure, he claimed, that London himself died not knowing it had been published.[23] McDevitt's lifetime collection was monumental. It so burdened the shelves of his bookstore that one day an entire wall of books, perhaps 20,000 in all, came crashing down. "It was like an earthquake," he recalled.[24]

In summing up his fortunes as a book dealer, McDevitt at age eighty-five might as easily have been describing his life story and the path of America's social progress.

"It is like chess: an accumulation of small gains," he said. "There have been no master strokes in my story."[25]

Long after McDevitt had moved on from Equality, years after the colony had been all but forgotten even in Skagit County, a few families remained on the wooded hillside amid the discarded hopes for a socialist century. Among the diehards were Henry and Josie Halladay, the salt-of-the-earth couple who arrived from the parched farmlands of northwestern Kansas in the fall of 1897. They stayed longer than anyone. In February 1931, in their fifty-seventh year of marriage, she died at home of stomach cancer; three months later he succumbed to heart failure.

Socialism never lost its hold on Henry, and Equality's demise dealt him a particularly harsh blow— "you might say catastrophic," a grandson recalled. "He had a dream that was completely destroyed."[26]

Destroyed, yes, but not completely.

Henry Halladay died at the outset of the Great Depression, amid bank panics and an industrial collapse that produced one of American history's great ironies: Wall Street magnates—apostles of unconstrained capitalism and champions of individualism—went to Washington on bended knee and hats in hand for a government bailout that amounted to state socialism. What followed in a decade of national recovery were radically new government programs—socialism for the rest of us, you might say. This became the foundation of today's social welfare state—Social Security, unemployment insurance, workers' compensation, food stamps, health insurance for the elderly, and other bulwarks against the sucker punches of life and the cruelties of capitalism.

These were the kinds of social safeguards that radicals like George Boomer raised hell for, that saints like Helen Mason prayed for, and that dreamers like Henry Halladay envisioned on their most hopeful days at the Equality colony.

Notes

Prologue

1. *Chicago Tribune*, June 20, 1897.
2. *Cleveland Plain Dealer*, June 22, 1897. He was referring broadly to any attempt to colonize Washington for socialism.
3. Harry Ault, "Account of the Ault Family's Travel to the Equality Colony in Washington State, April 1898," Harry E.B. Ault Papers, 1899-1956, Box 6, Folder 69. University of Washington Libraries, Special Collections. This and other Ault biographical materials, plus his Equality colony sketches and recollections, are in accessions 0213-001 and 0562-001, hereafter referred to as the Ault papers.
4. *Spokane Chronicle*, May 21, 1898.

1. A Radical For All Reasons

1. My portrait of George Boomer, here and in Chapter 7, is drawn mainly from his writings in numerous socialist newspapers, including *Justice*, *Uncle Sam*, *The Spirit of '76*, *The Appeal to Reason*, *Industrial Freedom*, and the *Peninsula Free Press*, as well as reported remarks by associates. Many mainstream newspapers published accounts of his activities, particularly during his years in Rhode Island, Maryland, Kansas, and Washington. Additional details in the *Anacortes American*, Dec. 17, 1908, and the *Everett Commonwealth*, July 14, 1913.
2. Boomer's weekly column, "Thoughts," in *The Appeal to Reason*, April 9, 1898. Nearly a century later, legal protection for a more radical form of flag protest—burning the banner—was established with a United States Supreme Court ruling in 1989 that destroying the flag was political expression protected by the First Amendment.
3. *Pittsburgh Post*, May 10, 1887.
4. The *Daily Tribune* in nearby Pittsburg, Kansas, reported that the townsmen who objected to Boomer's choice of words included Henry B. Orwig, who was preparing to lead a local group of volunteers for Army service in the just-declared war against Spain. The paper said the two had "an altercation" but did not elaborate. They knew each other: Orwig was drum major of the Girard marching band in which Boomer played the piccolo. There is no indication whether Orwig threatened Boomer.

5. My account of the response in Girard to Boomer's flag "rag" comment is derived from many newspaper reports, including the Fort Scott *Daily Tribune*, April 30, 1898.
6. Headline, the *Topeka State Journal*, May 2, 1898, p. 7. The article mistakenly referred to him as George E. Bowman, but there is no doubt that the person was Boomer. It apparently was an Associated Press story, appearing in numerous papers across the country with the same misspelling of Boomer's name, including the *Spokane Spokesman-Review* and the *New York Times*. A somewhat modified version that appeared in the *Daily Times* of Bath, Maine, said Boomer fled Fort Scott penniless; "Socialist friends advanced him money, and he left for Seattle."
7. The scarcity of telephones in Skagit County in the 1890s is from "The Telephone," Skagit County Historical Museum, La Conner, Washington.
8. The McDevitt comments are from his seven-part series, "Un-Lost Horizon: Shangri-La of Puget Sound," published in 1950-51 by *Searchlight* magazine, San Francisco. Copies are in the Harry E.B. Ault papers, 1899-1953, Accession No. 0562-001, box 4, folders 19 and 20, University of Washington Libraries, Special Collections. Also, from a lengthy article by journalist Robert de Roos, "An Interview with William McDevitt, LL.M," published in the Fall 1954 issue of the *Quarterly News Letter* of the Book Club of California.
9. There are two versions of Ayer's critique of the colony. The first, written on May 22, 1898, was published in the *Minneapolis Times* on June 13. The second, written several days after the first, appeared in the *Seattle Post-Intelligencer* on June 4.
10. Ibid.

2. Defying Human Nature

1. My account of the early days at Equality is based in part on Smith's *Equality Colony* manuscript, as well as LeWarne's *Utopias on Puget Sound* and McDevitt's *Searchlight* series, as well as contemporaneous reports in *Industrial Freedom*, *The Coming Nation*, and other newspapers. Most issues of *Industrial Freedom* have been digitized by the Washington State Library; some others are in the Frederick E. Smith papers at the Center for Pacific Northwest Studies at Western Washington University, hereafter referred to as the Smith papers. A microfilm collection of *The Coming Nation* is held by the Wisconsin Historical Society.
2. David Burgess, *Industrial Freedom*, Feb. 25, 1899.
3. *Spokane Chronicle*, May 21, 1898.
4. Hiram C. Crockett, the *Seattle Daily Times*, June 4, 1898.
5. The case of the bartender who shot himself is from Skagit County Death Returns, #493, George Arnkil, Anacortes, Aug. 19, 1902. Cause of death: "Shot himself." Contributing cause: "Rum & Women." An *Anacortes*

American news report on the suicide said Arnkil suffered from an "unrequited infatuation for a woman" and had been drinking for two days when he shot himself.

6. U.S. Census Bureau, Race and Hispanic Origin: 1850-1990.
7. *Inman News*, Inman, Nebraska, May 10, 1898. Chattel slavery: the system of servitude in which people are treated as property to be bought, sold, and owned for life. Formally abolished by the 13th Amendment to the Constitution, ratified in December 1865.
8. "Homeownership: A Housing Success Story," Frederick J. Eggers, *Cityscape: A Journal of Policy Development and Research*, Vol. 5, No. 2, 2001, U.S. Department of Housing and Urban Development.
9. A number of people were convicted of seditious conspiracy in connection with the January 6 attack on the Capitol to disrupt the peaceful transfer of power to a newly elected president. They included leaders of two far-right extremist groups: Stewart Rhodes, founder of the Oath Keepers, and Henry "Enrique" Tarrio, a former national chairman of the Proud Boys. Tarrio was sentenced to twenty-two years in prison, Rhodes to eighteen years. Upon entering office in January 2025, President Donald Trump pardoned Tarrio and commuted the sentence of Rhodes.
10. "Equality To-day," photo caption, *Industrial Freedom*, Nov. 12, 1898.
11. Pelton, *Industrial Freedom*, May 27, 1899.
12. "Shangri-La," is from McDevitt's *Searchlight* series; "an embryo garden," is from Pelton in *Industrial Freedom*, Oct. 16, 1897; "Satan's nest," *Bellingham Sunday Reveille*, Oct. 1, 1922; "Nest of socialist crime," *The Province*, Vancouver, British Columbia, May 1, 1907; and "a grand visionary," Ayer, *Seattle Post-Intelligencer*, June 4, 1898.
13. William Graham, of Colville, Washington, *Progressive Thought*, June 1, 1895.
14. Lermond, "How to Build a Commonwealth," *The Coming Nation*, Aug. 29, 1896.
15. *The Kansas Weekly Capital*, Sept. 10, 1897.
16. *Farmers' Alliance*, Lincoln, Nebraska, Sept. 6, 1890.
17. Boomer, *The News*, Providence, Rhode Island, Oct. 11, 1893.
18. Lloyd speech as delivered in October 1894, reprinted in *American Radicalism, 1865-1901*, by Chester McArthur Destler, 1963.
19. Lermond, "A Call to Arms," *Marion Headlight*, Marion, Kansas, Nov. 12, 1896.
20. "The Concentration of Wealth," *Political Science Quarterly*, Vol. 8, No. 4 (December 1893), pp. 589-600.
21. Indeed, the egalitarian world that Edward Bellamy imagined in his utopian novel, *Looking Backward: 2000-1887*, remains a fantasy. In his 2017 book, *Capital in the Twenty-First Century*, economist Thomas Piketty wrote that inequality of wealth in the United States had reached its highest point in two centuries. More recent Federal Reserve Bank

numbers show the trend holds. The Fed in 2019 found that three-quarters of household wealth in the United States was held by ten percent of families and the bottom fifty percent owned just one percent.

22. McDevitt, *My Father, Father Tabb, at Home and at College*, San Francisco. Recorder-Sunset Press, 1945. p. 33. Digitized by Google, original at University of California.
23. Jessie Mayer, a California school teacher, in *Industrial Freedom*, May 20, 1899.

3. A Bug Man And His Big Idea

1. Biographical details about Lermond are from his unfinished autobiography as published in the *Northeastern Naturalist*, Vol. 11, No. 2, 2004, annotated by Scott M. Martin; cited with permission from editor-in-chief Keith Goldfarb. Other sources include Lermond's articles in *The Coming Nation* and other newspapers; United States Census records; Boston city directories, and "I Knew Lermond," by William Clench, in *American Malacological Union News Bulletin and Annual Report, 1944-45*, courtesy of the Biodiversity Heritage Library, Harvard University.
2. "The Message of Jesus" text published in full in 1891 by Fleming H. Revell Co., New York, on file at the Library of Congress.
3. Herron letter, *The Coming Nation*, March 26, 1898.
4. *Annals of the Town of Warren, in Knox County, Maine*, by Cyrus Eaton, second edition, Masters and Livermore, Hallowell, Maine, 1877, p. 420. Digitized by Google; original at Princeton University.
5. My account of Omar Lermond's disappearance and death is from contemporaneous newspaper accounts, including the *Boston Globe*, July 17, 1884, the *Republican Journal* of Belfast, Maine, July 17, 1884, and the *Portland Daily Press*, August 11, 1884.
6. Lermond autobiography.
7. Ibid.
8. Willard's comments about Bellamy are from *Our Day*, Vol. 4, No. 24, December 1889, pp. 539-542.
9. Bellamy, "How I Came to Write *Looking Backward*," *The Nationalist*, May 1889. Also, "Edward Bellamy and the Nationalist Movement," John Hope Franklin, *The New England Quarterly*, Vol. 11, No. 4 (December 1938), pp. 739-772.
10. Daniels lecture titled "A Graduated Tax," in *A Crisis for the Husbandman*, adapted from Daniels lecture series delivered in 1889, published by Western Herald Print, Girard, Kansas.
11. Harris, "Edward Bellamy's Vision," *The Forum*, September 1889, pp. 199-208.
12. *Ranch and Range*, a Seattle weekly newspaper, Aug. 31, 1899, p. 3.
13. Lermond autobiography.

14. *Twentieth Century*, Nov. 14, 1895, pp. 13-14.
15. Lermond letter to Lloyd, Apr. 25, 1896, pp. 5-6. The Henry Demarest Lloyd correspondence, 1895-1897, is in the University of Washington Libraries, Special Collections, accession #4678-001; originals are held by the Wisconsin Historical Society.
16. Quint, *The Forging of American Socialism*, Bobbs-Merrill Co., 1953, 1964.
17. Lermond to Lloyd, Apr. 25, 1896. Lloyd correspondence, University of Washington Libraries, Special Collections.
18. Lermond to Lloyd, July 16, 1896. Lloyd correspondence.
19. Swift, "Is Our Republic to Fall?", *Public Ownership Review*, Vol. 1, No. 11 (December 1897). Herbert Baxter Adams papers, Johns Hopkins University, Sheridan Libraries, Special Collections.
20. Lermond, *The Coming Nation*, April 26, 1896.
21. Lermond, *The Coming Nation*, Aug. 29, 1896.
22. The exact peak of BCC membership is unclear. A reasonable figure is the 3,558 cited in *Industrial Freedom*, Dec. 31, 1898.
23. In March 1898, while Bellamy was living in Denver and shortly before he returned home to Chicopee to die, he partnered with Reed and Eugene Debs to create the New Nation Publishing Company. The first issue of its magazine, *New Nation*, published in June, carried Bellamy's obituary.
24. Bellamy to Parsons, April 8, 1896. Frank Parsons papers, MS 11, Yale University Library, Manuscripts and Archives.
25. My account of Parsons at the Kansas State Agricultural College is based in part on a letter to Parsons from representatives of the junior class, March 25, 1899, as well as the college's student newspaper, *The Students' Herald*, Sept. 28, 1899. Also, the Frank Parsons papers, MS 11, Box 1, Folders 7, 8, 10 and 17, Yale University Library, Special Collections. The account of Parsons' meeting with regents is from *The Manhattan Republic*, June 23, 1899.
26. *The Courier-Gazette*, Rockland, Maine, Sept. 4, 1898.
27. Debs, "How I Became a Socialist," *The Comrade*, New York. Vol. 1, No. 7 (April 1902).
28. My account of Debs' relationship with Lermond and their split is based on contemporaneous reporting in numerous newspapers, including: *Rock Island Argus*, June 17, 1897; *San Francisco Examiner*, June 19, 1897; *Chicago Tribune*, June 20, 1897; *Seattle Post-Intelligencer*, Dec. 9, 1897.
29. "Socialist Party Membership by States, 1904-1940," Mapping American Social Movements Project, Civil Rights and Labor History Consortium, University of Washington. https://depts.washington.edu/moves/SP_map-members.shtml The only state with more per-capita socialists than Washington was Nevada.
30. "Debs Talks About His Socialistic Colony Scheme," *The Evening News*, Benton Harbor, Michigan, June 17, 1897, p. 5.

31. The Rogers letter of June 7, 1897, is from the *Washington Standard*, June 25, 1897.
32. *Whatcom Reveille*, reprinted in the *Seattle Post-Intelligencer*, June 30, 1897.
33. Debs ran for president as a socialist five times, starting in 1900. He made his final run, winning nearly one million votes, or 3.4 percent of ballots, in 1920 while serving a prison sentence for violating the Espionage Act of 1917 by speaking against America's entry into World War I.

4. Equality is Born

1. My account of Pelton family history is drawn mainly from Jeremiah M. Pelton, *Genealogy of the Pelton Family in America*, 1892, as well as United States Census and Civil War records.
2. Details of the Grey Eagle affairs are from numerous sources, including an original copy of Ed Pelton's sworn statement to the Todd County court and the county grand jury indictment. Also, contemporaneous newspaper accounts, including the *St. Paul Globe*, Nov. 28, 1885; the Todd County *Argus*, Dec. 3, 1885; the *Little Falls Transcript*, Dec. 4, 1885, and February 19, 1886; and the *Alexandria Post*, Dec. 11, 1885; Todd County District Court records provided to author by the Gale Family Library, Minnesota State Historical Society; criminal court case number 637, State of Minnesota versus Jerry Woodman.
3. "Ed Pelton is Dead," *The Socialist*, Seattle, March 1, 1901, p. 3.
4. Pelton, *Industrial Freedom*, June 10, 1899.
5. Lermond to Lloyd, April 25, 1896, Lloyd correspondence.
6. Pelton, "On to Washington and the Cooperative Commonwealth," *The Coming Nation*, Aug. 7, 1897.
7. Pelton's search for a colony site is from numerous sources, including his "Historical Sketch of BCC," *Industrial Freedom*, Nov. 12, 1898.
8. My description of early Edison is based on numerous sources, including original land records on file at the Washington State Archives and an 1871 territorial census of the Samish precinct – before Edison became an official entity – in what was then part of Whatcom County.
9. Previous paths of the Skagit River is from an 1881 Annual Report of the Chief of Engineers, U.S. War Department, quoted in "Mid-19th Century Stream Channels and Wetlands Interpreted From Archival Sources for Three North Puget Sound Estuaries," Department of Geological Sciences, University of Washington, August 2000.
10. "Forest Survey Report No. 88," Pacific Northwest and Range Experiment Station, Portland, Oregon, August 1942, U.S. Department of Agriculture.
11. Bashford, "The Literary Development of the Far Northwest," *Overland Monthly*, Vol. 33, No. 196, April 1899, p. 319. University of Michigan Library, digital collections.

12. "Blanket Bill" Jarman details are from Miller and Miller, *Samish Island: A History, From the Beginning to the 1970s*, 2007, and Bancroft's *History of Washington, Idaho, and Montana, 1845-1889*.
13. *Far Corner, A Personal View of the Pacific Northwest*, The McMillan Company. 1952. p. 7.
14. Pelton, *The Coming Nation*, Oct. 16, 1897.
15. Pelton's land deal with Decker was for parcels in sections 26 and 27 of Township 36 North, Range 3 East of the Willamette Meridian, totaling 280 acres. The parcels were as follows: the east half of the southeast quarter and the south half of the northeast quarter of Section 27, (a combined 160 acres), and the south half of the southwest quarter and the south half of the north half of the southwest quarter of Section 26 (a combined 120 acres). The first owner of the 160-acre parcel, after it was surveyed by the federal government and placed in the public domain, was Samuel J. Brason, a local shingle mill operator. He paid $200 in 1873. The 120-acre parcel was first purchased by a Scotsman, John L. Morrison, who came west in 1842 in the first large wagon train to cross the Oregon Trail, led by the intrepid pathfinder Medorem Crawford. The BCC later upped its total holdings to 440 acres by acquiring 160 adjacent acres originally owned by George T. Stevens, a rancher who made his way to Alaska in 1898 to supply miners during the Nome gold rush. The Stevens property was the south half of the west half of the southeast quarter of Section 27 (40 acres); the north half of the west half of the northeast quarter of Section 34 (40 acres); and the east half of the northeast quarter of Section 34 (80 acres). General Land Office Records, Bureau of Land Management, U.S. Department of the Interior; Land survey records and tract books for Township 36 North, Range 3 East, on file at Washington State Archives, Olympia.
16. Lermond to Lloyd, Nov. 26, 1897.
17. The record of land sale, warranty deed No. 27754, and trust deed No. 27755, are on file at University of Washington Libraries, Special Collections.
18. Kenneth McKenzie, west half of northeast quarter and north half of northwest quarter of Section 12, Township 35 north of Range 3 east of Willamette Meridian.
19. "Exclusive" imagination is from Bige Eddy in his column, "Musings of a Mossback," *Industrial Freedom*, May 29, 1989. The local author who said Carey had "an ear for any idea that sounded a little radical" was Frederick E. Smith, *Equality Colony*, 1988.
20. Details of Coast Salish history and culture, from *Coast Salish Essays*, Wayne Suttles, University of Washington Press, 1987; Samish Indian Nation website, www.samishtribe.nsn.us; and National Archives "Pieces of History" blog, "The Birth of an Eternal Document: The Point Elliott Treaty." September 28, 2020. Also instructive is "Anarchism and the

Archeology of Anarchic Societies: Resistance to Centralization in the Coast Salish Region of the Pacific Northwest Coast," by Angelbeck and Grier, *Current Anthropology*, Vol. 53, Number 5, October 2012, pp. 555-556. Angelbeck and Grier argue that potlatching as practiced by the Coast Salish "facilitated the conversion of material capital into status," and, as importantly, ensured a redistribution of resources. "Consequently, any tendency for wealth to accumulate inordinately in the hands of a few was limited and controlled."

21. Smith, *Equality Colony* manuscript, Chapter 3.
22. Descriptions of Lewis's gardening skills are from an Ault sketch, "The Gardner," Ault papers. Also, Smith, *Equality Colony*.
23. 1871 Washington territorial census, Washington State Archives.
24. Pelton to Lloyd, Dec. 14. 1897, Lloyd correspondence.
25. Pelton, *The Coming Nation*, Nov. 20, 1897.
26. *Industrial Freedom*, May 7, 1898.
27. Smith, *Equality Colony* manuscript, chapter 16.
28. Smith audio tape interview, 1966. Smith papers. Frederick Smith had no direct exposure to the colony, since he was born several years after it dissolved.

5. Radicalism: From Hope to Despair

1. Cook, *The Corporation Problem*, G.P. Putnam's Sons. 1893, p. 253.
2. Editor's introduction to Richard White's *The Republic for Which it Stands: The United States during Reconstruction and the Gilded Age, 1865-1896*. New York: Oxford University Press. 2017.
3. Sinclair later regretted that it was the horrid meat products, rather than the despicable conditions under which they were made, that became the main target of public outrage. "I aimed at the public's heart, and by accident I hit it in the stomach," he said.
4. "Defects of the Wage System," Rehn, *Second Annual Report of the Bureau of Statistics of Pennsylvania for the Years 1873-74, Part Two*, July 20, 1874, pp. 586-596.
5. "Labor Force and Employment, 1800-1960," National Bureau of Economic Research, 1966. Also, "Explaining the Shift of Labor From Agriculture to Industry in the United States: 1869 to 1899," Frank D. Lewis, *Journal of Economic History*, Vol. 39, No. 3, (September 1979) pp. 681-698.
6. *Critics and Crusaders, a Century of American Protest*, Henry Holt and Company. 1947, p. 344.
7. My portrait of Joseph and Annie Billingsley is from numerous sources, including U.S. Census Bureau and General Land Office records, including Homestead Act records; records of the Buffalo County Register of Deeds; the 1907 Standard Atlas of Buffalo County, Nebraska, and

numerous Nebraska newspapers, including the *Gibbon Reporter*, the *Buffalo County Beacon*, the *Shelton Clipper*, and the *Buffalo County Sun*. Also, Joe Billingsley's Washington state death certificate; Skagit County Superior Court probate records of the Joseph Billingsley estate; Nebraska marriage records; "A Historical and Genealogical Register of John Wing, of Sandwich, Mass., and His Descendants, 1632-1888," by Rev. Conway P. Wing, 1888; and the two-volume *History of Buffalo County and Its People*, by Samuel Clay Bassett, 1916.

8. Billingsley's war experiences are difficult to document, in part because his unit, Company F of the 137th Regiment of Pennsylvania Infantry, played a small combat role during its nine-month existence. Military pension records indicate he was compensated as an "invalid," starting in 1896, but I could find no record confirming a service-related injury. He was mustered in at the rank of private on Aug. 28, 1862, and was discharged on June 1, 1863. The 137th saw action, but surprisingly little direct combat, during major battles such as Antietam and Chancellorsville. Sources: pension records of the Veterans Administration, Civil War muster rolls, and two books: *A Compendium of the War of the Rebellion*, Vol. 3, by Frederick H. Dyer, and *The Luckiest Regiment in the Army of the Potomac*, edited by Robert P. Broadwater.
9. "About This Way," *Gibbon Reporter*, July 23, 1896, p. 2.
10. Hayes diary entries are from "Diary and Letters of Rutherford Birchard Hayes," Vol. 4, 1881-1891. Ohio State Archeological and Historical Society, via Rutherford B. Hayes Presidential Library and Museum.
11. *1877: Year of Violence*, Chicago: Quadrangle Books, 1970, p. 10.
12. *Reading Daily Eagle*, July 24, 1877.
13. *Reading Daily Eagle*, July 22, 1877.
14. *Looking Backward: 2000-1887*, Bellamy.
15. "Pelton on Colonization," *Industrial Freedom*, Dec. 4, 1900. Smith papers.
16. Conant, "Industrial Consolidations in the United States," *Publications of the American Statistical Association*, March 1901, Vol. 7, No. 53.
17. *The Spirit of '76*, Feb. 25, 1899.
18. *The Buffalo Commercial*, June 29, 1899.
19. The Haymarket affair burdened Chicago with a lasting reputation for harboring anarchists, but the legal system's failings were largely forgotten. In his book, *The History of the Haymarket Affair*, Henry David concluded that the eight men were wrongly convicted. He found it impossible to establish who threw the dynamite bomb but leaned toward the theory that anarchism inspired the act, even if the demonstrators present that day did not commit it. William McDevitt, the Georgetown Law School graduate who became Lermond's legal assistant at Equality colony, recalled years later that a Georgetown professor and prominent Washington lawyer, R.

Ross Perry, told his class that the Haymarket convictions were a miscarriage of justice and that many others in the legal profession agreed.

20. *Living My Life*, Vol. 1, p. 10, New York: Alfred Knopf, 1931.
21. Debs, "The Martyred Apostles of Labor," *The New Time*, February 1898.
22. Cleveland veto message, Feb. 16, 1887, The American Presidency Project, University of California, Santa Barbara.
23. "Who Should Help Them?" *Post-Dispatch*. Aug. 24, 1893.
24. Parrington, *Main Currents in American Thought*, Vol. 2, New York: Harcourt, Brace and Company, 1927. Book 1, "Changing America," Part 1, "The Gilded Age," pp. 23-26.
25. "A Marshall Crushed," *The Evening Star*, May 4, 1894; "The Trial Today," *The Evening Star*, May 5, 1894; "Coxey's Testimony," *The Evening Star*, May 7, 1894.

6. 'On To Washington!'

1. Lermond, *Industrial Freedom*, May 7, 1898.
2. Helm letter dated Nov. 1, 1897, published in *The Anaconda Standard*, Nov. 19, 1897.
3. Biographical material about Dunckel is from census and land records as well as numerous newspapers, including *The Daily Deadwood Pioneer-Times*, Dec. 20, 1896 and Sept. 21, 1897; the *Black Hills Union*, Oct. 30, 1890 and June 3, 1892; the *Queen City Mail*, Spearfish, South Dakota, March 11, 1891; the *Daily Plainsman*, Huron, South Dakota, Jan. 13, 1893; *The Lead Daily Call*, July 7, July 22, and December 19, 1896; the *Black Hills Daily Times*, Rapid City, South Dakota, March 25, 1897, and the *Deadwood Evening Independent*, July 26, 1897.
4. George W. Quimby, letter of Dec. 5, 1897, to Henry Halladay from Verdigre, Nebraska. Freeland Cooperative Association files, University of Washington Libraries, Special Collections, Accession No. 2078-001.
5. William H. Wirling, *The Coming Nation*, Oct. 16, 1897.
6. Oliver Darr grandson, Oliver Smith, quoted with permission from Smith's daughter, Lorie Schaefer, who also shared documents and other materials related to the Darr family's experiences at Equality.
7. Goldman, *Buffalo Times*, Nov. 28, 1897.
8. Except for the period between 1902 and 1908, common law marriages in New York had been recognized since colonial times as valid if entered into within state borders, until they were abolished in 1933. "Common Law Marriage In New York State," *Columbia Law Review*, Vol. 30, No. 1 (January 1930), pp. 1-11. In his Equality Colony manuscript, Smith wrote that Horr and his partner Jenny "let it be known to the thin-skinned prudes of old Equality that for reasons of conscience they were not legally married." Their apparent common law marriage ended sometime shortly after the collapse of Equality in 1907. Details of her life are elusive, but it

seems highly likely that she was the "Jennie Bernstein" who committed suicide in San Francisco in June 1908 a few weeks after moving there from Seattle. Newspaper reports said the Russian-born woman poisoned herself with carbolic acid. A few weeks later, Horr memorialized a "Jennie Bernstein" in a poem in the inaugural edition of his San Francisco journal, *Freeland*. He did not mention their relationship but said she was a native of Russia, which aligns with the few available details of her personal background.

9. Lermond, *Lucifer, the Light-Bearer*, (a Chicago-based anarchist newspaper) Nov. 14, 1901.
10. *The Coming Nation*, Oct. 8, 1897.
11. Pelton quoted the Halladay letter in an article published in *The Coming Nation*, Oct. 9, 1897. Other details of Halladay's political views are from numerous Kansas newspapers, including the *Oberlin Times*, *Oberlin Herald*, and *Oberlin Opinion*, from 1881 to 1895.
12. Halladay injuries: *Industrial Freedom*, Oct. 1, 1898 and May 10, 1901.
13. George W. Quimby letter of Dec. 5, 1897, to Henry Halladay. Freeland file, University of Washington Libraries, Special Collections.
14. Norton biographic details are from "History of the People's Party with Special Reference to Illinois," Harold A. Neff, a master's thesis, University of Illinois, 1920; Timothy J. Orr, "On Such Slender Threads Does the Fate of Nations Depend," Gettysburg Seminar Papers, National Park Service; *Berdan's United States Sharpshooters in the Army of the Potomac 1861-1865*, Capt. C.A. Stevens, The Price-McGill Company, St. Paul, Minnesota. 1892.
15. *Ten Men of Money Island*, Chicago: F.J. Schulte and Company, 1891. Digitized by Google from original at Columbia University.
16. *Congressional Record*, June 22, 1894, pp. 6695-6696.
17. *Ten Men of Money Island*. Chicago: F.J. Schulte and Company, 1891, pp. 132-133.
18. His birth year was recorded differently over his lifetime. The 1850 U.S. census, taken in October of that year, listed him as three months old, indicated he was born in July 1850. His death certificate says he was born March 4, 1848. However, the 1900 census says he was born in March 1849, and his marriage license also indicates 1849.
19. Isaac Newton Halladay death, "Illinois Civil War Muster and Descriptive Rolls Detail Report," Illinois State Archives.
20. Benjamin and Mary Halladay letters to Syracuse (Nebraska) *Journal-Democrat*, 1878, 1883 and 1887.
21. *Daily Calamity Howler*, Sept. 28, 1891, and *Winfield Daily Courier*, Sept. 29, 1891.
22. *Progressive Thought*, July 1, 1895.
23. "Personal Notes on the Equality Colony, From Recollections of

Catherine Savage Pulsipher," the *Skagit River Journal*, Skagit County Historical Society, courtesy of Dan Royal, editor.

24. *Industrial Freedom*, reprinted in *The Socialist*, Sept. 29, 1901.

7. Boomer's 'Unremitting War'

1. Hicks, "The People's Party in Minnesota," *Minnesota History Bulletin*, Vol. 5, No. 8 (November 1924), p. 533. Hicks went on to assert that in the 1890s ordinary people came to the conclusion that only by banding together could they compete in a "mad race for prosperity." Thus rose the People's Party.
2. *A Son of the Middle Border*, St. Paul: Borealis Books, Minnesota Historical Society Press, 2007. pp. 336-341. Originally published by MacMillan, 1917.
3. Billy Boomer in 1886 wrote and published an insightful and amusing booklet on the history of his mother's side of the family, *The Goss Family, an Historical Romance.*
4. Details of George C. Boomer's war record are from numerous sources, including newspaper accounts, the 1890 Veterans Schedule of the U.S. Census (with a handwritten notation that he was shot in the right ankle on February 6, 1864), and *History of the Fourteenth Regiment, Connecticut Volunteer Infantry*, by Charles D. Page, Meriden, Connecticut, The Horton Publishing Co., 1906.
5. Boomer, "Grant's Deviltry in Louisiana," Auburn (Maine) *Clipper*, Jan. 9, 1875. Courtesy of the American Antiquarian Society.
6. Lewiston (Maine) *Daily Sun*, May 9, 1903.
7. *Wyoming Press*, Evanston, Wyoming, June 4, 1898.
8. Bruce Rogers, "George E. Boomer, Biographical Summary," *International Socialist Review*, Vol. 15, No. 11, (May 1915).
9. *Justice*, April 7, 1894. Courtesy, Rhode Island Historical Society.
10. "He Derided Old Glory," *Providence News*, May 2, 1898.
11. I was unable to confirm with full certainty that *Eastern Shore* was the newspaper Boomer sabotaged; no issues of the paper are known to have survived. It was published at Easton in Talbot County, Maryland. In a review of the region's other newspapers for the months of September and October 1896, including the *Easton Gazette*, the *Evening Journal* of New Castle, Delaware, and the *Smyrna Times* of Smyrna, Delaware, I found numerous references to the *Eastern Shore* and to Boomer as its manager in this period.
12. *The Appeal to Reason*, Aug. 14, 1897.
13. *The Socialist*, May 4 and May 25, 1902.
14. George and Mary Boomer had two sons, George L. Boomer and Richard D. Boomer. George died of tuberculosis in May 1902. Richard changed

his surname to Rathbun after his parents separated and Mary married John O. Rathbun in Massachusetts in November 1902.

15. The ad appeared in many newspapers, including the *Sacramento Bee*, Sept. 4, 1903.
16. Frostburg *Mining Journal*.
17. Frostburg *Mining Journal*, Oct. 24, 1896. Haroun al-Rashid was an 8th and 9th century caliph of Baghdad; "bustid" was late-19th century American slang for a ruined or disreputable person.

    No copies of Boomer's *Uncle Sam* paper are known to have survived.

    At times, Boomer's abusers got physical. In May 1912, a soldier reportedly pushed Boomer off his soap box to stop him from speaking on a Port Townsend, Washington, street; a War Department investigation ensued but the results were not made public. See the *Port Townsend Daily Leader*, Aug. 13, 1912.
18. Letter by Edmonds Mayor Hale E. Dewey to the editor of *The Commonwealth* newspaper in Everett, Washington, Jan. 19, 1912.
19. Puget Sound Cooperative Colony was started in 1887. In *Utopias on Puget Sound, 1885-1915*, author Charles LeWarne described it as "essentially a local movement derived from working-class agitations in Puget Sound cities." By 1893-94 it was in court receivership.
20. Boomer, "Let the Masters Fight Their Own Battles," *The Peninsula Free Press*, Feb. 27, 1915, p. 4.
21. *Inman News*, Inman, Nebraska, April 12, 1898.
22. David Barry, *Freeland* newspaper, Nov. 1, 1905, p. 1.
23. Smith was the author's second cousin; his mother, Mary "Blanche" (Morton) Smith, was a younger sister of the author's maternal grandmother, Anna (Morton) Freberg.
24. Handwritten draft of manuscript, "Equality Colony," Frederick E. Smith papers, Series 1, Box 2, Folders 1-2, Center for Pacific Northwest Studies, Western Libraries Archives and Special Collections, Western Washington University. The phrase, "colored with innocence, exuberance and tragedy," was dropped from the manuscript's final version.
25. Typed manuscript, 1988, Smith papers, Series 1, Box 2, Folder 5. Center for Pacific Northwest Studies, Western Libraries Archives and Special Collections, Western Washington University.

8. Living a 'Glory-radiant' Dream

1. The "I was not 'abandoned'" quote is from the *San Francisco Call-Bulletin*, June 12, 1953, p. 16. In 1873, while McDevitt remained in its care, the Foundling Asylum relocated to a larger building on 68th Street between Lexington and Third Avenue.
2. "Foundlings," *New York Herald*, Nov. 22, 1869, p. 10. Article mentions

that Sister Irene and three other nuns started the New York foundling "hospital" on Oct. 11, 1869.

3. McDevitt, *Searchlight* series. "My pristine enthusiasm," installment number two, May-June 1950. "Glory-radiant dream," installment number three, July-August 1950. University of Washington Libraries, Special Collections.
4. Names of some babies at the Foundling Asylum in its early years were mentioned in handwritten notes left by mothers or others. Hundreds of these notes have been preserved by the New York Historical Society, but none refer to William McDevitt. They give a sense of the desperate conditions of that time. One note writer asked that a newborn named Reginald be baptized and cared for, "for Christ['s] sake and not for the sake of the unhappy mother."
5. William McDevitt papers, MSS BANC 98/86, carton 1, folder 35, Bancroft Library, University of California, Berkeley. Hereafter, the McDevitt papers. It is an enduring mystery why, particularly during his years in Washington, D.C., McDevitt used the middle initial M.
6. This remark was quoted in the *San Francisco Call Bulletin* of June 12, 1953 from a McDevitt letter to the newspaper that unfortunately was not published in full. The remark as published was, "I am, I imagine, the sole survivor of the 'class' of 1869 at the New York Foundling Asylum, although I was not 'abandoned' by my mother but placed in the arms of the famous Sister Irene," referring to Sister Mary Irene FitzGibbon, who started the foundling asylum. Any details McDevitt might have added in the letter were not included in the portion quoted by the newspaper.
7. McDevitt to Mencken, May 25, 1955. H.L. Mencken papers, Manuscripts Division, New York Public Library.
8. For details of Sister Irene's role, see *The Foundling, The Story of The New York Foundling*, Martin Gottlieb, The Donning Co. Publishers, 2001. See also an article on the online publishing platform *Medium* by Caroline Baker, "Sister Mary Irene Fitzgibbon and The New York Foundling Hospital," Oct. 26, 2022. https://medium.com/@carolineannebaker/sister-mary-irene-fitzgibbon-and-the-new-york-foundling-hospital-2ad051c7c265
9. "My Old Plantation Days With Father Tabb," *Catholic World*, September 1949. McDevitt identified the head of the Frederick household only as "Aunt Mary," whose full name was Mary Ann Riordan, a dressmaker and staunch Confederate. McDevitt is listed in the 1880 U.S. census, taken in June, as living at the St. Patrick's orphanage in Baltimore.
10. During the Civil War, Gaitley was pastor of St. Mary's Catholic Church near Bryantown in southern Maryland, a hotbed of Confederate sympathy and a historic center of American Catholicism. His congregants happened to include Mary Surratt, who was convicted by a military

tribunal of conspiring in the Lincoln assassination. She was hanged in July 1865. By a coincidence of history, her son John Surratt studied for three years at St. Charles College, the prep school that Gaitley had attended earlier and that McDevitt would attend later. Gaitley seems to have tread carefully with the Surratts. At his funeral service in 1892, a friend of more than four decades, Cardinal James Gibbons, noted that "the unhappy and ill-fated Mrs. Surratt" and her family were members of Gaitley's congregation. "He steered his course between Scylla and Charybdis [mythical sea dangers from Homer's *Odyssey*] and never committed any act that would compromise his fair name," Gibbons said. Quoted in *The Baltimore Sun*, Dec. 13, 1892, p. 7. Also, a *Sun* story of July 1, 1891, reporting on the thirtieth anniversary of Gaitley's ordination, said without elaboration that during his pastorship at St. Mary's he "became intimately acquainted with the Surratt family."

11. St. Charles College was founded by the Sulpician Fathers, a society of priests founded in Paris in the 1640s; the Sulpicians also founded the first Roman Catholic seminary in the United States, St. Mary's, in 1791. Gaitley had attended St. Charles in the mid-1850s where he was a classmate of the future Cardinal James Gibbons, the ninth archbishop of Baltimore. The official St. Charles record of student enrollment spelled McDevitt's surname differently and gave him two middle initials. It listed him as William M.J. McDevitte of Baltimore. There is no question that this was William J. McDevitt. The enrollment record is titled, "A Complete List of the Students Entered at Saint Charles College, Ellicott City, Maryland Since the Opening, October 31st, 1848," archived by St. Mary's Seminary in Baltimore.
12. Tabb letter, circa July 1900, quoted by M.S. Pine in *John Bannister Tabb, the Poet-Priest*, published in 1915 for the Georgetown Visitation Convent, Washington, D.C.
13. "Personal production" was not meant in a strictly literal way. In his book, *My Father, Father Tabb* (1945, digitized by Google; original at University of California, Berkeley), McDevitt reproduced a portion of an article, "Father Tabb Centenary," written by a Tabb biographer, Francis E. Litz. In that article, Litz cites a Harriet "Hallie" Tabb letter to her younger brother John. Full quotation, p. 101: "While I give Willie credit for his natural ability, I look upon him so much as your *personal production* that I am almost as proud of him as of your poems."
14. John B. Tabb's parents, Thomas Yelverton Tabb and Marianna Bertrand Archer, were first cousins. Their great grandfather, Thomas Tabb, established the *Clay Hill* plantation in the 1730s or '40s, and it served as the Tabb family seat until it burned down in 1861.
15. McDevitt, *My Father, Father Tabb*. p. 92. McDevitt did not mention the given name of Mrs. Barksdale but said Tabb called her "Dussie." Also, p.

47: "She loved me like a mother, not, as I imagine, for my sake but for Father Tabb's sake. His 'son' was her 'son.'"

16. *Ibid.* p. 54. Tabb informally adopted McDevitt in 1884.
17. He said years later that he had been honored as class poet at St. Charles, a notable distinction given that his classmates included George Sterling, who would become one of California's most celebrated poets.
18. Gaitley's response to McDevitt's decision not to attend St. Mary's Seminary—disowned him and "chucked [him] out on his head"—is from unsigned notes, almost certainly written by journalist Robert de Roos, after his interview with McDevitt in San Francisco in 1954. The notes are in McDevitt papers, Bancroft Library, University of California, Berkeley, carton 1, folder 35.
19. Tabb letter to McDevitt, Oct. 13, 1889, reprinted in "My Father, Father Tabb," pp. 92-93.
20. His personal papers at the Bancroft Library at the University of California, Berkeley, include a short list of notable people from whom he took dictation during his lifetime. Helen Murphy Pernin was on that list. She created the Pernin shorthand system and operated the Pernin Publishing Company and Pernin's Shorthand Institute on Lafayette Boulevard in Detroit. The 1891 Detroit city directory lists McDevitt as a stenographer at Sloman, Berry and Duffie, a law firm.
21. Notice of his resignation as a "copyist" at the U.S. Geological Survey, and his salary of $720 per year, were published in the *Evening Star* on March 16, 1894.
22. In the third revised edition of his "Rite-it-Rite" shorthand instruction book, published in San Francisco in 1937, McDevitt cited praise by his former Smithsonian Institution boss, W.J. McGee, who was said to have asserted that McDevitt had done for shorthand "something comparable to what Darwin did for evolution." William McDevitt papers, 1905-1947, Manuscript Collection 1365, Kislak Center for Special Collections, Rare Books and Manuscripts, University of Pennsylvania.
23. Email correspondence April 15, 2026, with Carole Prietto, Georgetown Law Center archivist, Williams Library Special Collections, citing Law School enrollment record. Also, Georgetown Law School *Bulletin, 1893-94 and 1894-95,* courtesy of Williams Library Special Collections.
24. McDevitt years later said his essay was "adjudged the best paper" but he didn't win the $100 top prize because of a technicality. *San Francisco Chronicle*, Oct. 14, 1955.
25. Bachelor of Laws and Master of Laws records, including graduation programs, courtesy of Booth Family Center for Special Collections, Lauinger Library, Georgetown University.
26. Scrimshaw is a form of folk art in which figures or scenes are carved or engraved in bone or ivory. The author's real name was Douglas McCal-

lum, a Chicago activist who traveled with Coxey's "commonwealers" to promote his book.

27. Tabb letter to McDevitt, July 28, 1901. Tabb letters in William McDevitt papers, BANC MSS 89/86, Box 2, Folder 8, Bancroft Library, University of California, Berkeley.
28. It's just possible, also, that McDevitt had mentioned befriending John A. Joyce, a Union army veteran of the Civil War known to frequently feed a prodigious appetite for alcohol. In a booklet he co-authored in 1944 with Carl Browne, recounting the Coxey march on Washington, McDevitt said Joyce once told him of being invited to an Army veterans' reunion in Louisville and promised that the liquor would flow six feet deep. His reply: "Good Lord, men, I'm only five-nine!"
29. Tabb to McDevitt, Aug. 31, 1894. McDevitt papers, Bancroft Library.
30. In her 1922 book, *Father Tabb, His Life and Work: a Memorial*, Tabb's niece, Jennie Masters Tabb, noted a "peculiarity" of Tabb's: "his aversion to ever seeing again a young man whom he had loved as a youth." She didn't cite McDevitt by name, but her further description leaves little room for doubt it was him. She wrote that the young man had asked Tabb to come to Washington to visit him (McDevitt), but Tabb refused, saying he preferred to remember him as the boy he had loved at St. Charles, not the man he had become. In a similar vein, Tabb wrote in a 1901 letter to McDevitt: "It is as you *were* that I love you, and nothing would induce me to see you now changed as you are." In 1895 he wrote, "Never again can we meet as before."
31. Tabb to McDevitt, Oct. 16, 1894. McDevitt papers, Bancroft Library. To the best of the author's knowledge, Tabb never knew or met McDevitt's mother. He seemed here to be shaming McDevitt.
32. Tabb to McDevitt, Aug. 26, 1896. McDevitt papers, Bancroft Library.
33. Tabb to McDevitt, March 28, 1895. McDevitt papers, Bancroft Library.
34. McDevitt was drawn to revolutionary movements, although more as an observer than an instigator. In December 1897, shortly before he left the nation's capital to join what he hoped would be the beginning of a socialist revolution in "the other" Washington, he was busy getting in the mood. He attended a presentation at the now-defunct Columbia Theater by Maud Gonne, the Anglo-Irish actress, feminist, and revolutionary. She was a leading voice for establishing an Irish republic fully independent of Great Britain. Several members of Congress also were in the audience that day as she argued that innocent Irish were dying by the hundreds of thousands from "starvation and famine fever in a land of plenty which an alien government has reduced by systematic plunder." Her son, Sean, joined the Irish Republican Army at age thirteen. In 1974 he was awarded the Nobel Peace Prize for his work on behalf of human rights, including his efforts as one of the founders of Amnesty International and his leading role in establishing the Council of Europe.

35. The rail line was designated by the American Society of Civil Engineers nearly a century later, in 1994, as a Historic Civil Engineering Landmark, an honor shared with such engineering marvels as the Eiffel Tower and the Panama Canal.
36. McDevitt letter, *Industrial Freedom*, April 15, 1899.
37. A University statement published in the Seattle Post-Intelligencer of June 11, 1903, previewing faculty and other leadership changes for the coming academic year, said McDevitt was "not re-elected" as registrar. The job would hereafter be filled by a person "who has made a study of purchasing for such an institution," it said—oddly combining procurement with the management of academic records and student registration.
38. When London lectured at the Dietz Opera House in Oakland in March 1906, he was introduced by McDevitt.
39. Letters from Sinclair to McDevitt, 1910-1947; box 1, folder 1, William McDevitt papers, Manuscript Collection 1365, Kislak Center for Special Collections, Rare Books and Manuscripts, University of Pennsylvania.
40. Years after Sterling's death, McDevitt wrote in *My Father, Father Tabb* that he knew him "intensively although not extensively" in the San Francisco poet's final years.
41. *My Father, Father Tabb*, p. 80.
42. Richard Donovan, "Life with San Francisco," *San Francisco Chronicle*, March 26, 1942, p. 22.
43. It is possible McDevitt met Mencken when the Baltimore Evening Sun columnist came to San Francisco to cover the 1920 Democratic National Convention. McDevitt's poet friend and former St. Charles classmate George Sterling hosted a dinner party for Mencken during his stay. Mencken's *American Mercury* literary magazine published a good deal of Sterling's prose and verse, and Mencken was at the Bohemian Club in San Francisco for a Sterling-hosted banquet the night Sterling entered the eternal sleep by taking a fatal dose of potassium cyanide on Nov. 17, 1926. The events of that night are described by Joseph Noel in *Footloose in Arcadia*, p. 130.

    Among McDevitt's many communications with Mencken over four decades was an Oct. 28, 1948, letter in which Mencken thanked him for sharing a pamphlet on Richard Realf, an English immigrant poet who became a close associate of John Brown, the militant abolitionist who was executed for his attack on a federal armory at Harper's Ferry in 1859. "He seems to have been an unmitigated scoundrel," Mencken wrote of Realf, "but I agree with you that he was an interesting man."
44. In 1932, McDevitt sent Mencken, then editor of the *American Mercury*, a proposed article about his adoptive father, Father John B. Tabb. Mencken was not impressed. In a blunt but not unkind rejection letter, he told McDevitt the writing lacked discipline and direction. Using a fitting, if

unintended, metaphor for McDevitt's life, he added: "You wander all over the landscape."

45. The book, published in 1911, was written under the pseudonym Frank V. Webster for the Stratemeyer Syndicate as part of a series books aimed at young boys.
46. Payroll, Smithsonian Institution-Bureau of American Ethnology, Record Group 106. 1871-1952. 106.2 General Records of the Smithsonian Institution, 1892-1952.
47. "Josiah Warren and the Sovereignty of the Individual," by Ann Caldwell Butler, *The Journal of Libertarian Studies*, Vol. 4, No. 4 (Fall 1980), p. 438. Warren, born in 1798 in Boston, was an anarchist.
48. Quote from information paper presented to author during October 2025 tour of "Community House Number 2," New Harmony, Indiana.

9. Lermond Arrives, Trouble Follows

1. Details of Barton's mental health struggles are from numerous reports in Battle Creek, Michigan, newspapers from 1879 to 1897, courtesy of the Willard Library in Battle Creek.
2. "To Join The Brotherhood," *Tacoma Daily Ledger*, March 10, 1898.
3. In 1900, while living in Olympia, McDevitt became a card-carrying member of the Odd Fellows.
4. Lewis M. Ayer, who visited from Minneapolis in May 1898.
5. My account of Swigart's life story is from a range of sources, including newspaper reports in Ohio and Washington and student records of the Heidelberg College.
6. Swigart letter, reproduced in U.S. Senate, 64th Congress, 2nd Session, Report No. 1096, Feb. 20, 1907.
7. Newell, *Irrigation in the United States,* New York: Thomas Y. Crowell & Company, 1902, p. 3.
8. Cupples details are from newspaper reports, including *Freeland*, Nov. 1, 1905; *Bellingham Herald*, Oct. 10, 1910; Oroville (Washington) *Weekly Gazette*, Nov. 8, 1912, and the *St. Louis Post-Dispatch*, Jan. 9, 1914 and April 25, 1920. Also, William Jennings Bryan wrote about Cupples' "Arcadian Highway" plan in his Lincoln, Nebraska, monthly newspaper, *The Commoner*, September 1916, p. 4.
9. Kate Richards O'Hare, of St. Louis, was convicted of violating the Espionage Act for speaking against U.S. involvement in the First World War. Sentenced to five years in prison, she serve fourteen months at the Missouri State Penitentiary in Jefferson City before President Wilson commuted her sentence. She later was granted a full pardon.
10. Eisenhower's creation of the interstate highway system, "Eisenhower message to Congress," Feb. 22, 1955, Dwight D. Eisenhower Presidential Library.

11. "Equality Colony, New Organization for Cooperation," Bucyrus (Ohio) *Journal*, Jan. 28, 1898.
12. It's unclear how he came to know Lermond; he and his wife had donated small amounts to the BCC in 1896, and the following year the organization named him its master workman, even before he arrived at Equality.
13. *Discontent*, June 8, 1898, p. 1. Courtesy of Government Publications, Maps, Microforms and Newspapers, University of Washington Libraries.

10. A Teenage Rebel

1. Harry Ault is probably the best-known figure from the Equality colony, largely because of his prominent role in the Seattle labor movement of the early 20th century. My portrait of him relies on a range of sources, including newspaper reports, city directories, and his letters, but is built mainly on his unpublished memoir, "Early Memories," (also filed as "Autobiographical Notes") in the Ault papers. Also instructive was *Revolution in Seattle*, by Harvey O'Connor, Monthly Review Press, New York, 1964.
2. Ruhama Ault, "Freed From Some Anxieties," *Industrial Freedom*, Dec. 24, 1898.
3. This copy of the White House Cook Book, with "Equality Colony" ink-stamped inside, was acquired by Paul Peterson, who grew up in the neighborhood long after Equality disbanded but before all artifacts had disappeared. The heavily worn book's cover features images of the United States Capitol as well as the White House.
4. "Early Memories," Ault papers.
5. Ruhama Ault, *Industrial Freedom*, March 18, 1899.
6. Reference to the origin of the name of present-day Bratton township is courtesy of Dr. Benjamin B. Sunderland, Jr., professor emeritus of mathematics at Juniata College in Huntington, Pennsylvania.
7. Numerous copies of the *Young Socialist* are in the Ault papers.
8. "Ault to Lead U.S. Deputy Marshals," *Tacoma News Tribune*, Nov. 23, 1952.
9. Ault letter to Harvey O'Connor, Nov. 18, 1953, Ault papers.
10. In November 1919 a deputy U.S. marshal raided and shut down the *Union Record* and arrested him and three others on charges—later dismissed by a judge as groundless—of seeking to incite rebellion against the government. Robert C. Saunders, the U.S. district attorney in Seattle, who obtained the warrant authorizing the raid and arrests, called the raid "the beginning of a sweeping movement to quash radical publications in this country." In January 1920, a federal judge dismissed as baseless the sedition charges against Ault and his colleagues, declaring that the government's case was built on a flawed interpretation of law and did not merit prosecution.

11. Ault letter to Harvey and Jessie O'Connor, Nov. 18, 1953. Ault papers.
12. Ault, "You Can't Change Human Nature," Equality sketches, Ault papers.
13. George Savage, "Life and Adventures of George Savage and Family," written by George Savage and printed in 1964 by a daughter, Catherine Savage Pulsipher. Courtesy of Dan Royal of Mount Vernon, Washington. Savage details also in Smith's *Equality Colony* manuscript.
14. Savage letter of May 21, 1898, published in *Industrial Freedom*, June 4, 1898.
15. Wescott, "The Need of Unity," *Industrial Freedom*, July 23, 1898.
16. "Utopian Experiment in Skagit County Failed 50 Years Ago," *Seattle Times*, June 20, 1956.
17. This account of the Good Friday meeting is from McDevitt, "Getting Started at Equality," *Searchlight* series, September-October 1950, as well as Smith's *Equality Colony* manuscript, and *Industrial Freedom*.
18. Letter written July 7, 1898, published in *The Coming Nation*, July 23.
19. "The Greater BCC," *Industrial Freedom*, July 9, 1898.
20. Ibid.
21. *Industrial Freedom*, Aug. 6, 1898.
22. McDevitt, *Searchlight*, September-October 1950.

11. From Republican to Radical

1. My account of Burgess's experiences in Ohio, Iowa, Kansas, and Arkansas is based on his own extensive writings, land and court records in Arkansas and Washington, written recollections by daughter Eva Myrta Burgess Cooper, federal and state census data, city directories, dozens of newspaper articles, Quaker meeting and genealogy records, Smith's *Equality Colony* manuscript, and personal letters.
2. Bassett, "The Quakers and Communitarianism," *Bulletin of Friends Historical Association*, Vol. 43, No. 2, (Autumn 1954) pp. 84-99.
3. *Colonial and Revolutionary Families of Pennsylvania: Genealogical and Personal Memoirs*. Vol. 3, William Martin Bonsall, pp. 1340-1352.

   Anna Bonsall's ancestors apparently arrived in Pennsylvania shortly after William Penn, a fellow Quaker, established himself as governor of the province in 1682 and promoted it as a refuge for Quakers and other religious minorities.
4. Charles Bonsall was a son of Daniel Bonsall, who was a brother of Anna's father, Abraham Bonsall.
5. *When Coxey's 'Army' Marcht on Washington*, p. 9. [the use of "marcht" in place of "marched" reflected McDevitt's obsession with abbreviated spelling.] Carl Browne and William McDevitt. San Francisco. May 1944. McDevitt papers, MS Collection 1365, Kislak Center for Special Collections, University of Pennsylvania.

6. Bonsall family members in Green township in the early 1800s is from *History of Trumbull and Mahoning Counties*, Vol. 2, Chapter 12, p. 196. H.Z. Williams and Brothers, 1882. When the Bonsalls settled there, Green was part of Columbiana County.
7. The 1870 U.S. census lists Joseph Bonsall as residing in Burlington, Iowa, and his occupation as "principal" at a business college.
8. *The War Times*, Arkadelphia, Arkansas, April 29, 1863.
9. Cause #896, "R.A. Johnston & J. Weber vs. D. Burgess," Justice Court of Caddo Township, Clark County, and Clark County Circuit Court, Arkadelphia, Arkansas, August 1880. Source: Riley-Hickingbotham Library, Ouachita Baptist University. Although this was referred to in a local newspaper as a "celebrated" legal case, the newspapers and the available court records are silent on how it ended.
10. Eva Myrta Burgess Cooper, "A Sketch of My Life," written in 1973. A copy and permission to quote from it was provided by a granddaughter, Lora Leschner, who also shared family photos and letters.
11. As a state senator from nearby Huntsville, Arkansas, Murphy publicly opposed the state's secession from the Union in 1861. Three years later he became the first elected governor of Union-controlled Arkansas.
12. *St. Paul Republican*, Nov. 4, 1887, p. 4.
13. Eva Myrta Burgess Cooper, "A Sketch of My Life." She was known in the family as Myrta.
14. Marvin Sanford letter to Frederick E. Smith, June 30, 1969, Smith papers.
15. Burgess testimony, Skagit County Superior Court, Mount Vernon, Washington, Dec. 10, 1912. Full transcript on file at Washington State Archives in Olympia.
16. Eva Myrta Burgess Cooper, "A Sketch of My Life."
17. Burgess, *Industrial Freedom*, Oct. 22, 1898.
18. Hummel biographical information is from numerous New Ulm newspaper reports and his unpublished memoir, "Autobiography of William Hummel," cited with permission from a Hummel relative. Also, two obituaries, "Former Indian Fighter Is Dead," *The Oregon Daily Journal*, April 6, 1911, and "William Hummel Dead," *New Ulm Review*, April 12, 1911.
19. In his acclaimed account of Indian history in the American West, Dee Brown described the August 23, 1862 clashes at New Ulm. "It was a long and bitter battle, fought in the streets, dwellings, outhouses, and store buildings. When darkness fell, the Santees departed without a victory, but they left behind them the smoldering ruins of 190 buildings and more than a hundred casualties among the stubborn defenders of New Ulm."
20. The burning of New Ulm and the broader context of the war are from "The U.S.-Dakota War of 1862," Minnesota Historical Society.

21. *New Ulm Review*, Nov. 14, 1906
22. It's unclear when Hummel quit Equality, but it appears he lasted less than two years. He was back in New Ulm in time to be counted in the 1900 census. He and his wife Mary later moved to Portland, Oregon, where he died in 1911.
23. Maybell, *Civilization Civilized*, Denver: R.A. Southworth, 1889, Chapter 2, p. 7. Digitized from 1895 edition held by the University of California at Los Angeles; California Digital Library.
24. Burgess letter to Marvin Sanford, April 5, 1916. Marvin Sanford papers, 1896-1970. Call Number mssSanford. The Huntington Library, San Marino California.
25. Topolobampo colony was founded on Topolobampo Bay in the Mexican state of Sinaloa in 1886 by Albert K. Owen, a Pennsylvania engineer who envisioned a utopia built on what he called "complete social fellowship," achieved by "evolution, not revolution." The venture flopped. One of its members, George Washington Daniels, later moved to Arizona and became a financial supporter of the Equality colony. Sources include "Owen's Topolobampo Colony, Mexico," by Leopold Katscher, *American Journal of Sociology*, September 1906, Vol. 12, No. 2, pp. 145-175. Also, HistoryLink.org essay by John Caldbick, Dec. 2, 2019.
26. Pelton, *Industrial Freedom*, Sept. 24, 1898.
27. Boomer interview, *Anacortes American*, Dec. 17, 1908.
28. My account of Hogan's hijacking of the Northern Pacific locomotive in Montana was compiled from numerous sources, primarily contemporaneous newspaper accounts in Butte, Billings, Anaconda, Helena, and Forsyth.
29. *The Helena Independent*, May 15, 1894, p. 1.
30. "After the Coxeyites," *The Butte Miner*, April 25, 1894.
31. "Liscum Gets a Scoring," *The Anaconda Standard*, May 9, 1894, p. 5.
32. The unlucky bystander in Billings was Charles A. Hardy, who served in the First Massachusetts Cavalry in 1864-65 and suffered a gunshot wound in combat; Records of the U.S. National Homes for Disabled Volunteer Soldiers, 1866-1938.
33. The arresting officer was Army Lt. Col. John H. Page of the 22nd Infantry Regiment.
34. *Sanders County Signal*, Camas, Montana, June 30, 1922; Hogan's knowledge of Shakespeare is cited in same article.
35. *St. Louis Post-Dispatch*, Aug. 4, 1894.
36. *King Lear*, Act 3, Scene 4.
37. He was released from jail in August after serving three months of his six-month sentence; the local judge agreed to commute Hogan's sentence after the president of a Montana mining company offered Hogan a job.
38. *Industrial Freedom*, March 4, 1899.

39. During their years on Orcas and at Anacortes, William and Virginia Hogan were friends with Edward G. Cox, an English professor at the University of Washington who had a keen interest in all things Irish. He played the bagpipes and was a linguist with a special emphasis on Gaelic. He lectured at the University of Washington and elsewhere on Irish literature. He also was a yachtsman and in the 1920s served as treasurer of the Pacific International Yacht Racing Association. Boating was an interest he shared with Hogan, who had a cabin cruiser that he would take to Seattle to visit Cox. Cox and his sister Mabel Cox would sometimes come to Orcas to stay with the Hogans.
40. Throughout the 1920s and into the 1930s, the Hogans were nomads, traveling around the country in a motor home. The *Anacortes American* reported on June 30, 1932, that the Hogans had over the previous twelve years visited every state in the Union and used their motor home to live an "out-of-door existence." The 1930 census listed them as "lodgers" in the Atascadero, California, home of two other former Equality colonists: David and Inza Barry. The Hogans settled in Anacortes in 1932.

12. Rough Seas, Choppy Progress

1. Pelton, *Industrial Freedom*, Nov. 19, 1898, p. 3
2. Inza (Joslyn) Barry interview conducted and recorded in Atascadero, California, Feb. 23, 1966, by June Larrick on behalf of Charles LeWarne, author of *Utopias on Puget Sound*. Quotations used with permission from LeWarne.
3. Harvey O'Connor, *Revolution in Seattle*, Chicago: Haymarket Books, p. 17. Originally published 1964 by Monthly Review Press, New York.
4. *Port Angeles News*, quoted in *Spirit of '76*, Dec. 17, 1898, p. 2.
5. *Industrial Freedom*, Jan. 28, 1899, p. 2
6. *Industrial Freedom*, Jan. 14, 1899, p. 2
7. Harry Ault, "The Quartette," Colony Sketches, Ault papers.
8. The fire was reported in the *Mt. Vernon Argus*, Jan. 13, 1899. Half a year later, in its June 19, 1899, edition, *Industrial Freedom* referred to the fire that had "nearly demolished" the roastery.
9. *Battle Creek Moon*, Jan. 29, 1900.
10. The Tacoma *Daily Ledger* reported on March 14, 1909, that Barton was ordered committed to the insane asylum by Pierce County Superior Court Judge Miles L. Clifford. In addition to trying to talk an unidentified restaurant owner into "giving the girls higher wages," the *Daily Ledger* said Barton "labors under the delusion that he is a powerful athlete and a social demonstrator," adding, "He admits having been in an asylum before." The report made no mention of him being physically ill. On March 19, three days after Barton died at the asylum, the *News Tribune* and the *Daily Ledger* both reported that Judge Clifford approved a

request by "M. McNary," who claimed to be a friend of Barton's, to take custody of the personal effects he left at the asylum—the watch and cash. It's not clear who M. McNary was, but he or she may have had a direct connection to the asylum. A Mrs. Will McNary of Steilacoom had a sister named Agnes Webb, also of Steilacoom, who was described in news stories as a "traveling attendant" and "traveling matron" for the asylum where Barton died. This author's efforts in 2023 to learn more about Barton's three days at the asylum came to naught. Officials at what is now called Western State Hospital said they could release no information, including confirmation that he had been admitted and died there, except to a descendant. The Pierce County Superior Court Clerk's office told this author that a search of its archived 1909 records found no reference to Barton having been arrested or of Judge Clifford having ordered him committed to the asylum.

13. Equality For Women, Too

1. Helen M. Mason served as the BCC's treasurer and, as such, was a member of its board of directors.
2. *Industrial Freedom*, Aug. 6, 1898. The following summer Annie gave birth to another girl, Josie, who died at age three: *Mount Vernon Argus*, Sept. 5, 1902.
3. "Songs That Reach the Heart," *Appeal to Reason*, March 26, 1898, p. 3.
4. *Industrial Freedom*, Dec. 24, 1899, p. 4.
5. *Industrial Freedom*, Jan. 28, 1899, p. 4.
6. Helen Topman, "Some Truths," *Industrial Freedom*, Dec. 24, 1898.
7. *The Altrurian*, Pinon, Montrose County, Colorado, June 1, 1896. This Colorado venture, while not as ambitious in its political goals as Equality, followed a similar path to irrelevance. Internal conflict and financial pressures led to its demise as a cooperative colony.
8. In the 19th and early 20th centuries, use of the singular noun in a term like "woman suffrage" was the linguistic norm, as in the National Woman Suffrage Association. Today we refer to "women's suffrage." I use the older form in the interest of consistency.
9. *Topeka State Journal*, Sept. 1, 1898, p. 3. Also, "Populism and Feminism in a Newspaper by and for Women of the Kansas Farmers' Alliance, 1891-1894," Marilyn Dell Brady, Vol. 20 of *History of Women in the United States*, K.G. Saur, 1994.
10. "Gives Up Home," *Topeka Daily Capital*, June 12, 1900, p. 3.
11. "An Ideal Life," *Wichita Beacon*, Dec. 15, 1900, p. 3.
12. *Industrial Freedom*, Jan. 14, 1899, p. 4.
13. Sadie Smith Long, "Washington's Socialist Colony," *The Morning Oregonian*, reprinted in the *Daily News*, Santa Barbara, California, April 1, 1900.

14. Cooper, "Woman Suffrage—Cut Bono?" *The Overland Monthly*, Vol. 8, No. 2 (February 1872), pp. 156-165.
15. Sen. Benjamin Tillman, a South Carolina Democrat; *The Weekly Herald*, Newberry, South Carolina, Aug. 22, 1913.
16. U.S. Census Bureau, 1940 Census of Population, Part Two, *Occupational Distribution of the Nation's Labor Force, 1870-1940*, Chapter 8, *Comparative Occupation Statistics, 1870-1940*, Table 10, p. 128.
17. Miller. *The Strike of a Sex*. Chicago: A.B. Stockham and Company. 1896. pp. 21-22. Digitized by Google from original at Cornell University.
18. "A Correct View," a Burgess letter dated Nov. 2, 1900, from New Whatcom, Washington, published in the *Appeal to Reason*, Nov. 17, 1900.
19. Edwin J. Brown, the dentist, was expelled from the Socialist Party of Washington in December 1909. He later served as mayor of Seattle.
20. Charles D. Raymer. His Tacoma bookstore was at 1317 Pacific Avenue. He donated to the BCC cause.
21. "Equality Colony Woman's Column," *Industrial Freedom*, Jan. 28, 1899.
22. W.C. B. Randolph, *The Sun*, Shelby, Nebraska, May 5, 1899.
23. *Washington State Corrections and Jail Records, 1877-1970*, Whatcom County Government, Jail Records, 1890-1906, Register of Prisoners, p. 56.
24. Ibid.
25. Author email correspondence in 2023 with Clerk's Office, Whatcom County Superior Court, Bellingham, whose records indicated that the case file associated with the Temple matter was transferred without a recorded explanation to "Port Townsend," the seat of Jefferson County. The Jefferson County Superior Court office in Port Townsend subsequently told the author via email that no such transferred case file could be found.
26. 1900 United States Census. Register of Deaths, Humboldt County, California, 1898-1905, p. 287-288. The accidental drowning of Arthur Temple was reported in the *Ferndale Enterprise*, July 22, 1902; also recorded in Humboldt County death register.
27. Temple, "The Virden Affair and Some Remarks on War," *Industrial Freedom*, Nov. 5, 1898, p. 3.
28. Ibid.
29. *Wichita Citizen*, Wichita, Kansas, April 23, 1887, p. 1. This article was described as an extract from an article in the *Chicago News*.
30. *Trials and Triumph of Labor*. G.B. DeBernardi, Marshall, Missouri, Capital Parlor Print. 1890. "Portrait of a Workers' Utopia," H. Roger Grant, *Kansas History*, Vol. 43, No. 1 (Spring 1977).
31. *The Representative*, Minneapolis, Minnesota, July 28, 1897.
32. *Progress and Poverty*, 1879. George paid for the printing of his book through the San Francisco publisher, H.H. Bancroft and Company. Later

it was published commercially by D. Appleton and Company of New York.

33. "Bonds or Bondage," was among the government's widely used pitches. It appeared in many newspapers, including a version in the *Twin Bridges Independent* in Twin Bridges, Montana, Oct. 12, 1917, that added the warnings about becoming like Belgium. One such pitch in the Jackson (Michigan) *Citizen Patriot* of June 12, 1917, added that anyone lacking a good reason for not buying a Liberty Bond should "beat it to a lonesome isle in an unknown sea." The "selfishness" quote is from a Liberty Bond sales pitch published in many newspapers, including the Lewistown (Montana) *Daily News*, Oct. 14, 1917.
34. The case file for *United States of America vs. W.H. Kaufman*, District Court of the United States for the Western District of Washington, Southern Division, Cause #2439, is at the National Archives in Seattle, along with Kaufman's appeal, Cause #3237. The complete case file, including the government's Writ of Error, is at the National Archives in San Francisco.
35. *St. Louis Post-Dispatch*, Aug. 24, 1893.
36. *Industrial Freedom*, May 14, 1898, reprinting an article from the *St. Louis Post-Dispatch*.
37. Mason, *"Why Stand Ye Idle?"*, *The Union Signal*, May 26, 1892.
38. "Comparative Occupation Statistics for the United States, 1870-1930," Bureau of the Census, Sixteenth Census, 1940.
39. "Annual Report of the Secretary of Internal Affairs of the Commonwealth of Pennsylvania," page E3, Part Three, *Industrial Statistics*, Vol. 18, 1889.
40. "Annual Report of the Secretary of Internal Affairs of the Commonwealth of Pennsylvania," page E7, Part Three, *Industrial Statistics*, Vol. 18, 1889.
41. In a historical quirk, the person who donated some of the most valuable Equality colony documentation to the University of Washington was a half-brother of George Creel. His name was Herbert B. Creel, and he happened to be an ardent capitalist. He gave the records to the University of Washington Library in 1932, but little documentation of the donation has been found, leaving it unclear when, where, and how he gained possession of the records. Thank-you letters to Creel from the university's librarian at the time, Charles W. Smith, offer only the faintest clue about the donation. "I assume that we have now all of the material which you rescued," Smith wrote in July 1932 after receiving papers from Creel, a Seattle resident. "The Equality material is of important historical significance, and your cooperation is valued accordingly."
42. *Children in Bondage*, New York: Hearst's International Library Co., 1914, p. 20.

43. The Mason resignation letter is in the Freeland file, University of Washington Libraries, Special Collections.
44. Mason produced the pamphlet in St. Louis and had the copyright registered in 1896. It sold for five cents a copy.
45. Date and cause of Mason's death, King County death certificate. Author visited her grave at Mt. Pleasant Cemetery (section 1, lot 306) on Queen Anne hill in May 2025.
46. McDevitt, "Un-Lost Horizon," *Searchlight*, January-February 1951.
47. Details about Wescott's Chicago adventure are from *The Arena*, Vol. 9, February 1894.
48. "Cooperative Experiments in the United States—1. Equality Colony," *The Coming Age*, Vol. 1, No. 1, January 1899, p. 404-413. Digitized by Google from original at Wisconsin State Historical Society.
49. McDevitt, "Un-Lost Horizon," *Searchlight*, January-February 1951.
50. The historical record on the Postal Service's revocation of *Industrial Freedom*'s second-class mailing privileges is unclear. In its June 10 issue, the newspaper informed readers that it had been compelled to start paying third-class rates of postage, which it said meant a nearly 20-fold increase in costs. In his *Equality Colony* manuscript, Frederick Smith wrote that an unspecified "understanding" was then reached with postal authorities to allow a resumption of publication at second-class rates. In that era, the Postal Service sometimes punished newspapers it deemed excessively radical by withdrawing second-class mailing privileges. This, despite the fact that as a matter of public policy it had been the federal government's practice since the republic's earliest years to grant cheaper postal rates to newspapers as a way of encouraging the flow of information, thereby strengthening democracy. Why the BCC stopped publication entirely with the Nov. 1, 1901 issue is another puzzle. The editor at the time, Harry Ault, seemed caught by surprise. In that final issue, he said the paper was "slowly but steadily growing in influence," and predicted it "will soon be the brightest monthly paper issued by socialists."

14. Pelton's Last Stand

1. Burgess may never have said Equality was too tame for him, not in so many words. But that seemed to be his view, considering the path he took after leaving the colony in 1899. He became more directly involved in socialist politics by running for office numerous times and traveling around the region preaching the socialist gospel. He even adopted, perhaps unconsciously, some of the aggressive rhetoric of George Boomer. In June 1902, for example, he wrote that he had learned from speaking with farmers of eastern Washington that they were "beginning to realize that we are engaged in a moral combat"—one step short of what Boomer

called "war to the knife." The following year he began writing a regular column, "Slave Market Reports," in the *Socialist* newspaper in which he laid bare the hard truths as he saw them, namely that capitalism reduced ordinary workers to being slaves to corporate masters.

2. *Industrial Freedom*, Oct. 1, 1898, p. 3.
3. Pelton, "Equality's Struggles For An Existence," *Industrial Freedom*, May 27, 1899, p. 2.
4. Bige Eddy, *Industrial Freedom*, May 27, 1899.
5. William C.B. Randolph, "Ed Pelton Is Dead," *The Socialist*, March 1, 1901, p. 3.
6. Harry Ault letter to Bige Eddy, Dec. 19, 1953. Ault papers.
7. Pelton, *Industrial Freedom*, May 27, 1899, p. 2.
8. *Altrurian*, Pinon, Montrose County, Colorado, April 1, 1896.
9. Goldman, *Anarchism and Other Essays*. New York: Mother Earth Publishing Association, 1910. p. 57. Digitized by Google from original at Harvard College Library.
10. Pelton, *Industrial Freedom*, May 27, 1899, p. 2.
11. "Woman Turns Peppery 100 at Parkland," *The News Tribune*, Tacoma, Washington, Nov. 8, 1963.
12. Frederick Smith, in his *Equality Colony* manuscript, quoting from Pelton letter published in the Nov. 13, 1900, edition of *Industrial Freedom*, which is not in the publicly available collection.
13. Accounts of Pelton's death differed in some details, but it appears he was catapulted into the air and died from the fall. In *Equality Colony*, Smith wrote that it was a log—not Pelton— that was catapulted into the air, and that the log then struck Pelton, killing him. However, Smith's notes of his interview with Roland Lewis, Oct. 18, 1968, say Pelton was catapulted into the air and broke his neck in the fall. There is no publicly available Skagit County death record for Pelton.

15. Chaos and the Joslyns

1. "Cooperative Communities in the United States," *Bulletin of the Department of Labor*, No. 35, Vol. 6, July 1901, pp. 563-646. Digitized for Federal Reserve Bank of St. Louis. https://fraser.stlouisfed.org/title/bulletin-united-states-bureau-labor-3943/july-1901-477591
2. Ibid. pp. 617-618.
3. Smith, *Equality Colony* manuscript, Chapter 16, footnote seven, citing unpublished Harry Ault sketch, "The High Priestess."
4. Atascadero interview, Feb. 23, 1966, by June Larrick on behalf of author Charles LeWarne. Quotation used with permission from LeWarne.
5. *Southern Standard*, Arkadelphia, Arkansas, Feb. 12, 1881.
6. Atascadero interview, Feb. 23, 1966, by June Larrick on behalf of author Charles LeWarne. Quotation used with permission from LeWarne.

7. Details of Reuben Joslyn's military service are from Revolutionary War pension files, National Archives and Records Administration. Also, Reuben Joslyn (sometimes spelled Joslen) signed letter, undated; case files of pension and bounty land warrant applications from Revolutionary War veterans, National Archives.
8. Details of Phineas Joslyn's service in the War of 1812 are from "New York, War of 1812 Certificates and Applications of Claim and Related Records, 1858-1869," via Ancestry.com. His land claim in DeKalb County, Illinois, is from records of the General Land Office.
9. Details of the body snatching are from *Past and Present of DeKalb County, Illinois*, by Professor Lewis M. Gross, Vol. 1, pp. 83-86, Pioneer Publishing Company, Chicago, 1907. Also, "The Resurrectionists," *The Daily Chronicle*, DeKalb, Illinois, Nov. 27, 1963, p. 5.
10. Copy of Joslyn letter of June 18, 1869, provided by Kathy Bates-Lande, a descendant of Margaret Thompson Joslyn's older brother, John Heath Thompson.
11. U.S. Patent Office, Patent No. 168,931 issued Oct. 19, 1875. Application filed Aug. 6, 1875.
12. Margaret Joslyn patent, U.S. Patent Office, Patent No. 378,508, issued Feb. 28, 1888. Application filed Dec. 6, 1886.
13. Ely, "Pullman: A Social Study," *Harper's Magazine*, February 1885.
14. Olney, "The Regulars Reach Chicago," *The Times Leader*, Wilkes-Barre, Pennsylvania, July 5, 1894.
15. Inza's younger brother, Harry, killed himself with drugs and alcohol in November 1904 at age twenty-nine, three years after returning from Army duty in the Philippines, where he helped fight the insurrection that erupted after the U.S. government annexed the Philippines in late 1898. The annexation angered the very people whom the United States had liberated from Spanish rule; to apparent American surprise or indifference, the Filipinos rebelled at exchanging one foreign overlord for another. It may never be known whether Harry suffered anguish from the battles he witnessed as a member of the 42nd Infantry Regiment or from episodes of American atrocities against Filipinos that he might have seen or heard about. He died pitifully in a Salt Lake City jail. "Deserter Will Not Be Tried; Took Opium to Escape the Army," *Salt Lake Tribune*, Nov. 30, 1904, and "Buried By The County," *Salt Lake Telegram*, Dec. 2, 1904.
16. Postal appointment details are from "Appointments of U.S. Postmasters, 1832-1971," Skagit County, Vol. 76, p. 337.
17. Smith, *Equality Colony*, Chapter 15. A version of this episode is in Ault's unpublished sketch, "General Assembly," Ault papers.

16. 'Boy Bandit'

1. Alger may be best remembered as the target of intense public criticism for inadequately preparing the Army for war in Cuba in 1898 and for bungling its early execution. Most famously, he was blamed for what became known as the "embalmed beef" scandal—the sickening of troops fed spoiled meat. He was cleared of wrongdoing but resigned under pressure in August 1899.
2. "Alger's Timberland," *Seattle Post Intelligencer*, Oct. 30, 1889; "General Logan En Route East," *The Evening Telegraph*, Tacoma, Washington, Aug. 28, 1896; "Branching Out," *Fairhaven Herald*, Fairhaven, Washington, March 18, 1891; *Washington Standard*, Olympia, Washington, Aug. 10, 1888, and *The Eye*, Snohomish, Washington, June 22 and Aug. 17, 1889.
3. Alger biographical details are from Rodney Ellis Bell dissertation, "A Life of Russell Alexander Alger, 1836-1907," University of Michigan, 1975, made available at author's request by the University of Michigan Library. Also, *Russell Alexander Alger, Memorial Addresses, Fifty-Ninth Congress, Senate of the United States Feb. 23, 1907, House of Representatives Feb. 24, 1907*. Library of Congress.
4. My description of Bill Miner's background and prison record are from a variety of sources, including newspaper accounts and an article by Daryl C. McClary on HistoryLink.org, June 21, 2013.
5. Letter quoted with permission of Darr descendants and provided by Lorie Smith Schaefer, whose father, Oliver Smith, was a grandson of Oliver P. Darr. The identity of the letter's writer is unclear, but it seems not to be Oliver Darr; his name is written near the top, below an Equality Colony letterhead, suggesting it was addressed to him rather than written by him. Because the letter's final page is missing, there is no visible sign-off by the writer. It is dated June 25, 1900, by which time Darr and his family had moved to Puyallup, near Tacoma, as shown in the 1900 federal census, enumerated June 9.
6. The bungled train robbery and its aftermath were extensively covered by numerous newspapers in Oregon and Washington.
7. "Bad Man Nabbed," *Argus*, Mount Vernon, Washington, Oct. 16, 1903.
8. "Messenger Korner's Story," The *Salem Statesman-Journal*, Sept. 25, 1903, p. 1. The *Oregon Daily Journal*, Sept. 24, 1903, p. 2.
9. "Was Relative of James Boys," *Eugene Guard*, Oct. 13, 1903; "Owns His Guilt," *San Juan Islander*, Oct. 15, 1903.
10. "Ten Years For Robber," *The Sunday Oregonian*, Portland, Nov. 15, 1903, p. 24.
11. Ibid.
12. U.S. Census records; California prison and correctional records; "Harshman Given Twelve Years," *The Oregon Daily Journal*, Nov. 24,

1903; "Train Robber Now Talks," *La Grande Observer*, La Grande, Oregon, May 13, 1904; "Removed Several Bones And a Piece of Bullet From Convict's Brain," *The Capital Journal*, Salem, Oregon, May 11, 1904; Harshman death certificate.

13. Hoehn's prisoner file, including mug shot, personal details, court record and date of commutation, provided by Oregon State Archives.
14. Catherine "Katie" Archangel Shassey. She died in Skagit County in 1985.

17. 'Reign of Terror'

1. In 1904, King County had 189 saw mills, Snohomish County had 180, and Whatcom County, 166. Skagit County, with 115, was No. 4. Source: The *Argus*, Mount Vernon, Dec. 30, 1904, citing state labor commissioner report.
2. Smith manuscript, *Equality Colony*, Chapter 19.
3. *The Argus*, Mount Vernon, March 23, 1906.
4. David Barry in Whatcom County voter registration records is courtesy of Alison Costanza, Northwest Regional Branch, Washington State Archives, Bellingham. Details of his early life in New York are from federal census and local bank records.
5. "Shot by an Anarchist," *Tacoma Daily Ledger*, Dec. 12, 1901; the *Los Angeles Times*, Dec. 12, 1901. Horr conviction, "Iveagh's Assailant Convicted," *New York Times*, Feb. 6, 1902.
6. Horr quoted in the *Anacortes American*, Dec. 20, 1900.
7. *Butte Evening News*, June 2, 1908.
8. Lang, *Tomorrow is Beautiful.* New York: The MacMillan Company, 1948, p. 42. Lucy Robins Lang immigrated from Russia with her parents at age nine, grew up mostly in Chicago, and recalled in her memoir that Horr had fallen so hopelessly in love with her in San Francisco that he threatened to kill himself when she turned him down.
9. Horr's view of Hart is from Horr article in *Freeland* newspaper, Nov. 1, 1905.
10. Barry, "Some Incidents in the History of Equality," *Freeland*, Nov. 1, 1905.
11. Horr, "Freeland Colony vs. Hertzka Colony," *Freeland*, Nov. 1, 1905.
12. The poster, "Supremacy of the Individual," was reported in "Explosive Is Not Found," *The Seattle Star*, June 27, 1908. The article said police had raided the rented building in search of explosives but found only a variety of chemicals and laboratory equipment that one of the anarchists said were used to make a "pimple lotion." Horr was said to be in Montana en route to California.
13. "They Would Capture A State," *The Sun*, New York, Jan. 1, 1905, p. 16.
14. Horr remarks, "Freeland Colony," *The Demonstrator*, Feb. 1, 1905.

15. Smith, *Equality Colony* manuscript, Chapter 20.
16. Details of Horr's experiences in Texas are from the *Fort Worth Daily Gazette*, April 11, 1894; the *Waco Morning News*, Jan. 17, 1894, and the *Waco Evening News*, Nov. 7, 1893.
17. Goldman, *Living My Life*, New York: Alfred Knopf, 1931, Volume 1, pp.442-443.
18. "Freelanders Have Trouble," *The Argus*, Sept. 8, 1905.
19. "Freeland Fails to Arbitrate," *The Argus*, Nov. 11, 1905.
20. Skagit County Superior Court, Cause No. 4722, Section 10.
21. Reference to the odor of burnt hair and hide is from Smith, *Equality Colony* manuscript, Chapter 20. The identity of the person who set the barn fire was never proved. Smith, the local historian who studied Equality history for years, seemed uncertain who should take the blame. In his research notes he indicated that William E. Giles, who lived at Equality at the time, told him in 1969 that Henry Arnold, an Horr associate and anarchist, deliberately set the fire. Smith, however, did not mention this in his manuscript, perhaps because he found no corroborating evidence.
22. *The Tacoma Daily Ledger*, Feb. 8, 1906, p. 9.
23. "Trouble Among The Socialists," *Spokane Chronicle*, Feb. 22, 1906.
24. It cannot be ruled out that at least one murder *was* committed in this period. Many years later, Catherine Pulsipher, whose father, George Savage, used his portable sawmill to make lumber for the colony's early buildings, asserted on two occasions that a male colony teacher was murdered, perhaps in about 1905. She did not identify the teacher or the killer, and her accounts are unverified. In a 1966 letter to author Charles LeWarne, Pulsipher suggested that the killing was among rumors that "came to us after we left the colony." Separately, she wrote in a newspaper article (date not recorded) that anarchist newcomers to Equality — apparently Horr and his comrades — snatched a teacher who had urged their expulsion. She added in verse form, "None saw them beat him, but there was no doubt; because our tutor died." Pulsipher materials courtesy of Dan Royal.
25. Skagit County Superior Court, Cause No. 4823.
26. Roland L. Lewis, Skagit County Oral History Preservation Project, transcript at Skagit County Historical Museum, La Conner, Washington. Accession SKG77.
27. The true extent of violence at Equality in its final months is unclear and may never be known. George Peth, a son of John J. Peth, the farmer who purchased the Equality land at court auction in 1907, claimed in a 1979 oral history interview for the Skagit County Historical Society that "people started killing one another and used sandbags on one another," at the colony. He suggested this happened after Alexander Horr's arrival in 1904; he provided no names, dates or other details, and his claim is unver-

ified. "Oral History: George Peth on the Peth Family History," June 26, 1979, p. 31, *Skagit River Journal of History & Folklore*, 2020.

28. Judge Joiner decree, Skagit County Superior Court, Cause No. 4722, Summary, Jan. 8, 1906.
29. *Bellingham Herald*, April 25, 1907, p. 1.
30. Occupation of George D. Harding, U.S. Census, 1880 and 1900.
31. Julia Rowland Rhone, master's thesis, Western Washington University, "It Takes a Community: An Archeological Investigation of the 1897-1907 Equality Colony." November 2014. Her work contributed to the author's understanding of the geography and archeology of the colony.
32. Not all deaths at Equality were reported to county authorities. Ed Pelton is one example; his death does not appear on the county's death register. Pelton was buried at Equality, but some other colonists who died there were not. The post-Equality history of the cemetery is murky. The fact that today it rests on private property appears at odds with the June 17, 1907, Skagit County Superior Court decree governing the final sale of colony property, in which Judge George A. Joiner wrote that "the cemetery now located upon said property shall be excluded from said conveyance." He did not elaborate on that point; the cemetery land apparently was sold separately, later. Superior Court, Skagit County, Cause No. 4823, "Confirmation of Sale of Real Estate."
33. Ault, "Thirty Years of Saving the World," Ault papers.
34. Author examined the cemetery site twice in successive years, with permission of the property owner, who asked not to be identified by name or specific street address.
35. C.T. Conover, "Utopian Experiment in Skagit County Failed 50 Years Ago," *Seattle Times*, June 20, 1956.

18. A Dream Destroyed

1. *Industrial Freedom*, Nov. 12, 1898.
2. O'Connor, *Revolution in Seattle*. New York, Monthly Review Press, 1964, p. 8. O'Connor grew up in Tacoma. He worked for the Seattle Union Record during Harry Ault's editorship and later wrote books about Andrew Mellon and other leading capitalists. In 1955 he was convicted of contempt of Congress for refusing to tell Sen. Joseph McCarthy's Permanent Subcommittee on Investigations whether he had been a member of the Communist Party. O'Connor argued that as a private citizen his political affiliations were no business of the committee. His conviction was overturned on appeal in 1956.
3. O'Connor, *Revolution in Seattle*. p. 1.
4. "Image of Capitalism Slips to 54 Percent in U.S.," Gallup, Sept. 8, 2025. Among Americans polled by Gallup, 54 percent viewed capitalism favor-

ably, compared to 61 percent polled in 2010. Favorable views of socialism rose to 39 percent from 36 percent in 2010.

5. "Big Co-operative Scheme," *The New York Times*, Feb. 24, 1900, p. 11.
6. Lermond's letter to Einstein was reprinted in full in a newspaper article, "Must Attack War's Cause Einstein Told," *The American Guardian*, Oklahoma City, Oklahoma, Oct. 2, 1931. Einstein's reply was cited in an article, "Says Capitalists Not Main Cause of War," *Boston Globe*, Oct. 31, 1931.
7. Burgess testimony, Skagit County Superior Court, Cause No. 6441, Dec. 10, 1912. Washington State Archives.
8. "At a 'Boes' Dinner," Burgess letter, datelined Lothrop, Montana, May 30, published in *The Socialist*, Seattle, July 10, 1908. p. 2.
9. Ibid.
10. Goldstein, "The Anarchist Scare of 1908: A Sign of Tensions in the Progressive Era," *American Studies*, Vol. 15, No. 2 (Fall 1974), pp. 55-78.
11. Burgess, "Correspondence From Washington," *The Mountain Air*, St. Paul, Arkansas, Oct. 2, 1909.
12. Burgess, "Names Especially Remembered," *The Mountain Air*, St. Paul, Arkansas, Oct. 22, 1927.
13. John Joslyn died in San Luis Obispo County, California, in 1918.
14. Details of the Barrys' life in Atascadero are from local newspaper accounts and records of the Atascadero Historical Society. My description of the Drake scam and Inza Barry's involvement are based on newspaper accounts from 1915 to 1932, including "True Bill Is Found Against Drake's Heir," *Des Moines Register*, Aug. 9, 1915; "Drake 'Heir' in Jail," *Evening Times-Republican*, Marshalltown, Iowa, Dec. 6, 1920; "Myth Estate 'Donors' Split," *San Francisco Examiner*, June 11, 1927;"Drake Estate Lure Faces Court Action," *Sacramento Bee*, June 9, 1927; "Investors in 'Lost Estate' Claims Duped," *Oakland Tribune*, June 9. 1927; "Drake Estate Myth Exposed By State Corporation Dept.," *Los Angeles Evening Post-Record*, Dec. 2, 1931; "Drake Estate Sales Stopped By New Order," *Atascadero News*, Oct. 30, 1931.
15. The Inza Barry rebuttal letter was in at least two newspapers: "Replies to Story of Drake Estate," *San Luis Obispo Morning Tribune*, Dec. 17, 1931, and "Public Opinion," *Santa Maria Times*, Feb. 4, 1932.
16. *The Tribune*, San Luis Obispo, California, Sept. 13, 1963.
17. *San Francisco News*, June 16, 1959. Courtesy of Bancroft Library, University of California, Berkeley.
18. Tabb to McDevitt, Jan. 18, 1905. This is the last known Tabb letter to McDevitt. Tabb died four years later.
19. In 1936, Tabb admirers and former students organized "*The Forest* Memorial Association" to pay for the construction of a Tabb monument near the site of his birthplace on the former plantation. Contributors were mostly priests but included a number of former Tabb students who went

on teach at the University of Notre Dame. McDevitt's name is not on the list of contributors. Sources: *The Notre Dame Scholastic*, May 8, 1936, p. 9, and the John M. Cooney Papers; contributors list, Box: CJCO 2, Folder: 02, University of Notre Dame Archives.

20. A detailed accounting of McDevitt's corporate stock holdings at the time of his death are in the McDevitt papers at the Bancroft Library, University of California, Berkeley, carton 1, folder 37. This and other McDevitt items were provided to the author by Rebekah Kim, head librarian at the California Academy of Sciences Library and Archives, San Francisco. Additional materials from the McDevitt papers, including rarely seen portrait photos and other documents, were found later for the author by Sara Ferguson, a professional photo archivist and photographer.
21. The McDevitt papers ended up at the Bancroft Library at the University of California at Berkeley largely thanks to Victoria Sexton. She befriended him as a regular customer at his San Francisco bookstores in the 1930s and 1940s. In a letter dated Aug. 13, 1948, in which he addressed her as "My dear Miss Vee," McDevitt reminded her that he had proposed she become his "adopted daughter," with no obligation on her part other than being heir to his estate. She accepted, writing in a return letter four days later, "I am deeply conscious of having done nothing to merit the trust you place in me." The McDevitt papers include a copy of a notarized sworn statement of Aug. 27, 1948, in which he certifies that he has "adopted and made my legal daughter, Veronica J. Sexton." Additionally, on July 21, 1950, he signed a statement bequeathing to her "all and every kind of property, real or personal ... as well as every form of right or equity or dividend accuring [accruing] to me." In 1954 she invited him to live in an upstairs bedroom in her home in the city's Richmond district. He lived there until his death in 1959. Sexton donated his papers to the California Academy of Sciences, where she had been the head librarian; the Academy in turn donated them to the Bancroft Library.
22. Sexton's home, at 618 5th Avenue, was less than two blocks from Golden Gate Park, home of the California Academy of Sciences, where she was chief librarian.
23. The London story was titled "Two Gold Bricks." McDevitt wrote about this in a pamphlet, "Jack London's First," published in San Francisco by Recorder-Sunset Press in 1946, held by the University of Pennsylvania, Kislak Center for Special Collections, Rare Books and Manuscripts, Manuscript Collection 1365. McDevitt dedicated this pamphlet to "my good friend of 40 years ago, Mrs. Jack London," referring to Charmian London. In it, he says Jack London never knew his story was published because shortly after he submitted it to a New York publication called *The Owl* in the summer of 1897, he ran off to the Yukon to observe the Klondike gold rush. "While he was mushing into Dawson, his story was published in *The Owl* in September issue of 1897," McDevitt wrote.

24. "An Interview with William McDevitt, LL.M.," *Quarterly News Letter*, Vol. 19, No. 4 (Fall 1954), Book Club of California.
25. Ibid.
26. Bernard Halladay, letter to Frederick E. Smith, Dec. 12, 1970. Smith papers.

Bibliography

Collections consulted:

Herbert Baxter Adams papers, Sheridan Libraries, Special Collections, Johns Hopkins University.

Harry E.B. Ault papers, 1899-1956. Accession Nos. 0213-001 and 0562-001. University of Washington Libraries, Special Collections.

Freeland colony records, 1898-1906, containing documents from Equality colony. Accession No. 2078-001. University of Washington Libraries, Special Collections.

Rutherford B. Hayes collections. Rutherford B. Hayes Presidential Library and Museums, Manuscripts Collections.

Norman Wallace Lermond Socialist papers. Raymond H. Fogler Library, Special Collections, University of Maine, Orono.

Henry Demarest Lloyd correspondence, 1895-1897. Accession No. 4678-001. University of Washington Libraries, Special Collections. Originals at Wisconsin State Historical Society.

Wm. (William) McDevitt papers, 1892-1959. Collection No. BANC MSS 89/86c, and BANC PIC 1989-043. Bancroft Library, University of California, Berkeley. Includes photos credited in gallery, pages 121-130.

William McDevitt papers, 1905-1947. Manuscript collection 1365. Kislak Center for Special Collections, University of Pennsylvania.

H.L. Mencken papers, 1905-1956. Manuscripts and Archives Division, New York Public Library.

Frank Parsons papers. Call No. MS 11. Manuscripts and Archives, Yale University Library.

Marvin Sanford papers, 1896-1970. The Huntington Library, San Marino, California.

Veronica J. Sexton papers, 1925-1996. Collection No. BANC MSS 89/188c, Box 1. Bancroft Library, University of California, Berkeley.

Frederick E. Smith papers, 1865-1988. Center For Pacific Northwest Studies, Western Libraries Archives and Special Collections, Western Washington University. Includes photos credited in gallery, pages 121-130.

Books and Periodicals:

Allen, Frederick Lewis. *The Lords of Creation*. New York: Harper & Brothers, 1935.

Bakunin, Jack S. "Pierre Leroux on Democracy, Socialism, and the Enlightenment." *Journal of the History of Ideas*. Vol. 37, No. 3 (July-September 1976), pp. 455-474.

Bamford, Georgia Loring. *The Mystery of Jack London*. Oakland. 1931. Digitized by Google from original at University of California.

Bancroft, Hubert Howe. *History of Washington, Idaho, and Montana, 1845-1889*. San Francisco: The History Company, 1890.

Bashford, Herbert. "The Literary Development of the Far Northwest." *Overland Monthly*. Vol. 33, No. 196 (April 1899), pp. 316-320.

Bassett, T.D. Seymour. "The Quakers and Communitarianism." *Bulletin of Friends Historical Association*. Vol. 43, No. 2 (Autumn 1954), pp. 84-99.

Bellamy, Edward. *Looking Backward: 2000 to 1887*. Boston: Ticknor and Company, 1888.

—. *Equality*. New York: D. Appleton and Company, 1897.

—. "How I Came to Write 'Looking Backward.'" *The Nationalist*. Vol. 1. 1889. Digitized by Google; original at University of Michigan.

Bowman, Sylvia E. *The Year 2000, a Critical Biography of Edward Bellamy*. New York: Bookman Associates, 1958. Digitized by Google; original at University of Michigan.

Broadwater, Robert P. *The Luckiest Regiment in the Army of the Potomac*, an annotated diary of Corporal John A. Rhode of Company I, 137th Regiment of Pennsylvania Infantry. Lancaster, Pennsylvania: Quaker Hills Press Inc., 2007.

Bruce, Robert V. *1877: Year of Violence*. Indianapolis: Bobbs-Merrill Co., Inc., 1959.

Carnegie, Andrew. *The Gospel of Wealth*. Originally published in the *North American Review*, June 1889.

Cloud, Ray V. *Edmonds, the Gem of Puget Sound*. Edmonds, Washington: Edmonds Tribune-Review Press, 1953.

Coling, Jerome F. "The Historical Geography of Coalgate, Oklahoma." Unpublished master's thesis, University of Oklahoma. 1966.

Cook, William W. *The Corporation Problem*. New York: G.P. Putnam's Sons, 1893. Internet Archive; original at University of Illinois, Urbana-Champaign.

Collins, Brian. "Mid-19th Century Stream Channels and Wetlands Interpreted from Archival Sources for Three North Puget Sound Estuaries." Department of Geological Sciences, University of Washington. Aug. 1, 2000.

David, Henry. *The History of the Haymarket Affair*. New York: Russell & Russell, second edition, 1958.

Daniel, Pete. "The Tennessee Convict War." *Tennessee Historical Quarterly*, Vol. 34, No. 3 (Fall 1975), pp. 273-292.

Desmond, Matthew. *Poverty, By America*. New York: Crown, Random House, Penguin Random House, 2023.

Destler, Chester McArthur. *American Radicalism 1865-1901, Essays and Documents*. New York: Octagon Books, 1963.

Dick, Timothy A. "Yakima Project," U.S. Bureau of Reclamation, 1993.

Eaton, Cyrus. *Annals of the Town of Warren*. Hallowell: Masters, Smith and Company, 1851. Internet Archive; original in the Library of Congress.

Ely, Richard T. "Socialism in America." *The North American Review*, Vol. 142, No. 355 (June 1886), pp. 519-525.

__. "Pullman: A Social Study." *Harper's Monthly Magazine*, Vol. 70, No. 417 (February 1885), pp. 452-266.

__. "Report of the Organization of the American Economic Association." *Publications of the American Economic Association*. March 1886.

Fine, Sidney. *Laissez Faire and the General-Welfare State*. Ann Arbor: University of Michigan Press, 1956.

Flowers, Benjamin O. *Progressive Men, Women, and Movements of the Past Twenty-Five Years*. Boston: The New Arena, 1914. Digitized by Google; original at Stanford University Library.

Garland, Hamlin. *A Son of the Middle Border*. New York: The Macmillan Company, 1917.

George, Henry. *Progress and Poverty: An Inquiry into the Cause of Industrial Depressions and of the Increase of Want with Increase of Wealth*. New York: D. Appleton and Company, 1886.

Goldman, Emma. *Living My Life*. Volume One. New York: Alfred Knopf, Inc., 1931.

Glassgold, Peter. *Anarchy! An Anthology of Emma Goldman's Mother Earth*. Washington, D.C.: Counterpoint, 2001.

Green, James R. *Grass-Roots Socialism*. Baton Rouge: Louisiana State University Press, 1978.

Hayes, Rutherford B. *Diary and Letters of Rutherford Birchard Hayes*, edited by Charles Richard Williams, 1922. Vol. 4. 1881-1893. Ohio State Archeological and Historical Society, via Rutherford B. Hayes Presidential Library and Museums at Spiegel Grove, Ohio.

Hoe, Robert. *A Short History of the Printing Press*. New York: Hoe, 1902. Digitized by Google; original at Harvard University.

Hoffman, Charles. "The Depression of the Nineties." *The Journal of Economic History*. Vol. 16, No. 2 (June 1956), pp. 137-164. Cambridge University Press.

Holbrook, Stewart H. *Far Corner: A Personal View of the Pacific Northwest*. New York: The McMillan Company, 1952.

Holmes, George K. "The Concentration of Wealth." *Political Science Quarterly*. Vol. 8, No. 4 (December 1893), pp. 589-600.

Horr, Alexander. *Fabian Anarchism, a Fragmentary Exposition of Mutualism,*

Communism, and Freeland. San Francisco: Freeland Printing and Publishing Company, 1911.

Hoxie, Robert F. "The Rising Tide of Socialism: A Study." *Journal of Political Economy*, Vol. 19, No. 8 (October 1911), pp. 609-631.

Jordan, Ray. *Yarns of the Skagit Country*. La Conner, Washington: Skagit County Historical Society, 2016. Original copyright, Jordan, 1974.

Kent, Alexander. "Cooperative Communities in the United States." *Bulletin of the Department of Labor*, No. 35, July 1901.

Lang, Lucy Robins. *Tomorrow is Beautiful*. New York: McMillan Company, 1948. Digitized by Google; original at the University of California at Santa Cruz.

LeWarne, Charles Pierce. *Utopias on Puget Sound, 1885-1915*. Seattle: University of Washington Press, 1975.

—. "Equality Colony: The Plan to Socialize Washington." *The Pacific Northwest Quarterly*, Vol. 59, No. 3 (July 1968), pp. 137-146.

Litz, Francis A. *Father Tabb: A Study of His Life And Works*. Baltimore: Johns Hopkins Press, 1923.

London, Jack. *The Iron Heel*. New York: The Macmillan Company, 1908.

Madison, Charles A. *Critics and Crusaders, a Century of American Protest*. New York: Henry Holt and Company, 1947.

Markham, Edwin; Benjamin R. Lindsey, and George Creel. *Children in Bondage*. New York: Hearst's International Library Company, 1914.

Martin, Scott M., Norman Wallace Lermond. "Autobiography of Norman Wallace Lermond, Maine's Naturalist/Socialist." *Northeastern Naturalist*, Vol. 11, No. 2, 2004, pp. 197-228. Copy of autobiography also held in archives of American Malacological Society at Drexel University.

Maybell, Stephen. *Civilization Civilized*. New York: Lovell, Gestefeld and Company, 1892. Digitized by Internet Archive; original at University of California, Los Angeles.

McDevitt, William. *My Father, Father Tabb*. Washington, D.C.: Recorder-Sunset Press, 1945. Digitized by Google; original at University of California, Berkeley.

—. "Un-lost Horizon: Shangri-La of Puget Sound." *Searchlight*, eight installments, March-April 1950 to May-June 1951. Harry E.B. Ault papers, Accession No. 0562-001, box 4, folder 19, University of Washington Libraries, Special Collections.

__. "Jack London's First." San Francisco: Recorder-Sunset Press, 1946. Manuscript Collection 1365, Folder 4, Kislak Center for Special Collections, Rare Books and Manuscripts, University of Pennsylvania.

__. "When Coxey's 'Army' Marcht on Washington." San Francisco. 1944. Manuscript Collection 1365, Folder 4, Kislak Center for Special Collections, Rare Books and Manuscripts, University of Pennsylvania.

—. "My Old Plantation Days with Father Tabb." *The Catholic World*, September 1949. Serial archive listing, Internet Archive, volume 168, scanned from microfilm. Originally published by

McMahon, Darrin M. *Equality: The History of an Elusive Idea*. London: Ithaka Press, 2024.

Meany, Edmond S. *History of the State of Washington*. New York: The McMillan Company, 1909.

Miller, Susan and Fred. *Samish Island: A History, From the Beginning to the 1970s*. Mt. Vernon, Washington. 2007.

Morgan, Arthur E. *The Philosophy of Edward Bellamy*. New York: King's Crown Press, 1945.

Newell, Frederick Haynes. *Irrigation in the United States*. New York: Thomas Y. Crowell & Company, 1902.

Noel, Joseph. *Footloose in Arcadia: A Personal Record of Jack London, George Sterling, Ambrose Bierce*. New York: Carrick and Evans, Inc., 1940.

O'Connor, Harvey. *Revolution in Seattle: A Memoir*. Chicago: Haymarket Books, 2009. Originally published in 1964 by Monthly Review Press, New York.

O'Hara, S. Paul. *Inventing the Pinkertons; or Spies, Sleuths, Mercenaries, and Thugs*. Baltimore: Johns Hopkins University Press, 2016.

Parrington, Louis Vernon. *Main Currents in American Thought*. Vol. 2: "The Romantic Revolution in America, 1800-1860." Vol. 3: "The Beginnings of Critical Realism in America, 1860-1920." New York: Harcourt Brace, 1927.

Peffer, William A. *The Farmer's Side, His Troubles and Their Remedy*. New York: D. Appleton and Company, 1891.

Pelton, J.M. *Genealogy of the Pelton Family in America*. Albany, New York: Joel Munsell's Sons, 1892.

Pfaff, Christine E. *Harvests of Plenty, a History of the Yakima Irrigation Project, Washington*. Denver: Technical Service Center, United States Department of the Interior, Bureau of Reclamation, 2001.

Pollack, Norman. *The Populist Mind*. Indianapolis and New York: Bobbs-Merrill Company, 1967.

Piketty, Thomas. *Capital in the 21st Century*. Cambridge, Massachusetts: The Belknap Press of Harvard University Press, 2017.

__. *A Brief History of Equality*. Cambridge, Massachusetts: The Belknap Press of Harvard University Press, 2022.

Quint, Howard H. *The Forging of American Socialism*. Indianapolis: Bobbs-Merrill Company, 1953.

__. "American Socialists and the Spanish-American War." *American Quarterly*. Vol. 10, No. 2, Part 1 (Summer 1958), pp. 131-141.

Reclamation Record. Vol. 6, No. 6 (June 1915). U.S. Department of the Interior.

Rezneck, Samuel. "Unemployment, Unrest, and Relief in the United States during the Depression of 1893-1897." *Journal of Political Economy.* Vol. 61, No. 4 (August 1953), pp. 324-345.

Rosner, Peter. "Theodor Hertzka and the Utopia of 'Freiland.'" *History of Economic Ideas.* Vol. 14, No. 3, 2006, pp. 113-137.

Schwantes, Carlos A. "Free Love and Free Speech on the Pacific Northwest Frontier: Proper Victorians vs. Portland's 'Filthy Firebrand.'" *Oregon Historical Quarterly.* Vol. 82, No. 3 (Fall 1981), pp. 271-293.

Scontras, Charles A. *The Socialist Alternative: Utopian Experiments and the Socialist Party of Maine, 1895-1914.* Orono, Maine: University of Maine, 1985.

—. "Norman Wallace and His Quest for the Cooperative Commonwealth." *Maine History,* Vol. 42, No. 2, 2005, pp. 47-65. A publication of the Maine Historical Society and the University of Maine History Department. https://digitalcommons.library.umaine.edu/mainehistoryjournal/vol42/iss2/4

Scrimshaw, Frederic. *The Dogs and the Fleas, by One of the Dogs.* Chicago: Douglas McCallum and the Libby & Sherwood Printing Company, 1893.

Smith, James Allen. *The Spirit of American Government.* New York: The Macmillan Company, 1907.

Srinivasan, Bhu. *Americana: A 400-Year History of American Capitalism.* New York: Penguin Random House, 2018.

Stevens, C.A. *Berdan's United States Sharpshooters in the Army of the Potomac, 1861-1865.* St. Paul, Minnesota: Price-McGill Company, 1892.

Stiles, Henry R. *A History of the City of Brooklyn,* Volume II. Brooklyn. 1869. Digitized by the Internet Archive; original at Columbia University Libraries.

Suttles, Wayne. *Coast Salish Essays.* Seattle: University of Washington Press, 1987.

Tabb, Jennie Masters. *Father Tabb: His Life and Work.* Boston: The Stratford Company, 1922.

Quint, Howard H. *The Forging of American Socialism.* Indianapolis: Bobbs-Merrill Company, 1953.

Walz, Robert B. "Migration into Arkansas, 1820-1880: Incentives and Means of Travel." *The Arkansas Historical Quarterly.* Vol. 17, No. 4 (Winter 1958), pp. 309-324.

Weinstein, Allen. *Prelude to Populism.* New Haven: Yale University Press, 1970.

Wescott, Helen J. "Cooperative Experiments In the United States. 1.-Equality Colony," *The Coming Age,* Vol. 1, No. 1 (January 1899), p. 404-413.

White, Richard. *The Republic For Which It Stands*. New York: Oxford University Press, 2017.

Wooster, Ernest S. *Communities of the Past and Present*. Newllano, Louisiana: Llano Colonist, 1924. Digitized by Google; original at University of California, Berkeley.

Court Records:

Multiple lawsuits, 1905-1907, leading to dissolution of Equality colony. Skagit County Superior Court. Primarily, Cause #4722 and Cause #4823. Records of additional legal actions reviewed at Washington State Archives, Olympia, including Cause #6441, D. Burgess vs. Trustees of the BCC, Skagit County Superior Court.

David Burgess farm contract lawsuit. Justice Court of Caddo Township, Clark County, Arkansas, and Clark County Circuit Court. Cause #896. "R.A. Johnston & J. Weber vs. D. Burgess." Arkadelphia, Arkansas. August 1880. Riley-Hickingbotham Library, Ouachita Baptist University.

Indictment, conviction and appeal of William H. Kaufman. United States vs. W.H. Kaufman, Cause #2439, United States District Court, Southern Division, Western District of Washington, 1918. Reversal on appeal, Cause #3237, Circuit Court of Appeals for Ninth Circuit, 1919. National Archives and Records Administration, Seattle.

Ernest Pelton killing. State of Minnesota vs. Jerry Woodman. Cause #637. Todd County District Court, 1886-1888. Gale Family Library, Minnesota Historical Society.

Acknowledgments

Broad outlines of Equality colony history were never hard to find. Better hidden were answers to the questions I wanted to explore: Who *were* these people? What drew them to socialism, motivated them to join this would-be revolution in a wilderness, and made them think it could work? How did their ideas, hopes, and failures fit into the longer history of capitalism and inequality in America?

After seven years of research, this book represents my findings. Any errors of fact or analytical judgment are mine alone.

No story of this kind, so rooted in history, can be told without help. Mine began with Charles P. LeWarne. His 1975 book, *Utopias on Puget Sound, 1885-1915*, remains the most authoritative account of utopian, or communitarian, experiments in western Washington. Chuck and his wife Pauline twice hosted me at their Edmonds, Washington, home on a bluff facing Puget Sound to discuss Equality colony and its characters, to offer encouragement, and to share portions of his research. It was an honor to learn from a wise and true gentleman who served his community as a school teacher for thirty years.

By chance, LeWarne's initial interest in Equality coincided with that of Frederick E. Smith, a self-made historian born in nearby Blanchard shortly after the colony collapsed. Smith happened to be my first cousin once removed—my maternal grandmother's nephew. I never knew him, and I had no awareness of Equality until I stumbled upon an online mention of a Frederick E. Smith collection at the Center for Pacific Northwest Studies at Western Washington University while researching my Swedish ancestors in 2016. After years of study, including interviews in the 1960s with former Equality colony residents and descendants, Smith had nearly finished a book manuscript when he died in 1979. His sister Florence, with whom he had collaborated, completed it and printed a number of plastic-bound copies.

I owe thanks, also, to Suzanne Hawley of Shoreline, Washington, who shared with me her family's copy of the Smith manuscript, titled *Equality Colony*, and encouraged me to make best use of it. Suzanne is a granddaughter of Smith's older brother Philip. I considered publishing the Smith manuscript as is but ultimately chose to develop and tell the story my own way, placing it in a new historical context.

I also acknowledge and thank the staff at the Center for Pacific Northwest Studies at Western Washington University, particularly archivist Ruth Steele and assistant archivist Rozlind Koester. They indulged my requests, questions, and visits over many years. Thanks also to the staff at the Washington State Library, the Washington State Law Library, the Washington State Archives, the University of Washington Registrar's Office, and the University of Washington Libraries' Special Collections, especially librarian Allee Monheim.

I owe a big thank-you also to Julia Rowland Rhone, whose 2014 master's thesis on the archeology of the Equality colony gave me a better understanding of its physical layout. She shared a copy of her study, which brilliantly combined historical and archaeological research methods, including use of old and modern map overlays, to pinpoint the location of colony buildings and other structures. I also thank Julia for being one of several people who read all or parts of my draft manuscript and offered useful suggestions. Other readers included a long-time colleague, Jim Mannion, as well as Charles LeWarne and my wife Liz Burns, whose encouragement and love sustained me. Our talented daughter, Libby, designed the book's cover and adapted a map to illustrate Equality's location in the Puget Sound region.

A meaningful analysis of the history of an obscure episode like the rise and fall of the Equality colony is not possible without digging below the surface. It requires details—artifacts, if you will—that reveal more than bare facts. I wanted to know not just what happened at Equality but why. That's where old newspapers, court records, autobiographies, personal letters, diaries, memoirs, and research collections came in.

Newspapers in the late 19th and early 20th century were the life blood of a community. It was to my benefit that internet sites and many small, regionally focused on-line newspaper collections now make it possible to explore the lives of ordinary people from centuries gone by. Michael McCullough at the Willard Library in Battle Creek, Michigan, for example, enabled me to review newspapers that provided extra insights into the life of Robert Barton, the eccentric blacksmith. Likewise, assistant archivist Kristin Jacobsen at the Frances Willard House Museum and WCTU Archives in Evanston, Illinois, provided articles written by Helen M. Mason, the prohibitionist and former St. Louis school teacher.

I also extend thanks to public libraries in Tacoma, Washington; Easton, Maryland; Fayetteville, Arkansas; Fairfax, Virginia, Bellefonte, Pennsylvania, and New York City. Also, the Raymond H. Fogler Library at the University of Maine; the Riley-Hickingbotham Library at Ouachita Baptist University in Arkadelphia, Arkansas; the Beinecke Rare Book and Manuscript Library, Yale University; the Bancroft Library at the University of California, Berkeley; the Founders Memorial

Library at Northern Illinois University; the University of Pennsylvania Kislak Center for Special Collections, Rare Books and Manuscripts; the Lauinger Library's Booth Family Center for Special Collections at Georgetown University; the Sheridan Libraries at Johns Hopkins University in Baltimore; the University of Notre Dame Archives, and the University of Michigan's William L. Clements Library.

Thanks, also, to the Associated Archives at St. Mary's Seminary and University in Baltimore, and the Huntington Library at San Marino, California. Also, the American Antiquarian Society, the state archives in Arkansas and Oregon, and the California Academy of Sciences, whose head librarian, Rebekah Kim, graciously provided documents that deepened my understanding of William McDevitt.

Historical societies and their staffs are under-appreciated treasures. I benefitted from the help of many of these organizations. They include the Rhode Island Historical Society in Providence; the Gale Family Library of the Minnesota Historical Society in St. Paul; the Talbot Historical Society of Easton, Maryland; the Maine Historical Society, the Warren (Maine) Historical Society; the Wisconsin State Historical Society; the Skagit County Historical Museum in La Conner, Washington (especially archivist Mari Anderson-Densmore); the Madison County Genealogical and Historical Society in Huntsville, Arkansas; the Todd County Historical Society in Long Prairie, Minnesota; the Atascadero Historical Society in California, and the Buffalo County Historical Society in Kearney, Nebraska.

Index

About the Author

Robert Burns is a native of Stanwood, Washington. After earning a bachelor's degree in communication from the University of Washington in 1977, he began a 45-year reporting career with the Associated Press, retiring in 2022. He and his wife, Liz, live in Reston, Virginia. They have two grown children and three grandchildren.

Author's page: robertburnsbooks.com

Also by Robert Burns: *A Long Way Home: From Sweden to Cedarhome*. 2019.

www.ingramcontent.com/pod-product-compliance
Lightning Source LLC
Chambersburg PA
CBHW030907120626
46554CB00001B/41

9798994055809